Surviving *Utopia*

A Novel

Linda Jones Weber

SURVIVING UTOPIA

Linda Jones Weber

Book Cover Design and Interior Formatting by 100Covers

ISBN (Print Edition):979-8-3011828-5-3
ISBN (Hardcover Edition): 979-8-9918194-4-2
ISBN (eBook Edition): 979-8-9918194-3-5
ISBN (Audiobook edition): 979-8-9918194-5-9

Also by Linda Weber, **FINDING UTOPIA** © 2023
First Trade Paperback Printing.
Published by BookBaby
https://store.bookbaby.com/book/finding-utopia
Second Trade Paperback Edition
Published by Amazon KDP

For my brothers *Gordon Charles Jones* and *Jeffrey Donald Jones*
And my son *Ryan Donald Ladd* and my nephew *Parker Jones*
...keepers of the stories and sharers of the memories.

And for *Becky Beckett, Kristina Weber, Margie Callahan*, and *Edie Booth* for yearning for, and demanding a sequel to *Finding Utopia*. And for your tears, enthusiasm, and support—it meant the world to me.
The *Sisters Writes Read and Critique Group* for your unvarnished critique and encouragement. You have made me a better writer.

Author's note: This book is set in the 1920s and 1930s and authentically reflects language and comments in use during that time but does not condone it.

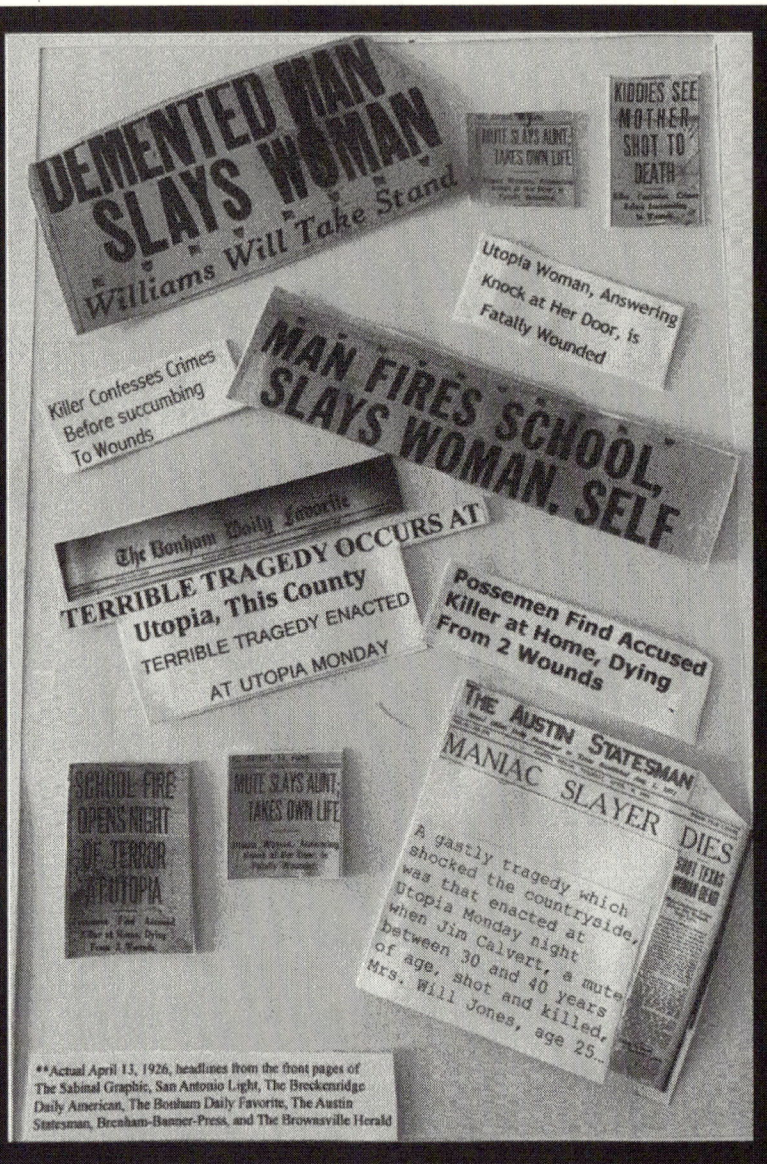

DEMENTED MAN SLAYS WOMAN
Williams Will Take Stand

MUTE SLAYS AUNT; TAKES OWN LIFE

KIDDIES SEE MOTHER SHOT TO DEATH

Utopia Woman, Answering Knock at Her Door, is Fatally Wounded

Killer Confesses Crimes Before succumbing To Wounds

MAN FIRES SCHOOL, SLAYS WOMAN, SELF

The Bonham Daily Favorite

TERRIBLE TRAGEDY OCCURS AT Utopia, This County

TERRIBLE TRAGEDY ENACTED AT UTOPIA MONDAY

Possemen Find Accused Killer at Home, Dying From 2 Wounds

SCHOOL FIRE OPENS NIGHT OF TERROR AT UTOPIA

MUTE SLAYS AUNT; TAKES OWN LIFE

THE AUSTIN STATESMAN
MANIAC SLAYER DIES
SHOT TEXAS WOMAN DEAD

A gastly tragedy which shocked the countryside, was that enacted at Utopia Monday night when Jim Calvert, a mute between 30 and 40 years of age, shot and killed Mrs. Will Jones, age 25...

**Actual April 13, 1926, headlines from the front pages of The Sabinal Graphic, San Antonio Light, The Breckenridge Daily American, The Bonham Daily Favorite, The Austin Statesman, Brenham-Banner-Press, and The Brownsville Herald

April 13, 1926   *   Crime Board**

PART ONE

TEXAS-ARIZONA

1926-1930

MAIZELLE CLARK
JONES
AUG. 17, 1902
APRIL 12, 1926

CHAPTER ONE
Maizelle

My death was unexpected—but not entirely unwelcome. The dark cloud of Jimmy Calvert had loomed over me for four long years. Now I was free of the fear and dread I faced daily.

It was difficult watching Will suffer and struggle with my loss. There were so many decisions I wanted to help with, but of course, that wasn't possible. In all those terrible days after I died, I tried to get through to him in every way I knew how. He was so numb from whiskey he couldn't feel me. He couldn't hear me. He couldn't see me. I only penetrated the fog once—the day he visited me at Jones Cemetery.

This altered state of being was new to me. I was at a loss to know what to do. I tried to hold him, but he slipped right through my arms. I spoke to him, but he thought it was someone else. When I asked him to promise to care for my babies, he begged me to show myself. That's how I knew he heard me, but I didn't know how to make myself visible. I made him promise, and he did. I said I had to go, and he protested and pleaded with me to stay.

At my graveside, I watched him stand and brush the dirt off his knees. The whiff of fresh soil surprised me. He looked so sad and lost. How could I leave him? How could I leave Charles and Aaron and W.E.? What would poor little near-blind Lynch do without me to watch after him? If I chose to go, my beautiful curly-headed Maisie would be cast adrift without a mother, much as I had been. No, leaving was not an option.

Drifting in this space above the world, I was as much a part of it as if I'd never left, and time meant nothing to me. My inclinations as a wife and mother were as strong as if I were beside my husband and children, yet I couldn't act on them. I saw and heard everything Will experienced but could do nothing to help or change the situation. Learning to navigate in this new state would take practice. It surprised me that I could smell, think, and see. I still had feelings, and I also knew everyone else's feelings. But I had no idea what physical actions were possible. I heard Will's thoughts and experienced the same emotions as him. He promised, and I trusted him to love and care for our children no matter what.

CHAPTER TWO

Will drove away from the cemetery and made his way to the Uptons', where his cousin, Bobby, and his wife, Emma, cared for W.E. Bobby had explained to Will that Emma had taken our second son because our boys were close of an age. Will's aunt Elizabeth took the two younger boys, Aaron and Lynch, because they weren't as rambunctious. The arrangement made me happy, but I was distressed that Charles and Maisie were not with the rest of the brood. I knew baby Maisie would be safe and loved by my sister-in-law, Eula. And my sister, Julia, adored Charles. I loved both those women with my whole heart, and under the circumstances, it was the right thing to do since neither had children of their own and would offer unconditional love to my first and last born.

I watched the reunion as W.E. raced out of Emma's house and leaped from the porch into Will's arms. He climbed him like a raccoon going up a tree and buried his sweet face in his daddy's shoulder, sobbing like nothing I'd ever heard.

"There now, big guy," Will said, "what's the trouble?"

"I didn't think you would come back," our six-year-old sobbed.

"'Course I was comin' back," Will said. "I just needed a little time to get used to missin' your ma." His voice rose, and I saw W.E. pull back to see if his daddy was crying.

Little W.E. reached up and brushed a tear away from Will's cheek with a tenderness that wrenched my heart. "It's okay to cry, Pa. Emma said so."

Will let our son slide down his bony frame and patted him on the head once he settled on the ground. "I hope so, son, 'cause I been doin' quite a bit of that lately."

"Can we go get Aaron and Lyn? I miss them, and I miss Maisie and Charles." He raised hopeful blue eyes and searched Will's face.

"Soon as I get your things and tell Emma I'm here for you. I'll have us all back under one roof again before you can say, 'Don't you do it.'"

"Why would I say that? I want you to do it."

"It's just an expression, Dubbya'E, never mind." He took our son's hand and walked to the house.

I felt the goodbye hug Emma gave W.E. with every fiber of my being. I would have given anything to be delivering that hug myself.

"You behave now, ya hear?" she said, stepping back and holding his thin shoulders in a firm grip. "You mind your pa and help him with your brothers. I don't want any reports comin' back that you quarreled with either of them. You're the big boy now, Dubbya'E, and you need to show your pa."

"Aunt Emma, is it still okay to cry when I'm missin' Mama?"

"Probably not. Your mama's gone to heaven now and cryin' over her isn't goin' to bring her back. Your daddy needs you to be strong for the young 'uns. If you want to cry, wait until they're asleep and do it into your pillow, okay?"

My towheaded little man puffed out his chest and gulped back tears as he slipped out of Emma's grasp. Oh, how my heart ached for him. If only I could make him feel or see me, just this once.

The second reunion of Will and our children was as heart-wrenching as the first. Aaron clutched Will's pant leg and cried, "I want Mama. Where's Mama?"

Will's jaw clenched, and he worked it like he was going to grind his teeth off. I saw he was on the verge of crumbling—something he couldn't allow himself to do.

Aaron stared at him and wailed. Will extracted him from his pant leg and turned him toward the porch, where Elizabeth waited with three-year-old Lynch on her hip.

"Let's go find your brother," he said, patting our four-year-old on the head as he steered him along with his other hand.

I watched in horror as Lynch lurched toward Will with his skinny arms outstretched, and Elizabeth lost her grip on him. I tried to stop his plunge, but I couldn't.

Will surged forward and caught my baby before he tumbled to the ground. He held our son close to his chest and patted him on the back. "There, there, Lyn," he said, "I've got you now."

Oh, how I loved him in that moment. I knew I could trust him.

"Mama," Lynch said, pulling back from Will's body. "Mama."

His demand was so clear. Will closed his eyes and pursed his mouth. I felt his hurt. How would he ever deal with my loss as long as he had these youngsters demanding my presence?

"Mama's gone, son. We all have to get used to the fact that she isn't comin' back."

"Bad man," Aaron piped up. "The bad man shot her."

"That's right, Aaron," Will said. "The bad man shot Mama, and that's why she can't be with us anymore."

Will's aunt Elizabeth stepped off the porch and reached for him. He sidestepped her advance and bent over to let Lynch down. Their eyes met, and he gave a little shake of his head. He wasn't in any condition to be consoled. "Sorry," he muttered, "not now."

Elizabeth put on a warm smile and said, "Let's go inside and gather their belongings—that is, if you're planning to take them with you."

"Yeah. I am. Dubbya'E's in the car. We have the dog and Charles's cat, and I'm headin' for San Antonio to get him and Maisie."

"What then?" she asked. "Are you planning to stay in San Antone or go to Del Rio to your folks?"

"Can't say as I know yet. If Charles wants to come with us, I'll take him, but if Eula wants to keep Maisie and raise her, I might let her do that. I think a girl needs a mother."

"And a father," Elizabeth said under her breath.

CHAPTER THREE

The car jiggled along the rutted highway to San Antonio, which wasn't much improved since the night Will and I eloped nine years ago in Bobby's Packard. The boys were unusually subdued as Will guided the car toward whatever would be their new life. I didn't know what he had planned, and I could tell from his face he didn't either. I knew I should leave—let Will take the boys, find Maisie and Charles, and gather them together again—but I couldn't make myself go. I drifted along with them, occasionally reaching out to touch the boys' faces, only to have them brush my hand away like they were being tickled with a feather. Once, Aaron reached over and smacked Lynch, saying, "Stop, Lyn. Stop ticklin' me!" Poor little Lynch cried and protested his innocence, and Aaron shouted, "If it ain't you, who is it?"

"Don't say 'ain't,'" Will admonished from the driver's seat.

"Sorry," Aaron mumbled. "He keeps ticklin' my neck and touchin' my hair."

"Do not," Lynch said. "Daddy, can I ride up front?"

"No, Lyn, you stay where you are until we get to San Antone. It's safer back there. And keep your hands to yourself, hear?"

Lynch leaned over the front seat and waved his little hands in Will's face to show him he wasn't guilty. I knew then I needed to leave the boys be, at least while they were riding in the car and Will was trying to get them there in one piece.

I worried about what awaited them when they arrived in San Antonio. I knew Julia and Eula were taking good care of Charles and Maisie, but what would happen when they saw their pa and their brothers? If Will tried to take them back, would it upset them more than if he left them where they were?

Will drove to Julia and Sam's house first. He had never been there but followed the directions she'd left with Elizabeth when she took Charles home after my funeral.

Sam saw them drive up and met him at the curb. He pulled Will aside as soon as he exited the car. "Good to see you, Will. I should warn you that Charles is having a difficult time accepting what happened to his mother. I hope you don't plan to uproot him again. Julia's taken to the mothering role like it was second nature. I do hope you will consider her feelings."

Pain and shock shifted from Will's forehead to his eyes and his cheeks before it settled in his jaw. He looked like he'd been hit between the eyes with a rock. He did that thing he does when he's upset. He clenched and unclenched his jaw multiple times in a matter of seconds. The muscles in his face tightened, and his forehead wrinkled. His body stiffened, and I could see he was desperate to hold back tears. If only I could have held him—just for a moment—until the pain passed.

Will gave a stiff nod to Sam, put his fedora on, and pulled it low over his brow.

"Dubbya'E, take the dog for a walk around the house. Aaron and Lyn, straighten yourselves up. It's time to visit your aunt Julia and see Charles."

The younger boys scrambled out of the car as soon as Will opened the door. Lynch called, "Char-es, Char-es." Aaron ran for the front door like the devil was on his tail.

Julia opened the door and her arms to gather my babies to her breast. They clung to her like possums on a jill. When she finally extracted herself and herded them inside, she said, "Where's Dubbya'E?"

Aaron said, "He's walking Barfy."

"Who's Barfy?" she asked.

"Our daaawwwg," Aaron said, in a that-was-a-stupid-question tone. "Charles's cat is in a box in the car."

"Oh my," Julia said under her breath, "I'd forgotten Charles had a cat."

"Where is he?" Aaron asked, looking hopefully at his aunt.

"Char-es, Char-es," Lynch said.

"In his room," Julia said. "Charles hasn't been feeling well, so don't expect him to play with you."

"What's wrong with him?" Aaron asked.

"It's hard to say. He misses your mama an awful lot."

"I miss Mama too. A bad man shot her, and Daddy says she's watching us from heaven now."

"Does he? That's comforting. I hope you can help Charles accept that she's still watching over you from heaven. I think it will do him good to see you boys. He's upstairs resting. Let's tiptoe so we don't scare him."

Will and Sam waited for W.E. to return with the dog before they went inside.

As Julia put her foot on the first step, Will and W.E. came up behind her. "Julia, I need to see my boy."

She jumped and stumbled backward, bumping into W.E. "Will! You startled me. I was taking Aaron and Lynch upstairs to Charles. He isn't feeling well. He's resting."

"What's the matter with him?"

"I think they call it melancholy, Will. He's grieving the loss of his mother. Let me take the boys up first. Once they've had a chance to see him, I'll bring them down, and you can spend some time alone with him."

"Julia," Will said more sternly than necessary, " I need my boy. I want him to come with us."

"Can we talk about this later? The boys are excited and want to go up to him now."

"He's my son, Julia. You took him without asking me, and now you want to keep me from him?"

"I took him because he wanted to come. As I recall, you were too incapacitated by alcohol to object or give permission. Now, let me take the boys upstairs. I'll come back for you in a jiffy." With that, my sister launched herself at the stairway, dragging Aaron with one hand and Lynch with the other. "Come on, Dubbya'E," she shot over her shoulder, "you might as well come now, too."

W.E. turned pleading eyes on Will. "Can I, Pa?"

"Yeah. Go. Tell Charles I'll be up to get him shortly."

Julia grimaced, and her shoulders tensed. I suspected this wasn't going to go well. Will wanted his boys together again, wherever that ended up being. Julia adored Charles, and since she didn't appear to be starting a family with Sam, I felt certain she would press to keep him. I was torn. Charles was the most fragile and sensitive of our five children, but he was also the mediator and the glue that held fights at bay and brotherhood strong.

Will spun on his heel and headed for the parlor, where Sam stood by the fireplace smoking a cigar. "You got any whiskey?"

Sam turned toward the voice. "Whiskey? Wouldn't you rather have a cigar? Seems early in the day to be starting on the whiskey."

"I need a drink," Will said.

I was crushed. I had hoped all those weeks he stayed drunk after I died had it out of his system.

"Julia wants very much to keep Charles, Will, and raise him here in San Antonio. He clings to her. When he has nightmares she comforts him as she would her own. I hope you won't make any rash decisions, considering the emotional state you're in." Then he moved to a sideboard and pulled out a bottle of whiskey.

Will clenched his jaw in that way he has where he slides it back and forth like he's chewing on a gristly cut of meat. "I don't need any lectures from you about what I need to do with my boys."

Sam handed him a short fat glass with two fingers of Southern Comfort.

He tossed the liquid back in a single gulp, set the glass down hard on the sideboard, and said, "I'd appreciate a refill."

"Sorry, Will, that would be against my better judgment." Sam stared his brother-in-law square in the eye. "Prohibition is still alive and well here, and whiskey's hard to come by. I've been as generous with you as I care to be."

I noticed how Will bristled. He used drink to relax. He had consumed all he had stashed at home and realized it wouldn't be easy to replace. The tension between Sam and Will made me dread the scene I imagined would unfold when Julia returned from alerting Charles that his pa was here. I didn't have long to wait. A plaintive voice rose from behind Will.

"Daddy?"

Will whirled and reached for Charles with both arms.

I watched with joy as father and son clung to each other like moss on a rock.

"I missed you, son. Your brothers missed you, too. You can come with us now."

Charles pulled back from Will's arms. "I don't want to leave Aunt Julia," he whispered, his eyes cast down. "She smells like Mama."

He sounded younger than his eight years. I'm not sure Will even realized he had missed Charles's eighth birthday during this time of grieving.

"I know you miss her, son. We all miss your mama." Tears rimmed Will's eyes. He turned so Charles wouldn't notice. "I'm goin' to be both ma and pa to you now, and I'll need your help with your brothers."

"Please, Daddy, don't make me leave. Why can't all of us stay here?"

"I don't expect Aunt Julia and Uncle Sam have room for five houseguests. Besides, they've done enough by taking you until I could come."

"Are we going back to Utopia? Back to our house?"

He sounded frightened—timid in a way I wasn't used to hearing from Charles.

"I don't want to go back. The man might come and hurt me."

"He won't come hurt you, Charles. They caught him. He's dead. But we aren't going back. I thought I'd take you boys and head down to Del Rio to my ma and pa's place. I think you'd like it there. They tell me there are lots of wide, open spaces to run and play. You can swim in a big river called the Rio Grande. You could see Aunt Minerva again and Granpappy and Granmama."

"I don't know them, Daddy. I want to stay with Aunt Julia."

"Of course, you know them. We lived with them when you were born."

"I don't remember." His chin quivered, and his eyes glistened.

Julia came into the room, the other three boys in tow. They all talked at once, pleading with Will to let them stay with Aunt Julia and Uncle Sam.

"Please, Daddy," W.E. said. "Charles likes it here. He says we should stay with Aunt Julia."

Will and Julia locked eyes. I must say, my sister appeared a little frantic. She desperately wanted Charles, but she had no intention of taking on any of my other offspring.

Will fluctuated between looking angry and confused. I knew he didn't have a clue what to do. If he had talked to his folks about staying with them in Del Rio, I missed the conversation. He'd never seen their house. He had no idea if there was enough room for them. His mother's arthritis had not improved with the move to the Gulf—that much I'd gotten from their letters. How could she be expected to take on a brood of this size when she struggled to walk from room to room? His expression told me all the questions, doubts, and overwhelming thoughts bounced willy-nilly through his head.

"Julia," he said, "I appreciate you takin' such good care of Charles until I got myself together, but I promised Maidee on her grave I would care for the kids. I can't do that if they aren't together. There's no chance I'll just leave my son with you and walk off. She'd come back and haunt me for sure."

Aaron said, "Daddy, what's 'haunt' mean?"

"Never mind, Aaron. I'll tell you another time. Right now, I need to talk to Aunt Julia and Uncle Sam, and I need you boys to go outside and wait for me. Get in the car if you want, and don't go where I can't see you. We'll be goin' to get Maisie in a little while."

Once the boys were outside, Will slumped into a chair, and Sam handed him another glass of whiskey. He drank it without even saying thank you.

I hated this. I hated it when Will drank whiskey, and I hated that he wasn't able to manage my death without it. Everything about this felt wrong. It was wrong of Julia and Sam to have taken Charles in the first place. It was wrong of Will to expect my sister to give up the one real connection with me she had left. And it was wrong of Sam to ply Will with alcohol.

"Will," Julia said, "Charles is struggling with terrible nightmares. He wakes up screaming at all hours. I don't think putting him through another change would be advisable when you're not sure it will be permanent. Let him stay with us until you're settled. We've enrolled him in school, and I'm no longer working at the bank, so I'm here when he comes home. He's lost without his mother."

"Don't you think we're all lost without her?" Will spoke sharply. "I need him to help me with the other kids."

"He can't, Will. He was the only one old enough to be sent for help. He thinks he failed her. He thinks it's his fault she died."

"It's not his fault. Your father turned him away when he came for help. He shut the door in his face. If anybody's to blame, it's Doc Clark."

"Papa's a broken man over this, Will. I doubt very much if blaming him for her death will do anyone any good. It wouldn't have changed the outcome if he had come when Charles asked. I'm told she was shot at close range and was barely able to say who had done it. There's no hospital in Utopia. She couldn't have been transported for five hours in a car to San Antonio. She'd have bled to death no matter who came to help. Maybe if you'd been home…"

Will jumped to his feet. "You think I don't turn that over in my mind twenty-four hours a day? It was me he was after, not her. If I'd been home, I'd be the one dead, not Maidee. At least then these kids would have a mother." He slumped back onto the chair and reached for the whiskey glass. Finding it empty, he looked at Sam.

Sam shook his head. "Sorry, Will. Those children need you in full possession of your wits, and another glass of hooch won't accomplish that."

"Will, please stay with us tonight. Let the boys spend some time together before you take them off to God knows where," Julia said.

"Where would we all sleep? Your house looks roomy enough for you and Sam and Charles. I can't see where you'd put three more kids and a grown man."

"I have it all worked out. You're tired from such a long drive, and a good night's rest should come as a welcome relief. If you go for Maisie tonight, you won't have anywhere to take her. She's safe where she is. Leave her be for now. We can discuss it in the morning."

"I'm not givin' up my boy, Julia. Charles belongs with his brothers. I'll stay one night, but we're leavin' first thing in the morning. No amount of discussin' is goin' to change my mind." Will stood and went to call the boys inside.

Sam turned to Julia and said, "I hope you know what you're doing. Where do you intend to put this brood of ruffians?"

"They aren't ruffians, Sam; they're my nephews. It's the least I can do to honor my sister's memory. I have a plan. Will can sleep in the parlor on the chaise, Charles and Lynch can sleep side by side at the top of the bed, and Dubbya'E and Aaron can sleep the same at the foot. It isn't like they haven't slept several to a bed in their own home."

I'd never heard Julia sound more self-assured than she did at that moment. Sam furrowed his brow and pulled his lips tight. Propriety obviously mattered a great deal more to him than to my sister. I wanted to reach out and touch her, thank her for accepting my little ruffians, as Sam called them. Will would make good on his promise to take all four of the boys and leave in the morning, of that I was certain. It would break Julia's heart. She thought she was giving comfort to Charles in his grief, but in truth, he gave her comfort in equal measure.

CHAPTER FOUR

Morning broke, and sunlight spilled into the room where Will spent a fitful night. He rubbed his eyes, made note of his blinding headache, and rolled off the narrow chaise onto the rug with a thud. The fall brought him to his senses, and he struggled to his feet as the looming hall clock struck six.

"Sweet Jesus," he muttered under his breath, "I need a drink."

I was relieved to know none was available. Under cover of night, Sam removed the liquor bottle from the sideboard and tucked it into a slipper inside his wardrobe. I realized my relief would be short-lived as my husband rummaged through the cabinet in search of anything to slake his thirst. His temples throbbed, and his hands trembled as he pulled things from the cabinet without coming up with the one thing he wanted. I felt certain he would find an excuse to quickly move on from Julia and Sam's hospitality, if for no other reason than to locate another source of drink.

Julia rustled about upstairs, and I knew she and Sam would soon emerge to try and persuade Will to let them keep Charles. They discussed their plan after they went to bed last night, and I can't say I entirely disagreed with their logic.

Will had no visible means of support. He had no place to live and no place suitable to raise five children. I thought it unlikely Eula and Fred Brown would take them all under their roof. The house did have three bedrooms, including the one in which Will and I first made love, but Eula had outdone herself to create a girlish space for Maisie in that room, and the other four, plus Will, couldn't possibly stay together in the spare room.

Will's sister, Edelene, was a newlywed and lived in a cramped little adobe house just outside San Antonio with barely enough room to turn around. Her place was definitely out of the question.

Julia and Sam had an indoor toilet off the kitchen, and Will used it before he washed up. He stared at the water as it swirled in the bowl before emptying, and I thought he would toss his stomach. We were both relieved when he managed to hold it down until he got his hands and face washed at the kitchen sink. He patted dry with his shirttail.

Julia walked in as he finished tucking his damp shirt into his trousers and pulling his braces onto his shoulders. "Mornin'," he said.

"Good morning, Will," Julia said in a bright voice. I recognized that voice. It was the one she always used with Papa and Leila when she wanted something and was almost certain they would object. "Would you like a cup of coffee?" she asked.

"Yeah. Sure," Will said.

Julia bustled around the small room, heating the kettle of water on her newfangled electric stove. The contraption fascinated Will enough to distract him while Julia busied herself putting some biscuits onto a plate on the table in front of him. When the fresh coffee arrived, he was both grateful and pleased.

"Thank you," he said and met my sister's eyes.

Julia saw her opportunity and jumped in. "Will, Sam and I have discussed your situation, and we feel it would be in Charles's best interests to remain with us and finish the school year. Only two weeks remain. It would give you time to visit your folks and see what the situation is for you and the boys."

"I promised Maidee I'd keep the kids together."

"I'm sure Maidee would want what's best for the children, Will, regardless of what you may have promised."

"I don't know, Julia. I know he's close to you. Now more than ever, it seems."

"Oh, he is, Will, and I'm close to him. It's unlikely I'll have any of my own, and I've always thought of Charles as half mine."

When tears threatened, Will turned away and lowered his eyes. He struggled to know what was best. Charles was our firstborn. The one who cemented our union and brought us such joy and pleasure. Letting him go—even to Julia—would break Will's heart all over again.

But a part of him wanted to let Charles go. He didn't want Charles to see him grieving, and he sure didn't want Charles to see him drinking like a fish. The desire for alcohol was strong in Will. It pulled on him in a way nothing but my presence ever did. Without me to temper his desire, the urge had grown stronger and stronger until his will to resist was gone.

He wanted to keep his promise to me, but the more he struggled, the more I wanted to say, 'let him go, my love. Let Julia be his mother. She's had a lot of experience raising children. She all but single-handedly raised Bowen and me after Mama died. She minded Jamie and helped Leila with her two after Papa remarried. If she wants him, let him go.' I felt so helpless. I didn't know how to communicate with him in this new state.

"No. I can't do it. At least I can't decide now. I need to talk to Charles, man to man. And I need to see my daughter and talk to Fred and Eula. They've always been my port in a storm, and I've never been in a worse storm than this."

"I understand, Will. But you need to remember that talking to Charles 'man to man,' as you say, will only make things worse. He already thinks he failed his mother. If he shows his grief in front of you, he will think he has failed your expectations as well. Give me these two weeks until school is out, then decide."

"I don't suppose you'd take Dubbya'E too? If Charles had a brother with him, I'd be a lot more comfortable with the idea."

"I can't. Sam and I have discussed that possibility, but it isn't practical. Charles is such an easy child, and Dubbya'E, well, he's a bigger handful than I think I'm prepared to inflict on my husband. Sam isn't a young man. He's agreed to take on Charles, but he's only willing to be a father to one."

"Could we get the boys up, please, so I can be on my way? I'll need some time alone with Charles to be sure this is what he wants. He might have changed his mind after seeing his brothers again."

Julia scrambled to her feet with a mile-wide smile on her face. It dawned on her at that moment that she had won, if not the war, then at least the skirmish. She rushed to the stairway and climbed with more determination than she'd had in a long time.

Four sleepy pajama-clad youngsters shuffled into Julia's tidy kitchen, rubbing the night sand out of their eyes. I longed for my routine morning hugs from each of them, something I knew I would never have again. Will glanced up from his coffee as Aaron and Lynch each sidled up to him and laid their blond heads on his thighs. Charles and W.E. pressed against his sides. He lifted his right arm and pulled W.E. close while he stroked Lynch's hair. Charles put his arm around Aaron and patted his back.

"Charles, we need to have a grown-up talk. Let Aunt Julia get breakfast for your brothers while we go in the other room. We can eat after they're finished."

Charles rubbed his cheek against Will's arm and nodded his head. He appeared anxious, and his eyes told me he dreaded what was coming.

Will lifted the youngest boys off his legs and gave W. E a gentle shove toward a chair. When he stood, he put his arm across Charles's shoulders and guided him out of the room. "Charles, I need to hear something straight from your heart. Your aunt Julia wants you to stay here and finish the school year. Is that what you want?"

Charles nodded his head but wouldn't lift his eyes to Will. His little heart was torn in two, deciding between his pa and his brothers and the comfort of my sister's arms. I wanted to tell him it was okay—I wanted to tell both of them it was okay. My sister placed a high premium on education, and if Charles stayed with her, he'd be assured of top schools and proper learning.

Will sat in a rather fussy chair in Julia's parlor. The sight of him trying not to slide off the edge of the embroidered satin cushion made me laugh. I think he heard me because he squirmed and searched the room with his eyes. He pulled Charles over in front of him so he could look him in the eye. "Son, I promised your ma I'd take care of you. I don't want to break a promise, and I don't want to make you do something you don't want to do. Understand?"

"Yes, Pa. But Aunt Julia takes good care of me, and she feels like Ma. I don't think Ma would mind if I stayed here."

"Well, I'll agree to let you stay until school's out, but I want you to promise me that when I come back for you, you won't give me any back talk about comin'."

A grin split Charles's face, and his eyes brightened like a new penny. "I promise, Pa. No back talk." His thin shoulders squared, and his chin jutted forward. He looked so relieved I wanted to shield Will from his joy. He had chosen, and the realization would stick in Will's craw like an unchewed nut.

"Well, then, it's decided. I'll come back for you as soon as I find a job and a decent place to live so we can all be together again."

There was no mention of the end of the school year, and my mother's intuition told me this would be a permanent arrangement. That only left the matter of Charles's cat. Will went to the car and brought the box into the house.

"What's that?" Julia asked.

"Charles's cat. You take my boy; you take his cat."

CHAPTER FIVE

Will had to pry Aaron's hands off the door jamb to put him into the car. He kicked, he bellowed "No," and he cried for Charles with everything his little being could muster.

W.E. put his arms around Aaron and did his best to soothe the tantrum. "It's okay, I'll be your big brother now," he said, sounding so grown-up.

"I want Charles!" Aaron screamed at him.

"It's only for a little while," Will said, the frustration showing in his furrowed brow and abrupt speech. "We have to let Charles finish school before we take him with us."

My boy wasn't having it. He pitched himself onto the floorboards and sobbed with a broken heart. I understood that his grief extended far beyond his desire to have his older brother close at hand. His grief was over losing me. This was a convenient moment to express it without crying for me when the adults around him had told him crying wouldn't bring me back. I suspected I would be in for many such occasions in the coming days and weeks if I chose to stay in this state of suspension. I tried, but I couldn't make myself go.

Will parked the Lizzie in front of Eula and Fred's house, and if I still had a human heart, I'm sure it would have skipped a beat. Seeing the house brought a flood of memories. I remembered the first time Will and I made love in the bedroom at the top of the stairs. I remembered

Will's sister teaching me how to cook breakfast and helping me learn my way around the kitchen so I wouldn't look a fool when Will and I set up housekeeping. I was still a week away from my fifteenth birthday. I have more sympathy for Papa now. I don't think he should have disowned me and shunned his grandchildren, but fourteen *was* young to run off and get married.

Fred came outside to greet Will and the boys. Eula stood on the porch with my darling Maisie in her arms.

When Maisie spied Will, she leaned toward him and stretched her chubby little arms to him. He took the sidewalk in two long strides and scooped her away from his sister and into his heart. Tears filled his eyes as he kissed her sweet face. His cheeks colored, and he glanced up embarrassed.

The boys gathered around Will, tugging on his pant legs and shirtsleeves, trying to squeeze in a hug on their baby sister. Maisie was overwhelmed by the sudden barrage of attention. She turned her face away and began crying.

Eula rushed down the steps and reached for her. My little girl snuggled her face into Eula's generous bosom as if she were inhaling the fragrance of a fresh rose.

Once the commotion subsided, Fred stepped up and pumped Will's hand. "Good to see ya, son," he said. "Glad to see ya made it down in one piece. Come on in. Come on in. Let's get some cake in these young 'uns. How'd ya like that, boys?"

The mention of cake did the trick. All three boys ran up the steps and into the house. Eula reached her free arm around Will and pulled him into an awkward embrace, pressing Maisie between them. The baby squirmed and fussed, and Will stepped back to let his older sister carry her inside.

I dreaded what would come next: the awkward silence as both Eula and Will tried to worry out how to approach my daughter's care. I didn't have long to wait, and it went more smoothly than Charles's situation at Julia's.

Eula put Maisie in her high chair and gave her cake to occupy her. Then she suggested to Will that he join her in the parlor.

The boys were entertained watching their baby sister pluck cake crumbs off her tray with fat little fingers and direct them into her mouth.

They took turns "helping" her and doubled over with laughter at her ineptitude before they settled on putting cake into their own mouths.

Will and Eula sat in the exact chairs she and I sat in the day she asked me to tell her all about myself. It brought another memory to the surface, and a wave of love swept through me, remembering the compassion she showed that day as I told her about my mother dying and Papa marrying Leila. These sudden feelings of love and sadness that keep invading me are disconcerting. How can I leave when I feel so connected to my old life?

Eula said, "Will, you might as well be my son. I practically raised you because Ma kept having babies faster than corn grows. And I loved Maizelle like my own daughter. Now circumstances have placed another baby in my lap, and I hope you realize it's the Lord's hand in this."

Will looked down, and again, tears welled. He shook his head side to side like he was saying no.

"Bless your heart. I'd never ask you to do something you didn't want to do. I understand that you love this little girl more than life itself, but if you let us keep her and raise her, she will be raised to know you are her father. She'll grow up around people who love you, and she will always know you love her."

Will hunched over and shook his head as teardrops plopped onto his pant legs. When he tried to speak, nothing came forth but a squeak.

Eula rose and put her hands on his back and shoulders. She patted him as if he were a small child. "I can't possibly know what you're going through," she said, "but I think you need time to get your feet under you again, and taking this baby would not be a good idea. She needs a mother, Will. I can give her that. You take the boys and go visit Ma and Pa. Take some time to decide what's best for all of you. I gather you left Charles with Julia and Sam. That must have been very difficult."

Will's shoulders heaved at the mention of Charles's name. Eula patted him again and returned to the chair opposite her younger brother.

Will dug his handkerchief out of his pocket and blew his nose. He continued to shake his head side to side. "I don't know what to do," he said. "I couldn't stay in Utopia without her, sis. She was everything to me. Everything."

"I know, honey, I know."

"She made me promise I'd take care of her babies."

"And you will." Eula spoke softly. "You will take care of them by doing what's right, and it might not be the same for each. If it helps, I think letting Julia and Sam raise Charles would be the best thing in the world for him. He's such a sensitive boy and has lived through something unthinkable for a child his age. He knows his aunt Julia better than he knows anyone on our side. I think you've made a wise choice."

"I didn't choose, he did."

"All the better," Eula said. "If he finds comfort being with her, it's the best place for him. Taking him away now would be cruel. You can't give him his mother back, but Julia is at least a familiar face."

"He told me she smelled like Maizelle." Will shook his head and swiped at his eyes. "I couldn't take him after he said that."

"Well, I'm sure I don't smell like Maizelle," Eula said with a shaky smile, "but I have soft bosoms, and Maisie likes to nestle into them."

A chuckle burbled up in Will's throat, and he raised his eyes. "I remember I liked to nestle into them too," he said with a wan smile. "Still do."

W.E. burst into the room, calling Will's name. "Pa, Pa," he shouted, "can we take Barfy for a walk?"

Startled out of the moment, Will stood and stuffed his handkerchief deep into his pocket as if holding it would be a giveaway that he'd been crying. "Slow down, Dubbya'E, slow down. This here's a city. Do you have a rope you can tie around his neck so's he won't run off?"

"Uncle Fred said he'd find us one. We won't get lost, Daddy, promise."

There it was again—W.E. used "Pa" to get his attention and then lapsed back to the childish name, "Daddy," to cement the deal. We wanted all the boys to call Will "Daddy" until they started school. So far, Charles and W.E. are the only two to graduate to the new form, and W.E. has not yet made a total transition. I liked hearing him call Will "Daddy." It seemed right somehow. There would be many years to call Will "Pa," but the years for Daddy were slipping past.

One thing was certain in my mind after Will's conversation with Eula. Charles would remain with Julia and Sam, and Maisie would stay with the Browns. I wasn't sure where Will and the boys would go, and I don't think he was either. But if they weren't all going to be in the same place, he would need my help. I would need to watch over them from great distances apart. It wouldn't be easy, but it would be necessary.

CHAPTER SIX

Will and the boys stayed with the Browns for three days. Fred didn't drink, so Will was anxious to find a watering hole where he could slake his thirst. The urge was getting stronger each day. He was agitated and tense. His hands quivered when he reached for things. When he was sleeping, I wiped his brow with my empty hand. I sang to him and told him how much I missed being with him. I tried my best to keep him at peace so he wouldn't give in to the pull of whiskey.

He let Eula put her arms around him during the day, and he cried a lot of tears onto her shoulder. I think the crying helped him. If he got over that part, he might be able to make a decent plan for his future and that of our boys. As it was, his brain was muddled with thoughts about where to get whiskey and where to go.

I figured in the end he would go to his folks in Del Rio. It seems people always go home in times of trouble. At least his folks would let him in. When I had trouble, my pa shut the door in my face. He did the same to poor Charles, and now my son thinks he failed me. He didn't. His grandfather did.

The car was loaded, and goodbyes were shared all around. Will herded our three boys into the backseat, then changed his mind and put Aaron up front. Aaron wasn't as distraught leaving his sister with Eula as he was leaving Charles with Julia, but he *was* gearing up for a tantrum if he didn't get to sit up front. Will wasn't taking any chances. It wouldn't surprise me if this competition between the boys lasted a lifetime.

Prohibition was a saving grace for me. Will had been opposed to the idea, but I welcomed it. Now, I was more grateful than ever. Will had polished off his entire homemade supply of moonshine in the weeks following my death. Now, he was stymied by a lack of outlets to replenish it. I suspected he thought his pa would have an ample stock laid up, and I was right. That's where he headed.

Will and the boys said their goodbyes to Eula and Fred. He held Maisie so tightly and for so long that she squirmed, whimpered, and reached for Eula to rescue her. The expression on his face and the set of his jaw told me this goodbye was the most difficult he'd ever given. Maisie was a piece of me, right down to her name. When he let her go, he would be letting go of me. The tears in his eyes and the turned-down mouth told me his heart was breaking. He steeled himself for the parting as he handed our plump little daughter to his sister for safekeeping.

The boys bounced in the backseat, excited about this unexpected journey to see the grandparents only Charles had met. I hoped the warm, moist climate of the Gulf Coast had worked magic on Mama Sarah's arthritis so she would be able to take my boys under her capable wing. I felt unsettled about how it would go.

Will and his pa had patched up their tumultuous relationship during the time we spent with them as newlyweds in the homestead house. Still, I worried that Papa Irvin would resort to his old ways of discipline, and Will would not stand for it. If Mama Sarah wasn't a whole lot stronger now than when she was raising her own, she wouldn't be able to stop him. This part of Will's promise to "take care of my babies" was not open for discussion. He promised me he would never strike one of our children—I expected him to extend that promise to his pa.

The drive to Del Rio was more than double the distance from Utopia to San Antonio. It was unlikely Will and the boys could make the trip in a single day. Not that Will wouldn't try, of that much I was sure. I was worried he wouldn't be mindful of the boys' hunger and need to use a privy or stretch their legs. We had never taken a trip of such a distance by automobile.

The train had always been the transportation of choice when anyone needed to go far. I'll admit I was more than a little curious as to how this journey would unfold. It was also the first time I felt torn; should I stay and watch over Charles and Maisie or continue with Will and the boys? I continued, because I needed to be certain the boys were safe, nurtured, and loved.

Will's ma, my mama Sarah, is one of the most loving women I've ever known. She seldom has a cross word for anyone, and she suffers her lot in life with a stoicism I admire. She bore ten children, of which my Will is number five. The three who remained at home when they left Utopia are now grown and gone. Even Minerva, who was ten when Charles was born, is married and on her own.

Mama Sarah finally had the time to enjoy a book or knit a sweater without the constant demands of children and a husband. Not that Will's pa had taken to doing for himself—that would have been an occurrence worthy of note—but looking after the needs of one other person is easier, no matter how you slice it. I prayed she would be up to the demands of three rambunctious little boys who needed more than just a bed to lie in and food in their stomachs. My boys needed the love and comfort of a mother, and Mama Sarah was the perfect person to give them what I no longer could.

Will drove as fast as the Lizzie would go. The boys were remarkably well-behaved for the first two hours. When he had to refuel, he made the mistake of letting the kids out of the car. They relieved themselves behind the building and then ran around the service stop like maniacs let out of a cage. They hooted, hollered, and begged for peanuts in a bag. Will caved in and bought the treats on the condition they would get back into the car and quit acting like hooligans. Will should have made them eat the proper lunch Eula packed for them before they got a treat, but he didn't. His common sense had flown out the window as they rolled down the highway toward the Gulf.

W.E. and Aaron got into another tussle over who got to ride in the front seat. W.E. shoved Aaron, and he toppled into the gravel, skinning his knees. He wailed and showed Will his bleeding knees as evidence he should ride in the front.

"No, Aaron, I'm going to put Dubbya'E up front with me where I can keep an eye on him," Will said.

"No, Daddy. He pushed me. It's not fair."

Will pulled his handkerchief out and spit on it to wipe the blood off Aaron's knees. "I know you don't think it's fair, but lots of things aren't fair. You just have to be a big boy about this."

Aaron stuck out his lower lip in a proper pout before he stomped to the car and crawled into the backseat. Lynch reached out and hugged his brother. "It's okay, Aaron, I won't push," my three-year-old soothed, melting my heart.

With not quite sixteen months between them, these two had an unusual bond. Aaron relaxed his jaw, and his lip went back where it belonged. Before long, they were humming down the highway again, the squabble forgotten.

Another hour passed without incident, and Will stopped for lunch in a grassy spot beside a stream. He unloaded Eula's full picnic basket, spread a coverlet on the ground, and told the boys to sit.

"Daddy," he heard, "Dubbya'E's goin' swimmin'. Can I go, too?"

Will lifted his head from the lunch preparations and stared at Aaron as if he couldn't quite understand what he'd said. His brow wrinkled, and his ears turned red when he realized W.E. was not on the blanket where he'd last seen him.

"Dubbya'E! Dubbya'E. You get back here." His head whipped back and forth, looking for our absent son. He lurched forward onto his knees and stood so fast it made him dizzy. When his head cleared, he ran toward the stream, shouting W.E.'s name.

"Help. Help." The cry was faint, but Will recognized the voice as he raced forward, stumbling on the uneven ground. When he reached the creek, he saw a head bobbing in the middle of the stream—first, it bobbed up, and then it disappeared. Will didn't even stop to take off his boots. He jumped into the fast-moving stream and lunged toward where he had seen W.E.'s blond head surface and disappear. He came up empty, took a deep breath, and dove again, frantic to find our son.

I was helpless, except to attempt to let Will know W.E. was fast moving downstream under the water. Something registered, and he turned and dove again. He disappeared for an eternity before breaking the surface, holding W.E. and scrabbling for the shore.

Swimming while carrying a child and wearing cowboy boots full of water was not easy. Will struggled against the swift current until he reached a place where his boot scraped against a rocky bottom. He planted both feet and held our son high over his head until he got him situated over his shoulder. The jostling made W.E. cough and spew water. I felt the relief that swept through Will as if I were in my own flesh and blood body.

"You okay, son?" he said, pounding W.E. on the back while trying to stay upright in the moving stream.

W.E. coughed again, and Will said, "Hold your head high. I'm goin' to make for the shore. I won't let go of you. You'll be okay. Hang on!" He took a hesitant step and found purchase on the stream bed. Another step, another solid footing. When he thought he was close enough to toss W.E. onto dry ground, he heaved him into the air and let him fly.

W.E. landed with a thud and began crying, "I want Mama."

"Well, you sure as hell weren't goin' to find her in the middle of a creek, now were ya?"

Will pulled himself up the bank and took our soaked, shaking boy into his arms. "You plannin' to pull any more stunts like that? Or are you ready to have a sandwich with your brothers?"

W.E. shook his head and then nodded. "I'm sorry, Pa," he said through his tears. "I slipped when I put my hand in to test the water."

"It's okay, big guy," Will comforted. "I've got ya now. Let's go eat before something else happens."

I was torn over whether to stay and hover over Aaron and Lynch during the excitement or help Will find W.E. I went to the creek with Will, and I'm glad I did. Aaron kept Lynch on the blanket and held on to him until Will returned. I burst with pride at how responsible Aaron was in the moment of panic and how gentle Will was with W.E. after he got over the shock of a near-drowning.

After they finished eating, Will put W.E. in the front seat and Aaron and Lynch in the back. This time, Aaron didn't fuss or complain, subdued after the shock of almost losing his big brother.

Will reached across the front seat and squeezed W.E.'s wet pant leg. W.E. slid his eyes over and met Will's. Will worked his jaw like he does when trying to hold back something important. The way he slips it back and forth sideways makes his ears wiggle. That always makes the boys laugh. A tentative smile tickled our wayward son's face, and Will squeezed his leg again. They didn't need any talking-to to know they'd had a close call.

Will had time to think on the long stretch of road that joined the Gulf Coast to San Antonio. He decided to leave the boys with Mama Sarah and head to Arizona to find work. The city of Tucson offered the best prospects for a mechanic. He'd make his way west, find a good job, locate a house near a school within walking distance, and bring them all together under one roof.

I thought it was a foolish plan. I wanted him to settle in San Antone and live where they could grow up with Maisie and Charles. He didn't know a single soul in Arizona. He was pulled by the reputation of Payson Dew Moonshine and its availability. It was much harder to find quality hooch in Texas, and Will clung to the notion he couldn't bear my loss without the comfort of whiskey.

The Lizzie ground to a halt in front of a small adobe house sitting alone on a dry patch of ground not far from the Rio Grande. A man with a strong arm might throw a stone from the front stoop and hit the middle of that wide river. Will took it in with a sinking feeling in his chest. How would his ma and pa be able to keep these energetic youngsters from falling in and drowning? If one of the boys fell into this river, there wouldn't be anyone to pull him out unless Will stayed. He didn't see how he could do that. He needed work, and it was clear there wouldn't be much work around these parts.

CHAPTER SEVEN

The little house looked bleak, sitting alone on parched ground. As the car came to a stop, Papa Irvin emerged from the open front door, bracing himself with a length of gnarled wood he'd fashioned into a walking stick. "Well, well. Look what the cat drug in," he said by way of welcome.

"Hey, Pa," Will said, lifting Lynch out of the backseat. "Is Ma here?"

"S'pose so," Papa Irvin said, "this here's her house."

"Mind if I bring the boys in to meet her?"

"'Course not. Let me give her a warnin', though. She might want to gussy up fer the occasion." Papa Irvin laughed and stomped his walking stick hard onto the ground. "I heared what happened to yer little woman a few weeks back. You gettin' on okay?"

"We're okay. Charles is with Maidee's sister in San Antone, and Maisie, our girl, is with Eula. I've got Dubbya'E, Aaron, and Lyn with me. I'm hopin' you can make room for us."

"We'll have to see about that. Yer ma ain't in any better health since the move than before. I'm not sure she'd be up to takin' on the raisin' of yer brood."

"Can we go inside? It's hot out here. The boys are tired after that long ride. Where's Ma?"

"In the kitchen. Come on. Place ain't much to look at, but it suits us."

"Daddy, he said 'ain't,'" Aaron piped up, tugging on Will's shirtsleeve.

"Shush, Aaron. Your granpapa can say whatever he wants. It's just you can't say 'ain't.'"

"Why?" Aaron asked. "Why can he say it, and I can't?"

"Just because," Will said. "Now be quiet and come meet your granmama."

Papa Irvin scowled and tightened his lower lip so his mouth formed an upside-down quarter moon. He didn't like criticism, and Will scolding Aaron for using the same speech as his pa was a direct rebuke. I held my breath lest this be the beginning of another upset between them. The moment passed, and Papa Irvin said, "Come on. Yer granny's been waitin' to meet y'all."

I breathed a sigh of relief as Will and his pa herded the boys into the cramped house.

W.E. was first through the door, but Aaron planted his feet, so Will had to push on his back to move him. Will had Lynch by one hand, and Lynch put his other hand on Aaron's back and pushed to match his pa's action. Finally, Aaron's feet gave, and they all tumbled through the doorway to meet Mama Sarah.

"Ma," Will choked. He let go of Lynch's hand and fell into his mother's arms. Mama Sarah wrapped him as tightly as she could with one free arm while she tried to maintain her balance with her walking stick in the other.

"I'm heartbroken, son," she said, "just heartbroken. That little gal was your whole world and everything in it."

A wrenching sob escaped Will's throat. He pulled himself free of his mother's embrace and dug for his handkerchief. The boys gaped open-mouthed. W.E. reached for Aaron and Aaron grabbed Lynch. They stood shoulder to shoulder like three little soldiers lined up for inspection. As Will regained his composure, he looked down and ruffled W.E.'s head of unruly blond hair. W.E. squeezed Aaron's hand hard and Aaron pulled away. Lynch puckered up and began crying. Nothing had ever been more upsetting to these boys than seeing their stoic father break down in tears.

"Ma," Will started over. "This here's W.E.—and Aaron—and Lynch." He touched each boy on his head as he introduced them.

"Where's our Charles?" were the first words out of her mouth.

"He's with Maidee's sister, Julia, in San Antone. They've got him in school for the next few weeks. Then I'll go for him and bring him down here."

Mama Sarah stared Will in the eyes. I knew that look. The one she used when she thought someone was trying to put one over on her.

Will looked away and said, "Boys, come meet your granmama."

All three boys shuffled reluctantly toward the hunch-backed woman with the heavy stick in her hand. She did appear frightening, even to me. But then she smiled and motioned for the boys to come for a hug. W.E. was first to brave contact, soon followed by his brothers. Mama Sarah said, "Y'all are fine-lookin' Jones boys, I'll say that. Your mama and daddy sure done good makin' children."

When Mama Sarah let go of the last of her grandchildren, she looked up at Will and asked, "Where's the baby?"

Will squirmed and shifted his eyes away. "In San Antone." His voice was flat, and I could feel his guilt as he tried to figure out how to explain. "Maisie's with Eula. She's settled now. We didn't think uprooting her again was a good idea."

Mama Sarah nodded. "S'pose not," she said, letting it drop. "You plannin' to be here awhile? There isn't much room, but we can squeeze ya in. Sorry, we couldn't make it back for her buryin'. Travelin' and me don't agree too good anymore."

"It's done, Ma. We can't change it now. No use talkin' about it, any more than talkin' about Maidee will bring her back. I came home because I couldn't stay in Utopia. I can't figure out what to do next. I need to find a job. I was thinkin' I might head over to Arizona and check things out. That is if I can leave the boys with you and Pa for a bit."

"I'm not sure, Will. I doubt I can manage lookin' after and cookin' for three little boys. I cain't hardly get around m'self."

Will looked crestfallen. His shoulders slumped, and his whole body appeared to shrink. "Dubbya'E's old enough to be some help to you. Aaron can keep an eye on Lyn. I'll talk to them about behavin'."

"It's not that, Will, it's just havin' the responsibility of fixin' meals and doin' laundry. Your pa won't help. I'll need to ask Minerva. If she can help with dinner, it might work. She don't live far. If she can help me, I'll give it a try, but I'm not promisin'."

"I'll stay and help out until they're used to things here. Then I'll look for a job and a place for us. I don't expect it to be permanent. I just need to know they're safe until I'm settled."

Will made up his plan while he talked. He didn't know a thing about Arizona, what work might be there, or if he could find a place to live.

It shocked him that his folks had settled in such a small house in bleak surroundings. If it hadn't been for the river, just a stone's throw away, and the lush greenery that grew along the banks, there wouldn't have been anything to recommend it. After the stately house they had enjoyed during all the kids' growing-up years, it was a real letdown. But Mama Sarah couldn't climb stairs, and anything bigger would have been near impossible to navigate in her condition. I understood, even if Will didn't.

The first few days went well. Will helped his ma in the kitchen and carried things to the table for her. His pa sat in the rocking chair in the living room and talked to the boys. Will collared W.E. to help in the kitchen and with sweeping up. Will's youngest sister, Minerva, married and pregnant as a cow, did agree to help with the afternoon meal each day. Anyone with two eyes could see it wouldn't last. She would be occupied with other obligations as soon as the baby came. Her husband wasn't very sociable, and it was clear—to me at least—that he wouldn't agree to Minerva dividing her time between her own family and Will's three. Helping her ma was one thing; caring for three rowdy little boys and a new baby would be quite another.

Watching Will struggle was hard for me. We'd always been a team, and I'd had Katherine to help me from when W.E. was born until Maisie came. She helped with laundry, canning, cleaning, keeping track of the boys, reading to them when I couldn't, meals—everything really. Will always came home to a house in order. He never thought about all Katherine and I did during the day, tending to a passel of children under eight. I was free to help Will with his projects on weekends and evenings because I had Katherine. Will was on his own.

CHAPTER EIGHT

Papa Irvin spent most evenings in a rocker on the low front porch. Will sat in the rocker meant for his ma and worked on puckering up his nerve to ask for whiskey. He had the jitters, and his hands trembled. He tucked them between his legs so his pa wouldn't notice and stared toward the Rio Grande. His mind raced, trying to find just the right way to say what he wanted until he blurted out, "Pa, you have any moonshine stashed around here?"

"Who's askin'?" Papa Irvin said, rocking without breaking rhythm.

"I'm askin', Pa." Will's voice had an edge to it, and Papa Irvin stopped rocking and looked askance at him.

I held my breath. I was nervous that they might get into an argument and spoil my boys' chance at being in a loving home.

"We heared you was hittin' the sauce pretty hard after yer wife died. It's best ya learn to manage without it…if you know what I mean. Now that crazy pro-bish-un thing is on us we all need to learn to go without."

"I haven't had a drink in six days. I'm just feelin' edgy this evenin' and was hopin' you'd help me out."

Papa Irvin went back to rocking without saying yes or no. I squeezed my eyes tight shut and implored him not to give in to Will's request.

The rocker stopped moving. Will's pa stood and walked around the side of the house out of Will's sight. He opened a small door underneath the house and pulled a bottle of 'shine out. He tucked it inside the bib of his coveralls and went back to the porch.

"Ya better not let yer ma see ya drinkin' this. Her fuse is short when it comes to 'shine," Irvin said, handing the bottle to Will.

Will stopped rocking and took the bottle. He slipped it inside his shirt and started toward the river. "Thanks, Pa," he muttered under his breath, "I'll be back in a bit."

Yellow dust blew up around Will's boots with every step he took toward the Rio Grande. When he reached the berm covered with lush greenery along the riverbank, he bent over and plucked a handful of grass to wipe it off. He made his way along the river atop the wide berm separating the scattered homes from the river until he found a small Montezuma cypress tree to offer some shade. He sat and pulled the whiskey bottle from his shirt. He turned it over and over in his hands. I knew he was trying not to open it, and in my heart, I also knew that he would fail. I felt that fullness in my chest I used to get when I wanted to cry but couldn't. There was no way to stop him, and nothing I could do to make the pain go away. The whiskey would put a damper on it for a time.

Will pulled the top off and tipped the bottle to his lips. He coughed and wiped his mouth with the back of his hand as the brown liquid slipped down his throat. That was all he took—one gulp. He sat and watched the water flow by. Unwelcome tears dropped onto his pant legs. Soon, his shoulders heaved, and his stomach contracted until a muffled sob escaped. The fast-flowing river dampened the sound. "Maidee," he said over and over. I reached for him and pulled him to me. A shudder filled his body, and his head came up. He looked around and called for me. "Are you here?" he asked. "Why don't you show yourself? You know I need to see you."

I let go and floated away. Letting him feel me in this way only added to his sorrow. I couldn't let him see me, and I couldn't let go of him. Soon, I would have to, but not today. Not until I knew Mama Sarah could manage the boys.

Will reached inside his shirt for the bottle and rolled it over in his hands. This time, he put it away without taking a drink. He stood and brushed the leaves and sticks off his pants, bent and plucked a stone from the ground, pulled his arm back, and hurled it toward the river. His jaw was tense, and his eyes brimmed. "Go," he shouted into the silence. "Just go and let me be." He spun on his heel and stomped away from the river toward the house.

When he reached the porch, Papa Irvin and Mama Sarah were rocking in unison. It was close to dark when Will said, "Where are the kids? I took a little walk. I wanted to see that river up close. Looks like if one of them fell in, they'd be a mile downstream before anyone could get to them."

"Could be," Papa Irvin said. "River's high this time a year. In another month, it won't be but a trickle on a sand flat."

"You'd better give 'em a good talkin'-to," Mama Sarah added. "Neither one of us could fish 'em out."

"Ain't no neighbors close enough to hear 'em neither," Papa Irvin said.

"They sleepin'?" Will asked.

"Uh huh. I put them in the twins' old room. There's two mattresses in there. I put Little Dubbya'E in one bed and Aaron and Lynch in t'other."

"That's good, Ma. We don't call him 'Little Dubbya'E' anymore— just Dubbya'E. We dropped the 'Little' when he started first grade."

"He don't seem to mind," Mama Sarah said.

"You lettin' me have Minerva's room?"

"Uh huh. She won't be needin' it. I put fresh linens in there for you, but it's not made up. Figured you could throw 'em on the bed good enough to sleep tonight."

"Thanks, Ma. I don't want you doin' anything for us we can do ourselves. And if you don't mind, I think I'll turn in."

"You need to, son. Come here and give me a hug first. It's been a long time since I put my arms around you. I like it."

Will held his breath and leaned down to hug Mama Sarah. He didn't want her to smell the hooch, so he offered his cheek for a goodnight kiss.

After Will turned in, Mama Sarah turned her attention to Will's pa. "Irv. I been ponderin' how we're goin' ta keep an eye on three little boys with as much energy as those three got. When ours were that age, we had a farm and all the chores that went with it to keep 'em occupied."

"Yep," Papa Irvin replied.

"I been thinkin' maybe we need to tell Will to take the little white-haired one and find another place for him."

"How so?" Papa Irvin said, knitting his eyebrows and looking askance at Mama Sarah.

"I don't think I'm up to managin' one that young again. It's clear he's near blind. Don't you think he'd be better off with Eula or Edelene? One of the girls?"

"Will wants to keep 'em together."

"I know, but he's already let Charles go to Maizelle's family, and Eula took Maisie. How's that keepin' 'em together?"

"It ain't. I s'pose he thought it was best."

"I want what's best for them too. I was thinkin' if we could get him to trade the little one for Charles, might be we could handle the other two."

"How d'ya mean, trade him for Charles?"

"Well, he said he was goin' back for Charles when school let out, so I thought if he took Lynch with him, he could get one of our girls to take him and bring Charles back to help with the other two."

Papa Irvin rocked and looked out at the night. Insects sang into the falling dusk, and a coyote howled for a companion. "Might could work," he said after a long silence. "We didn't come all the way down here to make more work for ya. The whole idea of leavin' Utopia was to make life easier. Raisin' somebody else's kids wasn't part of the plan."

"Will you speak to him then?" Mama Sarah asked.

I'd never heard her sound timid before. It took me by surprise. My biggest fear was that Papa Irvin and Will would get into a tangle, and the boys wouldn't be able to stay. If this was the conversation that needed to happen, I wished with all my might that Mama Sarah would do the asking.

A few more days passed, and Will didn't take any more of the 'shine. He hid the bottle so his ma wouldn't know but didn't offer to return it to his pa. I knew he wanted to drink more, but the security of knowing he had it seemed to keep him calm while he was with his ma and pa.

One evening in late May, Will and his pa were rocking together on the front porch. It was raining hard, and Will's usual evening walk to the river wasn't happening. I thought Papa Irvin seemed anxious. He kept glancing at Will with his forehead all wrinkled and his mouth turned down at the corners. Will wasn't in a talkative mood, and the only sound was the rain hitting the porch overhang and the creaking sound the rockers made against the porch boards.

Will pulled his tobacco pouch out of his pocket and rolled a smoke. He leaned over to light it, and the flame from the match lit up his face just the way I remember it from that first night we sneaked out to meet at Spanish Bridge. I got the same feeling of excitement I had that night. To me, Will was always the most handsome man in the world, even with his big ears that stuck out. His face was long and narrow, and his nose curved up at the end. His eyes were deep blue, and his eyelashes were long and thick. Seeing him in that firelight again brought it all back to me in a rush—our first spark when our arms touched, our first kiss, a river nearby—Utopia. I savored the memory and let myself drift in its intensity until Papa Irvin spoke and jarred me back to reality.

"Will," he said, "yer ma and me been doin' some thinkin' 'bout the boys and all. We want'a help ya if we can, but we got a problem."

"What's that?" Will asked. He stopped rocking and leaned forward over his knees, looking sidelong at his pa. He pulled on his smoke, knit his eyebrows, and set his jaw to working the way he does when he's upset.

"Yer ma don't think she can keep up with the little one."

"Lyn?"

"Yeah. He's more of a handful than she thinks she can manage. Ya know he's near blind, don't ya?"

"He does okay. The others help him."

Then Papa Irvin said something neither Will nor I had ever heard anyone say before. He said, "Son, he ain't yer boy, is he?" It wasn't the question that threw us so much as him saying, "son." He never addressed Will that way.

Will sat straight in the rocker and asked, "What do you mean by that?"

"He's Jimmy's boy, ain't he? Him bein' albino and all. That's what stirred Jimmy up so much, ain't it?"

"I don't know what you're talkin' about, Pa. Lyn is my boy, same as the others. If you're sayin' Maidee had a sweet spot for Jimmy and Lyn is his boy, you're wrong. Maidee and I loved each other and nobody else, hear? I won't have you suggestin' her bein' decent to Jimmy went beyond just bein' the kind-hearted woman she was."

"I ain't suggestin' she had anythin' to do with it. I'm thinkin' he took advantage of her, and this little blind beggar is the result."

"No. That's not how it is. Jimmy was lookin' for me, and I wasn't home. That's how he came to shoot Maidee. Lyn is our boy."

"You believe what you want, Will. Any fool with two eyes can see that boy ain't yours."

"So, you and Ma don't want to take him 'cause he looks like Jimmy? He's a good boy, Pa. A good boy."

"It's just yer ma don't think she can keep her eye on him and mind the others. If you bring Charles back to help her with Little Dubbya'E and Aaron, I think we can make it long enough for you to get your feet planted."

Will stood and walked into the rain. Papa Irvin watched until he was out of sight, then went inside and told Mama Sarah he'd told Will they couldn't keep Lyn. He never shared his suspicions with her, though. If she believed the same, she never let on.

"How'd he take it?" Mama Sarah asked.

"Not good," Papa Irvin said, "not good at all."

"Where is he?" she said.

"Walkin'," Papa Irvin said. "Walkin' in the rain. I 'spect he's thinkin' it over."

Will climbed the berm and found his tree. He pulled the whiskey bottle out of his pocket and uncorked it. He tipped it up and drank like it was water pouring down his throat. When he stopped to take in a breath, the sobs that wracked his bony frame were drowned out by the river and the rain. He stayed under that tree, letting the rain pelt him for a very long time. He hadn't thought about Lynch's birth since the day Katherine told him Jimmy'd ravaged me. He couldn't imagine it. He couldn't allow it to be true.

He kept going back to the scene in our house where I asked him to promise to take care of my babies. He asked himself why I didn't say "our babies"—why I said, "my babies." He mulled it over in his mind backward and forward, this way and that, until he finally collected himself and started back to the house. He had resolved that Lynch was our son and he would protect him no matter what anyone else thought or believed. "I will do this for you," he said to me.

My heart had nearly broken during Will's time under the tree. I loved Lynch, and he probably needed nurture and protection more than any of the others. I had trusted Will to keep his promise, and now I knew he would.

CHAPTER NINE

The morning after Will and his pa talked, he gathered the boys to him and told them they were going to walk to the river. Naturally, they were excited, pushing and jostling each other to scooch closer to Will. "Calm down, now." Will's sharp tone brought the giddy playing to an abrupt halt.

The air was fresh after the night's rain. A light fog rose along the pathway, smelling of honey mesquite, scrub pine needles, and wet earth. The kids skipped, hopped, and broke into a run at first sight of the Rio Grande. Will had put the fear of God into them about what would happen if they ever went that direction without him.

When they reached the berm where he spent his thinking time, he sat them all down under the tree and said, "Boys, I'm goin' to be gone for a while. I need to get your brother and bring him here to help your granmama."

W.E. piped up, "I'm helping Granmama, Pa."

"Yes, Dubbya'E, you are, and you're doin' a great job, but she needs help with more than kitchen work. She needs eyes in the back of her head to keep track of all three of you, and she doesn't think she's up to it without someone a little older to help out."

"I miss Charles," Aaron said.

"We all miss him. The thing is, I'm goin' to take Lyn with me when I go for Charles so as to make things a little easier on Granmama."

"I want to go too," W.E. said.

"Me too, me too," Aaron sang, jumping up and down.

Lynch crawled onto Will's lap and stroked his face with pudgy hands. Will pulled him close and kissed the top of his lily-white head. Our two-year-old snuggled against Will, and his thumb went into his mouth.

"We'll be back before you know it," Will said to the other boys. "I want you to promise you'll mind your granmama and granpapa. No whining. No complaining. Clean your plates and carry your dishes to the sink. When they say 'bedtime,' you stop what you're doin' and get ready for bed. Understand?"

Both W.E. and Aaron hung their heads, and Aaron's chin trembled. Will put his hand under it and lifted his face. "No cryin' now, you hear? This is just for a few days, and when I come back, I'll have Charles. Now, let's go see that big river I've been tellin' you so much about." He stood and let Lynch slide to the ground.

Aaron brightened at the mention of the river, and W.E. took off at a gallop down the face of the berm.

"Dubbya'E. Come back here," Will said, but momentum carried W.E. faster than his legs could keep up, and he plunged face down into the sandy loam at the bottom of the hill.

"See, Dubbya'E? This is exactly why your granmama doesn't think she can keep up with three of you." He dragged W.E. upright by the straps on his coveralls and let go of Lyn long enough to slap-brush the sand and dirt off W.E.'s clothes.

Aaron slid down the berm in one piece.

Will gathered the boys into a chain, holding hands as they continued to the water's edge. The Rio Grande flattened in this stretch, creating a matrix of sandbars and small islets as it wound through the riverbed, leaving the deeper, faster main channel farther out. Will moved the boys cautiously from one sandy island to another, letting them stop and play barefoot until they were caked with grit and mud. When they reached the fast-moving main channel, Will stopped and pulled them in tight. "This is the end of the line," he said. "You never, ever, ever, go past this spot, hear?"

They all nodded with wide-eyed fear. "Dubbya'E, watching Aaron while I'm gone is your job. Aaron can't swim strong like you, and even you almost drowned on me less than two weeks ago in a little creek not near as big as this. Can I trust you not to go near this river unless

Granpapa is with you? Even then, never go past this place. Granpapa is an old man. He might be able to fish one of you out, but if two of you ever got in that stream, you'd drown before he could figure out which one to grab. Do I have your promise?"

Aaron and W.E. nodded.

"Let me hear you say it," Will said.

"Yes, Daddy," Aaron said.

W.E. echoed, "Yes, Pa."

I swelled with pride hearing W.E. call Will Pa. It gave weight to his answer that he was old enough to make a grown-up vow.

The kids were exhausted from their day of lectures and play. Seeing the mighty Rio Grande was a milestone in their visit to Will's folks. Much had been made of the danger, and now they had seen it from two points of view—fear and fun.

When they returned to the house, Will filled the wash tub with water and bathed all three. Mama Sarah brought clean overalls for W.E. and Aaron, putting a new nappy on Lynch with a fresh cotton crawler. None of them wore shoes, so their callused feet would soon be dirty, but then, their feet were always dirty.

That evening, Will shared his plan with Mama Sarah. He'd take Lynch to Eula and ask her to keep him along with Maisie. If she refused, he'd go to Edelene and see if she and her new husband would take him. Edelene was twenty-six, newly married, and anxious to start her own family. Will wasn't sure she was the best choice, but he was running out of sisters. Asking Eula to raise two of his children might strain her goodwill, and getting Charles back from Julia without permanently setting her against him would be difficult. But he had made a promise, and he meant to keep it.

CHAPTER TEN

Will put Lynch in the front seat. He looped a long rag around him, tied one end to the door handle and the other end to his belt. If Lynch got the door open, he wouldn't fall out. He gave Lynch a stuffed teddy bear to hold, and off they went.

The first hour was uneventful. Lynch fell asleep and leaned against Will's side. When he awoke, he was hungry and tired of being confined. First, he tried to stand but couldn't because of the restraint. Next, he whimpered and tugged at the noose around his waist. Frustrated, as only a two-year-old can be, he threw a full-on tantrum, kicking and screaming, hammering Will on the arm and one leg with pudgy doubled-up fists. Will couldn't drive with all the bouncing and increasingly loud vocals, so he pulled off in the first spot that looked safe.

Extracting Lynch from the tie-down took a little time, during which Lynch continued to bellow and kick. Will was getting more frustrated by the minute. He grabbed Lynch's kicking legs and pressed them hard against the seat with his knee while he worked the knots on the restraint. When the contraption finally yielded, and Lynch felt freedom, he launched himself at Will, sobbing, "Mama, Mama, Mama."

Will lifted him gently out of the car and said, "Let's get your tears dried and have us something to eat, little man." The tenderness in his voice went a long way toward reassuring me that he loved our son.

Lynch immediately ceased crying and changed his refrain from "Mama" to "cracker."

A cracker was something Will could provide, as Mama Sarah had packed an ample supply for occasions such as this. Will tucked Lynch onto the back floorboard and burrowed through the wicker basket in the rear seat until he came up with the saltines.

Holding the white squares with one hand and Lynch's hand with the other, he walked toward a grassy area amongst a mostly dry and barren dirt-scape. The grass was sparse, coarse, and not particularly inviting, but letting Lynch stretch his legs and put something in his tummy was the smart thing to do.

Will and Lynch had almost reached the edge of the grassy area when Lynch pulled his hand loose and reached for something on the ground. "See," he said.

Will looked to his left and jerked our son off the ground by one arm. He jumped to his right and took off running. Lynch was inches from putting his hands around a coral snake—the quietest and most deadly venomous creature in Texas.

"Oh, boy," Will exclaimed as he ran for the car with Lynch reaching back and screaming, "I want, I want!" When he reached the safety of the car, he tossed Lynch through the open window onto the front seat. Lynch ramped up his fit and continued shouting, "Want. Want."

"No, Lyn, you do not want to pick up a coral snake," Will said, leaning through the window. His voice held such a tone that Lynch stopped crying and looked up at his daddy. "If that snake had bitten you, there wouldn't be any Lyn left to cry about it." He pulled his head out of the open window and went to the driver's side.

Lynch protested when Will put the restraint on him again. Will stopped, took him firmly by the shoulders, and said, "I know you don't understand what I'm doin' to you and why, but you need to stop kickin' and squirmin' so I can get this contraption hooked up again." Once more, the tone of his voice was enough to silence his son. "I'm not stoppin' until we hit San Antone, and I need you to behave."

Once Will was settled behind the wheel and rolling, Lynch leaned into his daddy's side and fell fast asleep. Will said to no one in particular, "Ma's right. She'd never be able to keep up with three of them without Charles's help. I can't even keep up with one. How'd you do it, Maidee?"

I smiled, knowing Will had a whole lot more to discover before he'd have any idea how much work it was to care for children. I loved him for trying, and as much as I had hoped he would let Julia raise Charles, I knew he was right to bring him back home.

Will went directly to Eula's. If she agreed to take Lynch and keep Maisie, his task at Julia's would be that much easier. If the two youngest could grow up together, and he could keep the three older boys together, he'd be able to make a home as soon as he found a job.

The minute Will hit the knocker Eula opened the door and reached her arms out for Lynch.

"Hi, sis," he said, "this little guy needs something warm in his tummy and a diaper change."

"I'll take him upstairs to change him. It's just about time for Maisie to wake up from her afternoon nap. Go on in the kitchen and pour yourself a cup of coffee. I'll be back with both of them in a jiffy."

Will did as his sister instructed. He leaned over the coffee cup and stared as it settled on him what a close call he'd had with Lynch and the coral snake. He rested his elbows on the table and put his head in his hands.

The door to the back porch opened, and Fred Brown walked in. "Will, my man. When the devil'd you get here?"

Will jumped and sloshed coffee onto the tablecloth. "Dammit," he said. "Sorry, Fred. You startled me." He pushed his chair back and reached for a dishrag to wipe the spill. "Lyn and I got here about five minutes ago. Eula's upstairs changing a diaper and getting Maisie up."

"Lynch, you say? Where'd you leave the rest of them?"

"They're with Ma and Pa in Del Rio. Well, outside Del Rio, but close."

"Everything okay?"

"Not really. Ma's health isn't strong and she doesn't think she can manage three boys unless she has Charles to help her. I've come to get him. The thing is, I have to find a place for Lyn. It's too dangerous for him at their place. The Rio Grande's too close, and he's at that age where they want to explore everything. On the way up here, I stopped to let him stretch his legs and he tried to pick up a coral snake. Neither Dubbya'E nor Aaron is old enough to be responsible for a near-blind two-year-old."

"Yee gawds, Will, a coral snake? One bite and he'd be a goner."

"Don't I know it. My heart almost stopped when I saw what he was reaching for. I swung him off the ground by one arm and hightailed it out'a there."

"Where you planning to leave him?"

Will hesitated a second before he said, "Here, I hope."

I saw the color drain from Fred's face, and so did Will. Sometimes folks don't need to say a thing to get their message across.

"I haven't talked to Eula about it yet. If you can't do it—take him, I mean—I'm going to ask Edelene."

"What about Julia? Maybe she'd be a better choice if you're taking Charles."

"No. I've been giving it a lot of thought, and I don't think I want to put him outside our family. He takes extra watching because his eyes are bad. I don't think Julia would take one this young anyway. Charles does for himself. Lyn can't."

"Well, your sister's got her hands mighty full with a one-year old. I'm not so sure she'd be ready to take on another. They're real close of an age, aren't they?"

"Yep. Only eleven months between 'em. Look, Fred, I know it's asking a lot, but Ma and Pa can't keep him. I don't know where else to turn."

"What's asking a lot?" Eula said, stepping into the room with Lynch by the hand and Maisie on her hip.

"I'll let Will tell you," Fred said. "I need to finish bringing in the groceries."

Eula looked from Fred to Will and said, "So, tell me. What's up?"

"I didn't mean to drop it on you like this. Fred has a way of getting things out of me before I'm quite ready."

"Drop what on me, Will? Spill it."

"I need to find a new place for Lyn. Ma and Pa can't take him. He needs too much watching, and Ma can't get around well enough to keep up with him. I was hoping for you and Fred to take one more."

"Oh, Will—" Eula nearly moaned his name out "—I've got my hands full with one and an ailin' husband."

"I know, sis. I wouldn't ask if I didn't think this was the best place for him. He'd be with his sister. They could grow up together. I'm takin' Charles back to Ma and Pa's to help with the other two."

"I need to think on it, Will. Fred hasn't had an easy time adjusting to a toddler in the house. I'm not so sure he could manage two."

Will looked down at the obvious coffee stain spread across Eula's clean, ironed tablecloth. "I spilled coffee when Fred came in. I was thinkin' about the close call I'd had with Lyn earlier, and he startled me."

"What close call? What happened?"

"Nothin' much. He tried to pick up a coral snake."

Eula's face blanched. She pulled Lynch closer. He screamed, "No!" and pulled his hand free. He ran to Will and climbed his leg like a squirrel up a tree. Will picked him up, sat him on his lap, and patted his head.

Eula found her voice and said, "Would you like to say hello to your daughter?" She moved toward Will. He slid Lynch off his lap onto the floor and reached for Maisie. He sat her on one bony knee and pulled Lynch onto the other. As he nuzzled Maisie's dark curly hair, he looked over the top of her head at Eula and said, "She looks happy, sis. You always were the best with the babies."

"Will Jones, sweet-talking me isn't going to change the facts. I'm forty-three years old, and Fred and I are pretty set in our ways. Adding one toddler still in diapers to our household was one thing; adding another might be more than we can handle. I'll talk to Fred about it and let you know what we decide before you head back to Del Rio."

"She's a sweet girl, isn't she?" Will said, sounding wistful and a little bit sad. Maisie rubbed her sleepy eyes and snuggled against his shoulder.

"Sweet as candy," Eula said, "and we both love her more than we thought it was possible to love someone else's child. She reminds us so much of Maizelle."

"I miss her, sis. I know it's best for her to be raised by you and Fred, but that doesn't mean I don't miss her every hour of every day."

"You could look for work here, Will. Why do you think you want to go to Del Rio?"

"I don't. I'm going to head over to Tucson and see how things look there."

"Arizona? Why would you want to be so far away?"

"I don't know. I just need to get out of the state of Texas, or maybe I just need to get Texas out of me."

"You can't outrun grief, Will. It takes time, is all. Wherever you land, it's going to land right next to you. It takes five times as long to drive from Del Rio to Tucson as it does to drive from Del Rio to San Antone. Don't you ever want to see your kids again?"

Will hung his head and buried his nose in Maisie's hair. Lynch scooted off Will's knee and crawled away as fast as his little legs would carry him.

Eula leaned over and grabbed him as he scooted past. She lifted him with one hand by the straps on his crawler and shifted him to her hip. He bucked backward, and she lost her grip. Lynch fell to the floor, bumped his head, and set up a howl I'm sure Fred could hear outside.

Will handed Maisie back to Eula and plucked Lynch off the floor. Lynch wailed between gulps of air he held until his face turned bright red. Will set him on the edge of the table and said, "Let's see if you're hurt or just insulted." He felt around the back of Lynch's head and found a sizable goose egg. His hand came back clean, so he knew there wasn't any blood. "There you go, big guy," he soothed. "It's just a little bump. You'll be all well in no time. Do you want me to kiss it?"

Lynch stopped howling long enough to listen to Will's soothing, and when he heard "kiss," he nodded. Will lifted him off the table and sat with him on his lap. He found the lump again and tipped Lynch's head so he could give it a loud slurpy kiss. When he looked up, he saw his sister's face and knew he was in deep water.

"Fred would never have thought to do that, Will, which is exactly why I'm not sure it would be a good idea to leave both toddlers with us."

"Please, Eula. My only other option is Edelene, and I don't have a good feeling about that. She just got married and wants to start a family of her own. Minerva is about to pop with her first, and I don't much care for her husband."

"Edelene's a darn sight younger than I am. I think she might be best."

"Just talk to Fred, like you said, and let me know before I go back."

Will and Lynch stayed with Eula and Fred for three nights. There were no more incidents to reinforce the Browns' reluctance to take on another of our children. Maisie blossomed with Lynch around. The two played together and chattered at each other like magpies in that peculiar language only toddlers understand. When Will left to get Charles, he had an agreement with his eldest sister and her even older husband to "try it" for a few months and see how things went. Will promised to stay in close contact with them and to come on the first train out of Tucson if anything warranted his immediate attention.

My heart swelled with emotion when Will took Lynch in his arms and kissed him goodbye. He held Maisie longer than she was in the mood for, and she fussed and reached for Eula. He gave her a quick peck on the cheek and let her go. If the children had to be separated, keeping the two youngest together made sense. When I asked Will to promise to take care of my babies, I didn't specify exactly how he should do that.

Truthfully, I thought his plan to keep Lynch and Maisie together was both creative and wise. There was no one else I'd rather have mothering them in my absence than Will's sister.

CHAPTER ELEVEN

Fred wandered out to the curb to collect the mail. Eula stood with Maisie on her hip, watching her brother load the car. As Will circled the car to climb into the driver's side, Fred called, "Wait! There's a fat letter here for ya."

Will turned with a scowl. "For me? Who'd be writin' to me here?"

"Looks like it's from Bobby Upton." Fred held the envelope out to Will.

"Bobby? I wonder why he wrote to me at your address," Will said, taking the envelope and staring at it like it was about to bite him.

Eula stepped close, and Fred crowded in as Will tore open the letter. He read to himself at first but then broke into a wide grin and shouted, "Hallelujah!"

"What?" Eula asked, "what's makin' you so excited?"

"Boyce Brody bought my garage!"

"Oh," Eula said, "that's wonderful news."

"It's terrific," Will said, "now I can start a shop somewhere near Ma and Pa."

"So, you think Del Rio is the right place to go into business?" Fred asked, his tone wary.

"As good as any," Will said. "Equipment is equipment, whether you're growin' lettuce or rearin' goats. There are more cars in Tucson, that's a fact, but if I stay in Del Rio, Ma and Minerva can help with the kids. I was goin' to Tucson to check out the business climate over there, and I still might. Del Rio doesn't have the kind of farmin' they do around Tucson. Can't say yet where we'll end up."

The words tumbled out as fast as they entered his head. I could tell he was undecided and trying to figure out his future on the fly; this was the most animated I'd seen Will since my death. I knew he missed the shop. He missed his tools. He missed his conversations with friends and customers. He missed the solitude of tinkering with a troublesome piece of equipment and making it work again. I was happy for him, even if I wanted him to stay in San Antonio near Lynch and Maisie.

The news changed everything for Will. He had money enough to restart somewhere else. He could now see a future where they all lived together under one roof. Choosing where was the only consideration, and W.E. and Aaron were settled in nicely with Mama Sarah and Pa Jones. Uprooting them again wouldn't be a good idea, and Will knew it; that he was even considering starting a business in Del Rio was proof of that.

Will bounced from one foot to the other. He tried to hug Maisie while she perched on Eula's hip, but she squirmed and twisted away. Instead of scowling and looking hurt, he laughed and tickled her. Her fat little legs flailed, and she pulled away from him, poking at him with her chubby little fingers.

"Y'all stop it now," Eula said. "I'm about to lose my grip." She turned toward the house.

"Let me hold her once more before I leave," Will said, reaching for his girl. He lifted her away from Eula, and the wail that went up could be heard a mile away. "Maisie, stop your hollerin'," Will said. "Daddy wants a goodbye squeeze and a kiss."

"No!" Maisie wailed her displeasure and pummeled Will with both her legs and arms. "Mama, Mama," she cried, reaching for Eula.

I could tell his feelings were hurt, but he put on a determined face and handed our daughter back to her aunt Eula. "No use gettin' her any more riled up, I guess," he said.

Selling the business hadn't done anything to alter the situation with the kids, but even a short-term agreement for Lynch and Maisie to be together in Eula and Fred's care was a comfort to both of us.

Lynch stood silently on the bottom step of the porch, taking it all in. His eyes danced side to side, and his head appeared to follow their movement. Suddenly, he screamed, "Daddy!" and stepped off his perch.

Will turned just in time to see Lyn fall. He took two giant strides toward the porch and scooped our boy into his arms. "What's the trouble here, big guy?" His voice had that calm, sympathetic tone, and Lyn looked at him with enormous tears pooling in his twitching eyes.

"Go!" Lyn said. "Go."

"Sorry, son," Will said, squatting down eye level. "I can't take you with me this time. You need to stay with Aunt Eula and Uncle Fred. Maisie needs your company. Be a good boy, now, and let Daddy go."

"No. Go," our youngest son insisted, and Will's heart twisted in his chest. I felt it as surely as if it were my own.

Fred ambled over and offered to take Lynch from Will, who extracted our son with tenderness and care, passing him into Fred's arms.

Will hurried to the car and climbed inside before any more emotional outbursts reached his ears.

CHAPTER TWELVE

Julia knew Will was coming. He had called her from his sister's the evening they arrived and they'd had a lengthy conversation. She had two days to prepare to part with Charles, the only one of our children with whom she had developed a bond. She and Sam had enjoyed having him with them. Julia told everyone, "He's an angel on earth."

Just two weeks shy of his eighth birthday when I died, he had matured much faster than anyone would have expected. I think when he went to Papa for help and was turned away at the door, it changed something inside him. He was always the quietest and most conciliatory of the boys, but the violent shock of my murder curled him in on himself in a strange way. On occasion, he reverted to the habits and behaviors of his childhood, but on others, he seemed far older than his years.

When Julia took him into the parlor and sat him down to explain he would be going to Del Rio to spend the summer with his brothers, he looked at her stone-faced. She reached for him to offer comfort and he pulled away. "I'll talk to your daddy about letting you come back to our place when school starts again," she said by way of compensation.

"I don't want to go to school here," Charles stated, his feet firmly planted.

"I thought you liked the school," Julia said.

"No. I like you, Aunt Julia. I want to live here."

"I don't have anything to say about that part of it. Your daddy…"

"Don't call him my daddy," Charles interrupted. "He's my pa."

"Sorry. I forget how grown-up you are now."

"I'm big enough to say where I want to live, too."

"Yes, I suppose you are, but you aren't as big as Will, and he's the one deciding for both of us."

"What if I just say I won't go?"

"The decision isn't mine to make. I want you to stay, but I'm only your auntie. Your pa has the final say."

"I'm not going," Charles said, on the verge of tears, and bolted from the room.

My sister was tempted to follow and console him, but she realized this was something he needed to work out for himself.

Will showed up at ten, looking for a quick departure ahead of a long drive back to Del Rio.

Charles refused to leave his room. His things were packed in a small suitcase, both the new clothes they had purchased for school, and the old, tattered coveralls and too-small shirt he had arrived in. Julia had even bought Charles shoes and socks, something our son seldom wore.

She met Will at the door and explained that Charles refused to come downstairs. "I don't know what else to do, Will. I've explained this all to him as best I could. I told him I'd ask you if he could come back when school starts."

"No. I appreciate the offer, but my ma needs him to help with Aaron and Dubbya'E. She's too infirm to manage without another pair of eyes on them. She's decided she can't handle Lyn. And she can't manage the other two by herself, so I need Charles."

"Lynch?" Julia asked. "What are you going to do with him?"

"Eula and Fred are keeping him with Maisie. We have an arrangement. I brought him with me on this trip. Now, I'll just get my son and be on my way."

"His room is at the top of the stairs on the left. I hope you have better luck reasoning with him than I did."

"I'm not in any mood for reasoning this morning. I'll drag him down here by his ear if I have to," he said as he stepped past her and climbed the stairs.

He caught the fear in Julia's eyes and stopped in his tracks. He turned to her and said, "He's my son. I know how to make him mind. I'm not going to hurt him, so wipe that look off your face. If he thinks he has an ally in you, it will make it harder on all of us."

When Will emerged from the bedroom, his arm around our boy's shoulders, both of my men had smiles on their faces. When they reached the bottom of the stairway, Charles turned to my sister and said, "Aunt Julia, thank you for letting me stay with you. I love you, and I love your cooking. I'll be back, and I promise to write to you. Pa says we can visit again soon." He threw his arms around her waist, gave her a fierce hug, and then bolted for the door. With that, Will and Charles stepped out of the house and into the car.

Julia put the suitcase in the backseat and waved to them as they drove away. Sam was at work, and she fled inside, where she dissolved in tears that didn't stop until he arrived home at five fifteen that evening.

What I thought didn't matter. My sister's heart was broken, and there was nothing I could do. For his part, Sam was just happy to have her all to himself again.

CHAPTER THIRTEEN

Charles had said his piece to Julia exactly as Will instructed, and things would never be the same. Charles wasn't ready to grow up so fast. Conscripted into responsibility for his two younger brothers, taken from my loving sister—who guided him through these past months of trauma and grief—never understanding why he had to go to his Granmama and Granpapa's place, all affected him in a way from which he would never recover. He huddled against the passenger door and wept all the way to Del Rio.

Will pushed Charles's arm with his handkerchief and tried to make conversation. He asked how school was in "the city." He asked if the other kids were nice to him. He asked if he liked Julia's husband, Sam. The answers were "fine," "not really," and "no."

When he asked why Charles wanted to stay with them if he didn't like Sam, he said, "I don't know."

Will shared his news that the garage had sold and he would be looking for a place to start another one and give them a home together.

"I don't care," Charles said. "It won't be the same without Ma."

Will gave up, and they rode in silence the rest of the way.

Ma and Pa Jones were excited to see the only child of ours to whom they felt a personal connection. Previously instructed, Charles was gracious and hugged each of them. They remarked on how tall he'd grown as if they expected him to be the same size as when they left for the Gulf and he wasn't yet two.

Mama Sarah said, "Charles, you will have Auntie Minerva's old room when your pa leaves on his scouting trip to Arizona. That will give you a place to get away from your responsibilities sometimes."

Charles said, "Pa's going to Arizona? How come?"

Mama Sarah looked at Will, and Will looked at his feet. "Well," he drawled, "there might be a little change in plans afoot."

"How so?" Mama Sarah asked.

"I got a letter from Bobby while I was at Eula's. The garage sold, and I got a check. I may see if there's a spot around here to open another one."

Papa Irvin clapped Charles on the back as if he hadn't heard Will and said, "How'd ya like to see the rest of the place?"

His grandson mumbled, "I guess so," and let his granpapa guide him out the door.

Papa Irvin said, "Sarah, you help Will figure out an answer to this here boy's question while we're gone. Then ya can explain it to me too."

W.E. and Aaron both jumped in with, "Can I go, too?" and Granpapa left with all three boys.

Will and his ma sat in the kitchen and stared at each other across the table. "Well," she said, "this puts a whole new wrinkle in the cloth, don't it?"

"Maybe, maybe not," Will said.

"Did I or did I not hear you say you would look for a spot around here to open a new shop?"

"You heard me right. I just haven't decided if I want to settle here or if I still want to check out the opportunities in Tucson."

"It would please your pa and me mightily if you settled here. I can't be much help with the boys except to squeeze 'em and love 'em, but I've got plenty of that to go around."

"I thought I needed to get away from everyone who reminded me of Maidee," Will said. "I'm not sleeping. I'm not eating proper, and all I do is think about her. But now, with money to get a fresh start, I'll have something to take my mind off losin' her—at least part of the time."

"Those young 'uns need you, Will. I make a pretty good substitute mother, but I can't do the things with them that boys need. They need a pa."

"Okay. I'll see if I can find a building to buy around here first. As soon as I get established, I'll get the other two and bring in a girl to help. If you and Minnie, with Charles's help, can look after them until I have my feet under me again, I'll stay."

Mama Sarah reached across the table and put her hand over Will's. He lifted it and squeezed hers. Physical affection was uncommon between these two, but I knew my loss had drawn them closer than they'd ever been.

"Pa will be happy, Will. He won't say it, and he prob'ly won't show it, but he enjoys havin' the boys' company."

But Will was a man of his word, so he got up bright and early and headed out to scout the area for two things: a place to establish his business close to his folks' house, and a house within walking distance of a school. I could hear every thought, every doubt, and every reason to reject each place he looked into. I soon realized that when a man's heart isn't into an idea, his head can make it troublesome to live with.

Del Rio had a population of nearly eleven thousand people. To Will and the boys, it was a huge city. Will struggled with his decision and his commitment to his ma to look for a place to establish his shop. He was looking forward to getting away by himself, forgetting he had responsibilities, and being able to drink himself rummy without guilt.

The summer heat arrived with a vengeance, and the air was thick with humidity. Will drove up one street and down the next, eyeballing the general area and the relative prosperity of each business.

On Elm, he saw a small building standing apart from the others at the end of a long block with a vacant lot adjacent. He stopped the car and got out. The building wasn't occupied, and there was a "For Rent" sign on the inside of the front door window. He jotted down the number on his matchbook and tucked it into his shirt pocket. Then he walked around the structure taking mental measurements and trying to see inside the dirt-obscured windows.

He returned to the car and rolled the windows down for relief from the heat. He counted cars that passed the location on both streets of the intersection. He made note of the number of people going in and out of nearby businesses. After an hour of observation, sweat dripped off his forehead and down his back, so he drove back to Ma and Pa's to use the telephone.

Mama Sarah looked up from her knitting when he walked into the house. She noticed the bounce in his step and the bright expression on his ordinarily solemn face. "You had a good scouting trip then?" she asked.

"Yep. Looks like I found just the spot for the garage. I have to call the number on the sign. Mind if I use the telephone?"

"Be my guest," Mama Sarah said, attempting to sound casual instead of jubilant, which was how she felt. She went back to her knitting, pretending to be disinterested, but her ears tuned in to the conversation Will was having, and when he hung up she couldn't keep silent. "Is it good news or bad?" she asked.

"It's good, Ma. The place I found is available. It's on the corner of Elm and Second. I counted over sixty people going in and out of businesses in the area, and there was a steady stream of automobiles on both streets. It's only a block off Sycamore and about a mile walk from the school. I think I could make it there."

"That is good news. Is the building available to buy or only rent?"

"It's only for rent, but the owner said he'd consider selling if I stay at least a year. That's good for me because it would give me time to make sure the location is right. I'd hate to buy something and then have to sell it and move."

"But if you rent and it doesn't work, will you have enough money to establish somewhere else? Ownin' is always best."

"Thanks for the advice. I need to meet the landlord at the building in half an hour. I'll be back in time for lunch."

The rest of the summer of 1926 passed quickly. Will was engrossed in establishing his new repair shop, Mama Sarah and Minerva shared responsibility for the boys, and Charles was quick to reestablish his close relationship with Ma and Pa Jones.

I worried that shouldering such responsibility so soon after my death would break Charles. He was always a sensitive child and the most seriously affected by my loss. I spent as much time as I could muster energy trying to ease his burden. I discovered that Charles was more likely to recognize it and respond if I hovered over a spot of trouble or danger. I tried hard to impress myself on him in the same way I did Will. It wasn't as effective with Charles, but my presence kept him more alert.

The boys found swimming holes along San Felipe Creek near Will's new shop. To his credit, Charles never let Aaron or W.E. out of his sight. They could play in the shallow water and cool off, which helped keep them in good humor instead of finding reasons to squabble. Everyone missed Lynch, but Charles was pragmatic enough to realize that their summer would have been very different if he'd been there. W.E. and Aaron could swim, and Charles was big enough to haul either of them out of the drink if they got in trouble.

There were often several little brown children at the swimming hole who spoke a different language, and the boys played with them as they would with any of the white children who came by. It never occurred to them that it might be frowned upon by the adults in their lives, and fortunately, no adults discovered their breach of etiquette. All three boys learned a few words of Spanish and made new friends.

Mama Sarah's health was getting worse instead of better. When fall was upon them, she pulled Will aside and said, "Son, I can't keep apace of these young 'uns anymore. Minerva's about to pop, and she won't be around to help me with cookin' and laundry. Now that school's about to take up, I think you need to find another way to care for the boys."

"Aw, Ma, I'm just gettin' the shop goin' good. I haven't had time to look for a place to live, and I don't know a soul to help out with the kids. How long can you give me?"

"Me and Minnie talked about it this mornin'. She thinks she can manage through November, but you need to find a place and a helper before her baby comes. As for me, I'm as good as useless as it is. Even finding somebody to do the laundry would be a big help. I can't get around like I used to, and once Minnie isn't here anymore to load the washer and turn the mangle, I won't be able to do any of it alone. I can't stand long enough to hang the clothes to dry or take them off the line."

"I'll put an ad in the paper to find us a helper. Charles can load and turn the ringer for you until we get someone. He can help with the cookin', too, after he gets home from school."

"He already has too much on his skinny little shoulders, Will. He needs some time to be a boy yet."

"Well, it's nothin' like what Pa expected of us when we were kids."

"That's a fact. But look what it done to your feelin's for him. Kids should be responsible and learn to work, but all work and no play ain't right. He's a good boy, Will. He's still grievin' his mama. Let him settle into school and make friends. You can afford to hire someone to help."

"I heard ya, Ma. I'll do what I can."

Finding help proved much harder than Will anticipated. There just wasn't another Katherine in this world. Several Mexican ladies applied but couldn't speak much English, and the boys had such limited Spanish it was impractical.

Mama Sarah was anxious to get back to a less stressful life, and November had come and gone with no solution in sight. The boys were settled into their new school and, from all appearances, were making a good adjustment.

Minerva looked like she could drop her baby any minute, and Will could sense her anxiety when he picked the boys up from her house each day at dinnertime. He had to find someone soon.

One evening in early December, after the boys settled into bed, Will walked out to the berm above the Rio Grande and sat under his favorite tree. From this vantage point, he could see the area where his shop stood, the roof of the boys' school, and the meandering San Felipe Creek that bisected the town.

As he gazed into the distance, he noticed a spiral of smoke rising from near the shop. He watched it absentmindedly as it snaked into the night sky. Suddenly, he saw a lick of red flame tickling the inside of the column of smoke, and his attention shifted to full alert. Something near the shop is burning.

Once the thought gelled, he scrambled to his feet and raced back to the house. He ran past Pa, sitting on the front porch smoking a cigar, and said, "There's a fire downtown. I got to go."

"What's your hurry?" Pa said. "Ain't your shop, is it?"

"Could be," Will said. "That's what I've got to find out."

"Want me to ride along?" Pa asked.

"No," Will said. "No need in both of us takin' off. Probably nothin' serious. If I don't come right back, you'll know."

Will drove toward the smoke spiral with increasing foreboding and anxiety. The night of my murder pierced his brain like it was yesterday. The night sky glowed red by the time he reached Elm Street. The memory of the blazing Utopia School burned through him like a river of lava. When he approached the intersection of Elm and Second, he knew with certainty that the fire was coming through the roof of his shop.

"No! No! It can't be!" The roar of grief and sorrow that erupted from him was unlike anything the bystanders had ever heard. He stopped the car and collapsed against the steering wheel, sobbing.

Someone approached and tapped on the window. "You okay?" a voice said out of the darkness, penetrating the wall of emotion.

"Get away! That's my shop. Everything I have is in there."

"Sorry," the voice said. "It's a total loss. You should just go on home and come back in the morning after the fire department is finished mopping up."

"Maidee. Maidee. Maidee." Will cried and called my name.

"Mister, are you sayin' somebody's in there?"

"What?" Will faced the man with a puzzled expression.

"I thought I heard you calling someone's name. I wondered if you thought there was someone in there. In the fire, I mean," the man said.

"No," Will said. "No one is in there. She's here with me." He started the car and drove back to Ma and Pa's place.

It didn't seem possible that after all Will and the boys had been through, they would have to go through another tragedy of such magnitude.

The fire and the loss of his shop hit Will with a force no one could have expected. When he closed his eyes at night, all he saw were images of the Utopia School blazing into the night sky; all he dared remember about the night I died. The loss of the shop, his tools, his money, and his livelihood became a substitute for his loss of me. He wept, drank his pa's hooch, wandered the berm above the Rio Grande, and smoked endless cigarettes.

When he sobered up enough to remember he had three boys counting on him, his response was anger. He was short-tempered with Charles and W.E. and even swatted Aaron's behind when he didn't move fast enough to suit Will. I was at a loss. If I tried to impress myself on him when he was drinking, he struck out at the night with a verbal fury that he could not contain. He blamed me for leaving him. He blamed me for the boys' quarreling and fighting. He blamed me for his ma's nagging that he "get right and get a job so's these boys can have a home."

The worse he got, the worse the tension in the Jones household. Then, one day, Mama Sarah said, "Will, I cannot cope with these boys another minute! They fight. They cry. They won't allow me to comfort them. I know you've got troubles, but so do I. I'm old, tired, and wore out trying to take care 'a young 'uns."

Will said, "I know, Ma. I been thinkin' I need to go on to Arizona and get established there."

"So, your solution is to go off and leave these kids with me when I've just told you I'm at the end of my rope?"

"I heard you, but if you can get along for a few weeks, I promise I'll take them out of your hair."

"It won't work, Will. I can't mind them the way they need mindin'. Pa does his best, but his fuse is short, and I don't trust him not to fall into his old ways of mindin' children. He don't see what harm a strap does if it gets the point across."

"Please," Will said. "Just give me a few weeks. I need to get far away from everything that reminds me of her. These kids remind me of her every minute of the day. I have to be where I can get my head clear."

"You sure can't tell yer pa that," she said. "He don't think you got much in the way of a head."

"I know, Ma"—his voice dripped sarcasm—"I'm not a total bone brain."

"Yer pa sure thinks ya are. Plus, a drunk."

Will raised his eyes to meet hers. "I guess I've earned that. I'll leave in the mornin' before the kids and Pa get up. It'll be easier on ever'body that way."

Before Charles went to bed that night, Will sat him down at the kitchen table and said, "Son, I'm heading over to Arizona in the morning. I'm leavin' you in charge. I know it's a lot of responsibility. You need to help your granmama as much as you can, but the most important thing is to keep track of your brothers and see to it they don't get into any mischief. Can I count on you for that?"

"I guess so," our sullen boy said. "How long will you be gone?"

"I'm not sure. I plan to find a job, get us a place to live, and come straight back for you and your brothers."

"Why do you have to go to Arizona? Why can't you stay here? Why can't I go back to Aunt Julia's?"

"I don't know, son. I'm looking for something, and I'm not even sure what it is. I'll find a decent job and get us a house. Then, I'll come for you. That's all I can promise right now."

"Pa, why'd Jimmy shoot Mama?"

"I'm not sure. He might have been mad at me. I wasn't home when he came lookin' to settle the score. He shot your ma instead."

"Aunt Julia said he's dead. Did you shoot him?"

"No. The law hunted him down. I don't know who shot him. Best we not talk about it anymore. What's done is done."

Will sneaked two big bottles of moonshine out of his pa's stash and made good on his promise to be gone before the boys saw daylight.

CHAPTER FOURTEEN

Seven hundred forty-two miles and three days later, Will rolled his Ford Touring car into the fast-growing settlement of Tucson, Arizona, bone-weary from the long drive and his attempts to sleep for a few minutes each time he stopped to gas up. He favored the sheltered side of stations along the vast stretches of desert in Texas and Arizona for the patch of shade they offered.

Each time Will crawled into the rear seat to get some shut-eye, it reminded me of our pre-wedding night spent in the backseat of Bobby Upton's Packard, spooned together like clams in a shell and trying with all our might not to do something we might regret.

Whenever Will stopped, he pulled a bottle of the 'shine out and took a swig. Never more than a single gulp, but enough to concern me. I watched him drive slowly up and down the streets of Tucson, looking for a likely place to stay. Eventually, he saw a small sign in the window of a large white house that read, "Room for Rent." He stopped the car and approached the front door.

A woman answered, and he inquired about the possibility of a week-long room rental. She looked him over carefully before she said, "I only rent by the month."

Will said, "I'm not sure I'll be here a month. I need to find a job before I make that kind of plan."

The woman introduced herself as, "Mrs. Richey—Faye," and extended her hand.

My husband shook her hand and said, "I'm William Jones, ma'am—Will. I'd be obliged if you could let me a room for a week. If I find work right away, I'll pay for the rest of the month and stay at least that long."

When their hands touched, I knew that Faye Richey would let Will Jones rent a room. My heart clutched. Which would be worse—Will seeking comfort in the arms of another woman or the bottle? I knew he was struggling against the bottle; I didn't know if he would struggle as hard against the warmth of another human being.

"It's against my better judgment, Mr. Jones, but I suppose I can make an exception if you give me your word you will stay once you find work," Mrs. Richey said.

I tried to take comfort in the "Mrs." part of her introduction and hoped there was a Mr. Richey somewhere. There wasn't. Once Will moved his belongings from the car into the room she showed him at the top of the stairs, he found her in the kitchen and let her know he was going to take a long nap before he set out looking for work.

She said, "The kids will be home from their music lessons in about an hour. I'll try to keep them from disturbing you."

"You have kids?" Will asked.

"Two," she said, "Favel, my boy, is five, and Rosemary, my girl, is six."

"I have a boy almost five and another who'll be seven in December," Will said.

"Oh?" Faye Richey said. "Are they with their mother then?"

"No, they're with my folks. Their mother died."

Faye lowered her eyes and her voice when she said, "I'm sorry to hear that. Forgive me. I didn't mean to intrude."

"I mean to bring them to Tucson as soon as I get settled."

"I'm widowed myself, Mr. Jones. My husband's two years gone now. I know how difficult it is."

That was all they needed to know about each other. Will went upstairs and took his boots off before flopping exhausted onto the bed. He didn't rouse until Mrs. Richey tapped lightly on his door to let him know the evening meal would be served in fifteen minutes.

At first, Will didn't remember where he was. Then he chided himself for sleeping through the better part of the day. A day sleeping was a day he wasn't hunting for work. He went downstairs and found the dining room set for four. Favel and Rosemary were already seated and stared curiously at the new boarder. Will nodded to each of them before sitting at the end of the table closest to the door.

Faye came in from the kitchen carrying a large serving dish in each hand. Will scrambled to his feet and rushed to take them from her. She smiled and said, "Thank you, I appreciate it. They are heavy." Then she turned to the children and introduced them to Will.

He nodded to each of them and said, "Pleased to make your acquaintance."

The children looked down at their plates, expressionless, while their mother served potatoes, carrots, and tender roast beef before passing the bowls to Will.

Will thanked Mrs. Richey, and the four of them ate in silence. When Will finished he pushed back from the table and said, "That was delicious. I appreciate it. I need to take a walk tonight and get the lay of the land around here." It never occurred to him to offer to help with the dishes; he never had when he was married to me. Why would he start now?

Will searched for work all week. He was a stranger. He didn't know anyone. Sure, he said he was a mechanic, but what proof did he have? If he had owned his own garage, why was he pounding the streets looking for a job? In many of the places he stopped, both whites and Mexicans spoke Spanish. He wasn't sure he would ever fit in.

Will felt defeated when he went to Faye Richey and told her he couldn't commit to a full month since he hadn't found work yet. It didn't surprise me, but it did surprise Will when she said she'd let him stay another week if he wanted.

In the middle of the second week of job hunting, he stopped in at a wrecking yard and inquired. The owner was a burly guy with an enormous belly that hung over his belt. He had a hard time getting into tight places, and it turned out that a lot of tearing apart cars and equipment involved tight places.

Will was rail-thin, muscular, and lean. Not only that, but he was also willing to do any kind of work they had. Mr. Blake wanted Will to start right away—on the spot. The wage wasn't high, but it was enough for Will to get by and send a little to Ma and Pa Jones for the boys' keep.

He worked the remainder of the day for Mr. Blake, then hurried back to Mrs. Richey's to pay for the remainder of the month. He found her in the kitchen preparing the evening meal and startled her when he spoke. "Mrs. Richey—Faye," he said.

She jumped and dropped a spatula on the floor. She reached for it at the same time as Will and their hands touched. "Oh, Will," she said, "I didn't hear you come in."

Will blushed, and his prominent ears turned bright red. "Sorry," he muttered as they stared at each other. "I have the money for the rest of the month."

Faye Richey smiled a broad, warm smile and said, "That's wonderful, Will. I'm happy you will be staying for the month. I'm sure Favel and Rosemary will be happy too. They don't like the constant turnover of new people in and out of the house. Does this mean you found work?"

"Yes, ma'am," a flustered Will said.

I knew what was happening, even if they didn't. Will was alone and lonely. Faye was in the market for a new husband. I couldn't bear to watch what was unfolding here and decided to return to Del Rio and see how the boys were getting along.

Mama Sarah and Papa Irvin were having quite a time with the addition of three energetic boys to their otherwise quiet lives. Charles was surly and ill-tempered much of the time. He missed me, and he missed his aunt Julia. The happy, entertaining toddler they had known in Utopia now shouted instructions at W.E. and Aaron rather than the gentle commands they'd been used to. He bossed his brothers around, told them where they could and couldn't go, and tattled to his granpapa whenever they stepped outside the lines he had put in place.

Papa Irvin would step in with his brusque discipline and threaten the strap. Mama Sarah would intercede on behalf of the kids, and Papa Irvin would stomp off in disgust. Everyone was suffering emotional distress of one sort or another. Will had made his pa promise never to take the strap to his boys, and Papa Irvin had agreed. Mama Sarah had to remind him of that promise, putting herself in the line of fire for his wrath. No one was happy with the situation.

I will give Mama Sarah credit, though, for giving all the boys as much love as they would allow. Charles declined to be hugged for the first month they were there, kept his arms plastered to his sides, and pulled away from her at the first opportunity. He was sullen and unsmiling most of the time. One night, a little more than a month after they arrived, she found him sitting behind the house, crying. "Charles, whatever has happened?" she said. He shook his head and looked away, refusing to answer. "Charles, I can't bend down to where you are to comfort you. I want you to stand up here and let me see your face." She waited, and Charles didn't move. "Now."

Charles stood and faced her with his chin tucked and his eyes downcast, tears cutting rivulets through the dust on his cheeks. Mama Sarah took her free hand and lifted his chin to look him in the eye. "Charles," she said very kindly, "I love you. I helped bring you into this world, heard your first words, and watched you take your first steps. I know you miss your mama, and I know you wanted to stay with your aunt Julia, but sometimes life doesn't work out the way we want. It looks like we're goin' ta be together for a while, and it would be a lot easier for both of us if you'd try to accept things as they are."

"Why'd he have to leave?" Charles shouted at his grandmother. "I hate him!"

"I'm sure you feel that way right now, but you still love him in your heart."

"No. I don't!"

"Come here, son," she said, reaching to gather him in. She balanced on her walking stick, put one strong arm around Charles, and pulled him to her. Something broke in him then, and he collapsed against his granmama sobbing.

"I want my ma back," he said between gulps of air. "I want my pa to come home."

Mama Sarah let him cry. She stroked his hair and patted his back. She let go long enough to pull a corner of her apron up and wipe his tears. "I know you do, Charles. We've asked a lot of you when you weren't ready to handle it. I wish your pa would come back too. I know helpin' me and lookin' after your brothers takes more effort than you've got to give right now. I can't speak for why he thought he had to leave. You all have broken hearts, and ever'body deals with sadness in their own way. What do ya say we check the mail and see if we have a letter from him today?" And they did. Mama Sarah gathered all three boys around as she opened the letter. She read it aloud.

Dear Charles, W.E., Aaron, Ma and Pa,

I found a job working in a wrecking yard.
I am living at a boarding house run by a Mrs. Richey.
I get two meals a day and a room.

Mrs. Richey has two children about the same age as
Aaron and W.E. The girl is called Rosemary, and the boy is Tavel.

I am enclosing some money to help with keep. I don't know
when I will be back to see you again. Right now, I'm only earning
enough to pay for my room and send a little to you.

I haven't had enough spare time yet to find a place where we can
all live together, but I will soon.

I hope you are being good and minding Granmama and Granpapa.
Write to me: C/o Mrs. Faye Richey
Number 17, Stone Street,
Tucson, Arizona.
I hope you write soon. I miss you.

Love,
Pa (Will)

"Read it again, read it again," W.E. and Aaron chorused. Charles, standing beside Mama Sarah's chair, looked glum and laid his head on Mama Sarah's shoulder. She reached over and patted his cheek. "See there, Charles, your pa hasn't forgotten you."

I was now satisfied that the boys were well cared-for and in as settled circumstances as I could hope for, so I went to San Antonio to check in on Maisie and Lynch. Will's sister, Eula, and her husband, Fred, struggled to manage two toddlers so close in age. Without his older brothers to help him get along in the world, my youngest son fell a lot, bumped into things in these unfamiliar surroundings, and spent as much time crying as he did sleeping. He took most of Eula's attention, leaving Maisie to fend for herself.

At twenty-two months, she walked, babbled, and got into everything she could reach or climb. Fred made a wooden playpen to contain her, but when they put her inside she crawled around, explored the four corners, pulled herself up, and scrambled over the rail, landing with a thud on the wood floor. After a brief bout of crying, she crawled away from the contraption, stood, and ran to the kitchen.

They tried putting Lynch in the playpen, but he screamed and kicked and cried until they relented and let him out of his prison.

Eula found that tending to two toddlers was a full-time job. She had difficulty cooking without one or the other hanging on to her hem begging to be held. She tried distracting them with a cookie but soon discovered that was a poor idea. They each learned to say "Cookie, Nana, cookie" and chanted the phrase while tugging repeatedly on her hemline.

After four months, she told Fred she had to have help. "I am too old and too impatient to raise two toddlers."

"Call your sister and see if she can spell you," he said.

Edelene, being the second youngest sister, seemed like a logical choice. She agreed to come daily for a few hours to give Eula time to catch up with laundry, cooking, and housekeeping. She played with the children, and they behaved well under her care. It would have been perfect if she hadn't gone home at night.

CHAPTER FIFTEEN

The telegram that arrived right after Christmas was a lethal blow. Edelene didn't waste any time telling Will he needed to make other arrangements for the care of Charles, W.E., and Aaron.

Fred had had a heart attack. It was out of the question for Eula to continue. She had Fred to care for, plus Lynch and Maisie. Edelene's telegram read.

> All four boys in San Antonio. Ma ill. Stop
> Fred heart attack. Stop
> Eula needs help. Come home. Stop
> Edelene.

Will answered the telegram thus:

> Train to SA 6:20 A.M. Saturday. Stop
> Meet me.

And he did take the train. But before he went, he asked Faye Richey to marry him. She agreed immediately, and they planned to marry the day he returned.

He was unsure what faced him in San Antonio. To be fair, he had almost put the responsibility of caring for the boys out of his mind. As far as he knew, they were all in good hands. He didn't even know the boys had been returned to San Antonio and had no idea how they got there.

He had never even kissed Faye Richey. They spent hours in the evenings talking after her children were down for the night, but it had never moved beyond that. Will wasn't ready for a new romance, and he certainly wasn't ready for another marriage. If I'd thought his hasty decision was anything other than needing someone to help with the boys, I might have been jealous. As it was, I just told myself it wasn't uncommon for widowers to seek companionship and support from a new wife. It didn't mean he cared less for me or that he was finished grieving my loss.

If things in Del Rio had remained stable and Fred Brown hadn't had a heart attack, I don't think they ever would have gotten around to getting married. But things did happen in Del Rio. Mama Sarah's health took a turn for the worse, and she sent Will a letter telling him he needed to come for the boys. He didn't respond to her as fast as she thought he should, so she contacted Edelene and told her to come take the kids. By the time Will got around to writing to his ma, Charles, W.E., and Aaron were already in San Antonio with Edelene.

In this state I'm in, emotions are difficult to describe. I feel love, compassion, sympathy, disappointment, longing, and guilt for being relieved of the constant anxiety of living in fear of Jimmy. I never expected him to kill me, but I lived in fear of another violent attack like the one that had produced Lynch. Death was a relief in so many ways. Yet, I felt guilty for leaving Will to manage the children on his own, and I felt appreciation for the members of his family who were willing to help him.

Mrs. Richey had set her sights on my husband, and he was responding. Mrs. Richey and Will spent most evenings washing up the dinner dishes together and sitting on the screened porch, visiting until after dark. Will never helped me with the dishes. I knew it was an excuse to spend time with his new lady friend, and it would most likely come to a screeching halt if they married. I was happy with the arrangement because it kept Will's mind off the sauce, and his drinking had slowed considerably.

The night he proposed to her was just such a night. He held the telegram in his lap, fiddling with the edges, folding, and unfolding it again and again.

Faye watched him, her eyes shifting from the telegram in his hands to his face scrunched up with worry, until her curiosity got the best of her. "Bad news?" she asked.

"Could be," Will said.

"Are your boys okay?" she asked.

"Think so," he answered. "I need to go to San Antone and get them."

"San Antonio? I thought they were in Del Rio."

"Me too. This telegram says different."

"What happened?"

"Not sure. Says my ma took a turn for the worse, and my sister Edelene went to Del Rio and got the boys. They're at her place now. She says I need to come get them."

"I'm sorry. What will you do? You don't have anywhere to live except your room here, do you?"

"Nope."

They sat in silence while Will fingered the telegram.

"I was thinkin'…" he said, then closed his mouth and his eyes.

"What? What were you thinking?"

"I was just wonderin' how you'd feel about marryin' me and lettin' me bring three of them here to live."

"I don't know…I mean, I hadn't thought of anything like that…"

"I know it's sudden, but I've been thinkin' on it for some time now."

"You have? Oh my, Will. I think it would be splendid!"

"Is that a yes then?"

"Yes, it is," and with that, she jumped out of her rocking chair and threw her arms around Will's neck.

I'd never once felt jealous of anyone or anything with Will, but I admit I was jealous in that moment.

Faye appeared thrilled at the prospect of a man around to help with things. She hastily planned where she would put everyone. "I'll put Favel in with Rosemary. They're young enough that it won't hurt them to share. Your boys will need to share the room you've been renting. We'll need another bed in there. We can put the two youngest in one bed and the older boy in the other. You…" she paused and looked up to catch Will's eye "…can move your things into my room. We'll settle everything as soon as the justice of the peace says the word."

Will's face turned the color of a man caught cheating at cards. As always, his protruding ears went red first. And the rest followed. He nodded as though he'd been struck dumb. I'll admit I took a perverse pleasure in seeing him so uncomfortable.

Faye said, "I'm not sure how we'll make ends meet now that I won't have rent from the room."

Will said, "I've been sending money to Ma, Pa, and my sister to care for the kids. I think it will more than replace what you'll lose." Then he stood and put his arms around Mrs. Faye Richey.

She melted against him, and they shared their first awkward kiss. If he'd expected a spark, he didn't get one. She looked flustered, stepped away, and said, "I can hardly wait to tell Favel and Rosemary they're going to have a new daddy."

"Do you want me to be there?" Will asked.

"Not unless you want," Faye said. "You need to pack. You're facing an early start in the morning." She turned to leave and then turned back. "Will, should we plan to be married at the justice of the peace's office as soon as you come back?"

"Yeah. I won't be gone long. Just up and back on the weekend. I'll arrange to be off work tomorrow and Monday. We'll get the license first thing Monday. You can make an appointment for late in the day."

Faye flashed a big smile and scooted on inside, humming happily.

Will's relief was evident. I don't think he'd given much thought to taking on two more young children and being a father to them. It seemed to me Faye and Will had very different motivations for this union.

CHAPTER SIXTEEN

Edelene met Will's train with Lynch by the hand. Charles, W.E., and Aaron were behind her, holding hands in a chain like Will taught them when they went to the mighty Rio Grande. My heart swelled with joy when I saw them all together like that. The only one missing was our little girl.

Edelene and Will had never been close. He was seven years older and had moved out to live with Robert and Elizabeth Upton when she was too young to be of much interest to him. She was two years older than me. I knew her from school, but we were not pals. I saw panic in her eyes and her body was tense as a watch spring.

"Will! Will! Over here," she hailed him as he stepped off the train.

Will looked around until he spotted her waving with her free hand, nearly lifting Lynch off the ground in her need to attract his attention. He nodded to her and touched the brim of his fedora. He took one step toward her before the line behind her broke into a gallop and consumed him in hugs with cries of "Pa" and "Daddy" tumbling over one another.

"I missed you, Pa. Why were you gone so long?"

"Daddy, Granmama can't keep us anymore."

"Are you taking us home now?"

Their voices filled the air as the three eldest clamored for Will's attention.

"Now, just a doggone minute," Will said, trying to extract himself from three sets of anxious arms. "Calm down. Let's get situated. Then we'll talk." He moved toward Edelene and lifted Lynch off the ground in a bear hug. "How's my boy?" he said, looking at Edelene for the answer.

"He's fine, Will. I've had him for the last month. Since Fred's coronary. Eula had her hands full with Maisie and caring for Fred when he came home from the hospital."

"How's he doin'?" Will asked.

"It was touch and go for a few days, but he seems stronger every time I see him. We all pray he's going to be okay. Whatever would Eula do if he didn't make it?"

"So, she asked you to take Lyn? Is that permanent then? She's keepin' Maisie, and you're takin' Lyn?"

"No. I mean, no, I'm not taking Lynch. She's planning to keep Maisie, but she can't manage both, and since I was helping, she asked me to take him off her hands. I can't keep him. I'm expecting one of my own in another month. It's too hard to keep track of him now, and I'd never keep up once the baby comes."

Will's shoulders slumped, and his face drooped with disappointment. He hadn't told his new wife-to-be there would be four little boys. He wasn't counting on taking Lynch. He put his arms around the shoulders of the older two and pulled them to his side. Aaron hugged his leg.

He took a deep breath and said, "Well, this is goin' to take some talkin'. We'd better go to the house so I can sort things out."

"I brought our car. When he found out I was expecting, John bought it and taught me to drive." Edelene bubbled with her good news and enthusiasm.

I felt sorry for Will, but I knew he needed to face this if he was ever going to keep his promise to me.

The sorting out didn't take long. One visit to Edelene's immaculate, fancy home told Will all he needed to know. The beautiful furnishings and breakable whatnots sitting everywhere would never survive his boys. Fred and Eula told him they had decided Maisie was enough at their age. Edelene was pleasant to the boys when Will was around, but the tide turned when her husband, John Gaddis, arrived home in his fancy solicitor's suit and spit-polished street shoes.

John was an officious man of substantial girth and wealth. Will tried to make conversation with him but was rebuffed. Edelene cooked a respectable dinner, and to Will's surprise, the boys sat quietly and cleaned their plates of every bite. Even Lynch, who was new to the household, seemed to understand that misbehaving would not work well here.

Every delicious bite of pulled pork tamale stuck in Will's throat. I'd rarely seen him so tense and uncomfortable. What he had come to ask them to do was out of the question. With every bite he swallowed, the knot in his gut got harder. By the time he finished eating, he had resolved that he would be taking Charles, W.E., Aaron, and Lynch back to Tucson with him on the morning train. If Faye objected, he had no idea what he'd do.

When dawn broke, Will rousted the boys, shushing them so they wouldn't wake Edelene's husband. He hustled them outside to relieve themselves behind the house so the loudly flushing toilet wouldn't wake Edelene and John. He sneaked a few pieces of bread from the kitchen and herded the boys to Fred's waiting car for the drive to the depot.

Despite Eula's protestations, Fred had insisted he was strong enough to drive them. Jovial, even at this early hour, Fred greeted Will and each of our boys by name. His warm smile penetrated their sleepy eyes and soothed their anxious souls. It was the last soothing they would receive for a long time.

Fred's car rumbled into the station, and Will unloaded four groggy little boys and their meager bundles of belongings. He thanked Fred for keeping Maisie and said he'd stay in close touch.

Charles was first to step onto the railcar. He turned and reached out a hand for Aaron to pull him aboard.

W.E. stretched his leg as far as possible and gripped the metal rails to lift his body onto the steps.

Will was behind him carrying Lynch and saw that W.E. would fall backward if he didn't get an assist pronto. He lurched forward as W.E. slipped, and put his knee into his brother's back to shove him up the steps onto the train.

W.E. let out a yelp of surprise, and Charles grabbed his coverall strap and pulled him aboard. W.E. shook himself free and shouted, "I can do it myself!"

He was so incensed I thought he was going to jump off the train and back to the platform, but Will climbed aboard, set Lynch down, and took W.E.'s shoulders in a firm grip. "Of course, you can do it yourself, Dubbya'E. We only tried to hurry you a little so other folks could climb aboard. Now straighten up here and act like a man."

When Will talked like this to our boys, my heart swelled. He was gentle and firm at the same time. Managing the boys had been my job, and when they were at Mama Sarah's and Papa Irvin's, she was gentle, and he was harsh. This mix of styles was exactly what W.E. needed. Will steered him toward the door to the passenger car and gently nudged him through the opening. They were followed by Aaron and Charles, with Lynch in tow.

What a grand adventure this would be to ride on a train all the way to Tucson. They had no idea what awaited them.

CHAPTER SEVENTEEN

I was only mildly jealous of Will and Faye during the first six months of what she expected to be wedded bliss. Will resumed drinking heavily, and their lovemaking amounted to nothing more than the awkward fumblings of two people who didn't love each other and were just doing what they thought was expected. It embarrassed me to watch them, so I spent most of my time watching her children and my four boys wrangling over whatever one had that the other wanted. Putting those two sets of children together was like trying to mix water and oil—as soon as you thought you had accomplished something, it broke apart again.

Will was pleasant enough to Faye and her children, but when you don't love someone deep in your heart, it's hard to convince them that you do. Gone were the long evenings in conversation on the front stoop. Just as I suspected, Will no longer helped clear up after dinner. His first drink of the evening now occupied that special time and was followed by his second, third, and fourth.

Being with the boys again was difficult. The reminder of what we'd had together as a family had shattered beyond repair. Charles and W.E. squabbled and jockeyed for control. Favel and Rosemary were naturally possessive of their mother's time. Will was short-tempered when the children argued and left most of the dispute-settling to Faye.

Perhaps the worst was when he and Faye went to bed at night and he showed no interest in her. As a woman, I knew she longed for a man's touch and the warmth of a willing body next to hers. Will's lack of affection was a direct response to his feeling that he was somehow betraying me. I did my best to let him know I understood why he married Faye, but my influence on him had grown weaker with time.

Lynch and Aaron required more attention than Faye was willing to give. The three eldest children were in school during the day, leaving Favel, Aaron, and Lynch to vie for her attention. Favel and Aaron now took up where Charles and W.E. left off, trying to establish who was king of the mountain.

Charles made the transition from one school to another without difficulty, but school wasn't going well for W.E. He didn't like the confinement of a classroom. His eyes wandered, he fidgeted in his desk chair, and one day, he fell on the floor with a thud. The teacher snatched him upright by his shirt collar and marched him down the hall to the principal's office.

Seated opposite the man at an imposing desk, W.E. fought back tears.

"What's your name, young man?" the principal asked.

"Bill Jones," W.E. responded, as he had decided W.E. was too long for a name.

That wasn't the name on the file before the principal, so he asked again. "I said, what's your name?"

"Bill Jones," came the second grader's defiant and belligerent response.

The principal came out from behind the desk and grabbed W.E.'s hand, flattening it on the wood surface where he soundly rapped it with a wood paddle.

W.E. yelped and pulled his hand back.

"Unless you want me to do that again, you'd better tell me your name this time."

"Bill Jones," W.E. said as tears slid off his reddened cheeks.

"Young man. I have a file here that lists your name as William Echols Jones, Junior. Is that your name?" Suddenly, he looked chagrined and said, "Oh, is Bill a short version of William? I thought you were called W.E.—that's what it says here."

The principal lost that round and was embarrassed for his behavior, so he sent W.E. back to class with a stern warning to "sit up straight and keep your eyes to the front, understand?"

The experience did not humble W.E. His hand hurt, and his ego was a little dented, but he was back in class with no further punishment—a clear victory in his mind.

From that day on, W.E. went by Bill. I had a hard time getting used to it, but in Arizona, it wasn't common to use initials for names like we did in Texas, and W.E. had taken some teasing. Fitting in is important to children—my boy was no exception.

The ribbing was harder on me than it was on him. I suffered when someone teased him, and I wanted to smack that principal just as hard as he hit my son. The only time "Bill" had been struck was the whack on his bottom I gave him the morning after I was ravaged, and he ran away from me and hid under the rabbit hutch. I thought Jimmy had grabbed him and reacted badly. The memory still caused me anguish.

The school sent home a notice of the infraction, and Will had to give W.E. a talking-to. He sat him down and said, "Dubbya'E, why don't you tell me what happened here?"

"Pa, I don't want to be called Dubbya'E anymore. None of the kids here use initials for names. You already took Will, so I decided I want Bill."

"Okay. I guess if you want to be called Bill, we can manage that. But what happened to send you to the principal's office?"

"I fell out of my desk."

"How'd that happen?"

"I was trying to look out the window to rest my eyes, and I slipped."

"Dubbya'E—I mean Bill—it's important to pay attention to the teacher when you're in school. You can rest your eyes at recess and home. When you're in class, you'd best keep your eyes on the teacher."

"I'll try, Pa, but she's boring. I hate school."

"I didn't much take to school either when I was your age, but it's important, and it would have been very important to your ma, so try harder."

Faye made the mistake of inserting herself into the conversation, and that was the beginning of the end. "Not just his ma, Will. It's embarrassing to me, too. I think you should give him something to remember this by."

Will turned on her and said, "If I want your opinion, I'll ask for it."

Faye fired back with, "It will be a cold day in Hell when you ever ask my opinion about anything."

"Since when do I need your opinion to talk to my son?"

"Since you decided I'd make a good substitute mother to your four waifs. If you don't want me involved with their upbringing, you should take them and find another place to live."

"If that's what you want me to do, that's what I'll do." Will stomped off, calling Charles, Aaron, and Lynch. When he had rounded up all four boys, he said, "Get your things together. We're moving in the morning."

When he and Faye went to bed that night, she tried to reason with him, and he rebuffed her. "Where will you go?" she pleaded. "You don't have anyplace to take four youngsters."

"I'll live in my car if I have to. Anything would be better than this. I thought I could make this work, but I can't. I don't love you, you don't love my boys, and your kids pay about as much attention to me as a buzz-fly."

"I'll try harder to learn to love your boys," she said.

"It won't work, Faye. Either you love something, or you don't. You know this marriage was a bad idea, and so do I. You'll have your house, and you can rent the room again. Get a divorce if you want or leave it the way it is. I won't ever marry again, so it doesn't make any difference to me."

Will took the boys and moved them out of Faye's house the next day. He didn't have a place, so he took them to the wrecking yard and fashioned a makeshift shelter in the back end of a gutted-out delivery van.

The boys were relieved. It was like a permanent camping trip with their pa. The old car seats Will flattened out for beds were as comfortable as the beds they'd left behind. Faye let Will take the blankets they'd been using, so they had covers.

I worried about their safety, of course. There were so many things they could injure themselves on in that mess of torn-up cars and equipment. I was back on full-time mother duty. I couldn't leave, even to check on Maisie.

CHAPTER EIGHTEEN

The weekend passed while the boys explored every square inch of that boneyard of old cars and broken-down tractors. "Pa, look at this," or "Can I have this?" rang out with great regularity. Will went to the grocery and bought bread, peanut butter, and a quart of milk. He had no way to keep it from spoiling, so he let the kids take turns having swigs until the bottle was empty. He used his pocketknife to spread peanut butter on the soft white bread, and that's what they ate for every meal.

Monday morning, he rousted Charles and Bill out of bed and dug through boxes to find clean clothes. Charles got his shirt on backward, and Bill buttoned his crooked. Will was all thumbs trying to straighten them out. I chuckled to myself, remembering how awkward he was unbuttoning my bodice the first time.

He got Aaron and Lynch up, and with all four boys in the car, he drove to the school. "Charles, you pay close attention here to where we're going. You and Bill are going to walk home when school's out."

I had a moment of panic when I heard that. What if they got lost? Tucson was a city, not a ranch.

When Will's boss showed up to open the office, Will met him at the door, holding Aaron's hand and carrying Lynch. "Well, well, well. What do we have here? You discover these two in that car we towed in on Friday?"

"No. These here boys are mine. I have four. The other two are in school—for now."

"For now? Does that mean you're bringing them here too?"

"For now. Me and Faye's decided we can't make this work with six kids in the house. She told me to take 'em and get out. I didn't have anywhere to go 'cept here. I made a shelter in the back of one of the old, gutted vans. We slept here last night. Hope you don't mind."

"Hell, Will, you and four young 'uns wasn't part of the bargain. I can't have you around all this dangerous equipment with little guys underfoot. How can you watch them and still work?"

"I'm not sure. I'll just have to try it for a few days and see how it goes. When the oldest two get home from school, they can keep track of these two. I might have to take a day off to look for a place. I can't see this working for long."

"Take whatever time you need. Just don't quit on me. I never had a man who could work as hard and as long as you. I'd hate to see you go. You might want to check out the orphans' home south of town."

That planted a seed in Will's mind. Technically, the boys weren't orphans since he was still around, but if he couldn't care for them, maybe it was the same. Mr. Blake was right. Getting anything done with a four- and five-year-old underfoot didn't work. If Will sat them down in a patch of shade and said, "Stay put," they weren't where he left them the next time he turned around. He spent more time hunting them than he did deconstructing cars. When he thought it was time for Charles and Bill to get home and they didn't show up, Will panicked. He tossed Aaron and Lynch into the Lizzie and sped out of the wrecking yard, bouncing through potholes like a rubber ball. Both kids tumbled onto the floorboards and shouted at Will to slow down. He lightened up on the throttle and aimed the car in the general direction of the school.

They rode up and down every street he thought it possible they could have taken. He craned his neck and searched vacant lots and back alleys. He stopped at the school and took Aaron and Lynch inside with him to see if the boys were still there. The secretary in the front office assured him they left with the other students and were last seen walking east. Will raced back to the wrecking yard, and there they were, looking lost and confused.

I wasn't sure Will's heart could take it. His first reaction was to be overjoyed that they were found, safe and alive. His second was less admirable.

"Charles and Dubbya'E, where in the H-E-double L have you been? I've been up and down every street between here and the school a half dozen times. I don't know how I could have missed you. You scared the bejeezus out'a me. When school's out, you come home. Straight home. No stoppin' to jawbone with strangers and no goin' to play at another kid's house. Understand?" The fierce look he gave them put an exclamation point on it.

Even if he hadn't given them that look, the timber of his voice alone would have frightened them into compliance. "Yes, Pa," Charles said, his eyes wide with terror.

"Yes, Pa," Bill said, sounding disgusted.

"What's the matter, Dubbya'E? You find something wrong with that order?"

"No, Pa, but I ain't Dubbya'E no more. I'm Bill."

"Okay, *Bill*. Just so's you know, no son of mine says 'ain't,' and it's 'anymore,' hear?"

"Yes, Pa," Bill said, chin to chest.

Will fixed peanut butter on bread for all the boys. They ate it and looked up expectantly, hoping for more. Will hauled a jug of water from the office and passed it around to help wash the bread down. "I think you'd better go to bed early and get a good night's sleep so you can get up in time to walk to school in the morning."

"I don't have to go to school," Aaron said, "so I don't have to go to bed early."

"Yes, Aaron, you do. We're all going to bed. Tomorrow, I'm going to find us a place to live."

CHAPTER NINETEEN

The hollowed-out back of the old delivery van provided shelter but was stuffy with five inside breathing the same air. Will had a fitful night amid a lot of blanket-pulling, "Stop stealing all the covers," and "I'm not, you are," disturbing his sleep.

When dawn broke, Will climbed out of the rig and rolled a smoke. He leaned against the automobile just the way he had on the night we eloped and had a little accident. Memories like this invade my serenity from time to time, and I struggle to remain here where I can watch over Will and my babies.

When he finished his cigarette, he snuffed it out with the heel of his boot, same as always. Then he grabbed a box of clothing and sorted through it to find something clean for Charles and Bill to wear to school. Both boys had dirt and grease on their clothes from playing in the boneyard of old cars and equipment. The shirts he pulled out were the last of the two each owned. There was no place here to do laundry, and he didn't feel inclined to go back to Faye and ask her to launder their clothes. He'd have to check and see if there was a laundress in the area—if such a thing existed.

After their morning ritual of stale bread slathered with peanut butter and a drink of water from the jug, Will put all four boys in the car to drive the two eldest to school. "I'll be here to pick you up when school's out today," he said, scowling at Charles. "Make sure you have Bill with you."

"Okay. Pa, are you going to find us a place to live today?"

"Yes. See you at three."

Aaron and Lynch jumped up and down on the rear seat, and Will said, "I told you not to bounce on the car seat." His voice was tense, and I knew he was anxious. He is often too stern with the boys for my taste when he's in that sort of mood.

"Sorry, Daddy," Aaron said, and Lynch cackled and jumped again.

"Lynch, do I need to stop this car and paddle you?" Will barked.

Lynch promptly dissolved in tears and buried his face in the car seat.

"Sorry, Lyn. I didn't mean to make you cry. Just please stop bouncing."

His voice was softer and meant to smooth Lynch's hurt feelings, but it didn't work. Lynch ramped up the volume and kicked the back of Will's seat.

"That's enough, Lynch! Any more of this, and I'm stopping the car." Lynch screamed and kicked the seat again. Will stopped the car, and the tantrum came to an abrupt halt. "That's good, Lyn. Are you finished? If you're finished, we can go find us a new place to live."

With that, he drove south of Tucson looking for the Arizona Children's Home. He passed the old building that housed the Sisters of St. Mary's Home for Children, now empty and boarded up. He'd heard about the orphan trains that brought displaced Irish children from the east to be placed here as house slaves and servants with Mexican families. He didn't want that for his boys.

He craned his neck, searching for the building his boss had described. A few miles south of the city limits, he spotted a sprawling yellow wood structure that appeared likely. When he got closer, he could see the large white sign that spelled out Arizona Children's Home.

Will turned down the long drive and stopped. He pulled Lynch out of the backseat and told Aaron to wait. Once Lynch was situated and his nose wiped, Will told Aaron to get out and walk beside him. He took Aaron's hand, and they made their way up the long walk and a flight of five steps to the front door. He knocked.

A woman wearing a nun's habit answered the door. "Yes?" She quickly realized that this tall, thin man was carrying a small, towheaded boy, and had another slightly older child by the hand. "Oh," she said, "are you here about placing the children?"

"I wanted to speak to someone about that," Will said, his voice cracking. He sounded so guilty and unsure of himself that it made my heart ache.

"I'll get the director," the nun said. "Please, come inside and wait here for her."

Will waited. He waited for what seemed to him a very long time—time enough to change his mind about being there at least twice. When the director, an older woman with well-coiffed white hair, appeared, Will was inclined to bolt for the door.

"Hello," she said, extending her hand. "I'm Mrs. Bailey."

"William Jones," Will said, shaking her hand.

"And these handsome youngsters would be yours?"

"Yes, ma'am. This is Aaron," he said, giving Aaron a little shove forward, "and this one's Lynch."

"They are lovely boys, Mr. Jones. How might we be of help?" She leaned down and patted Aaron's head.

"Well, I wondered...I mean, I heard...that is, I was told..."

"Yes?" Mrs. Bailey said. "Would you like to come into my office and tell me what you've heard?"

Will stammered, "I...I...I guess so," before saying, "I think maybe we should go."

"Oh. I'm sorry," Mrs. Bailey said, "I didn't mean to offend. I thought it might be easier for you to tell me the purpose of your visit if we were in a more private place."

"It might," Will said. "Okay, let's go to your office."

As they walked down the long corridor, Will took in the surroundings. They walked past what appeared to be classrooms with many little children looking with rapt attention at a nun. They walked past several rooms with decent furniture where adults might sit for conversation. They walked past a door that led to another corridor that said, "Dormitory." And finally, a spacious dining room with several tables set with white tablecloths, napkins, and flatware. It all appeared very nice, very orderly, and inviting. When they passed a long wall from which heavenly odors of cooking food emanated, Will's stomach growled.

Once they were seated in Mrs. Bailey's office, Will relaxed slightly. It was clean, well-ordered, and had comfortable furniture. Mrs. Bailey directed Will to a sofa where he could keep both boys with him. She sat opposite in an easy chair. "Now, Mr. Jones," she said, "why don't we begin again? What is the purpose of your visit today?"

"We don't have anyplace to live," Will blurted. "I've got two more, older than these two. They're in school. We're living in a wrecking yard.

Their mother died in April of twenty-six. They've been with relatives. I married again, but it didn't work out. I don't know what to do."

"I see," Mrs. Bailey said with sympathy. I could tell this was a story with which she was all too familiar. "So, do you know what the Arizona Children's Home is? What we do here?"

"Not really. My boss said it was an orphans' home. I know my boys aren't technically orphans because I'm still alive, but I wondered if they might stay here for a time until I can arrange something else."

"It's possible, Mr. Jones. It's possible. The thing is, we take children, presuming they will be available for adoption by worthy families. Is that something you are willing to consider? It would mean giving up your parental rights."

"No. I don't want to give them up. I promised Maidee—my wife—I'd take care of them. I can't let them be adopted. Couldn't they just stay for a while? I could pay for their board."

"In our experience, even parents with the best intentions find it difficult to pay board. It's usually much better to find a wife and try to make a home for your children yourself."

"No. That's not going to happen. I'm never getting married again. I tried it, and it didn't work. If they can't stay on a temporary basis, I think I should just take them and leave."

"Of course, that's your decision. However, we could be a temporary solution if you are willing to let them stay and pay for room and board. If someone comes along and falls in love with one of them, we will let you know an adoption request has been made. If you refuse, you need to remove all of them from our care immediately. Also, if you fall behind in the board payments, we make the children available for adoption. In that case, we give you three days' notice."

Dazed, Will hung his head and wrinkled his forehead. He worked his jaw like he does when he's upset or pondering something difficult. Mrs. Bailey let him sit like that for some time before she broke the silence. "Would you like to take a tour of the facility?"

Will looked up and blinked his eyes. "Yeah, sure," he said. "If I left them like you said, would I have to give up my rights?"

"Not immediately, no. Only if you let the payments lapse and don't come for the children before we can arrange an adoption."

"Okay. I'd like to look. Do you have a school here?"

"Yes. It's a Catholic school run by the order of the Sisters of St. Mary's. They are excellent teachers and very compassionate with the children."

Will was impressed with the cleanliness of every part of the orphanage. The dormitories were tidy, and all the beds looked clean and properly made. The facility had indoor plumbing, toilets, and deep claw-foot bathing tubs. The kitchen was efficient, and the food smelled delicious. The classrooms could not be disturbed, but Will could see through the windows in each door how attentive the children were. He was impressed and agreed to bring Charles and Bill and their belongings right after school let out. It would be easier to leave Aaron and Lynch if the older boys were with them.

"Mr. Jones," Mrs. Bailey said as Will started down the steps, "if you would like to take supper with your boys this evening before you leave them, we would welcome you at the table."

"Sure," Will said, "that's right kind of you. What time should we be here?"

"Five P.M. sharp," Mrs. Bailey said. "The children are always anxious for the evening meal after a long day in class."

"We'll be here," Will called over his shoulder as he herded Aaron and Lynch into the car.

CHAPTER TWENTY

At three P.M. sharp, Will pulled up to the school to collect Charles and Bill. Aaron leaned from the rear seat window and shouted, "Charles," as soon as his older brother stepped out the big double doors.

I watched my son's eyes light up, and he ran to the car. Charles clambered into the front seat with his pa. He turned a bright face to Will and said, "Pa, I get to be in a play!"

Will's smile faded, and he said, "That's exciting, son, but I don't think you'll be going to this school after today."

Charles was crestfallen. His thin shoulders slumped, and he turned tear-filled eyes to Will. "Why not?"

"Well, the place I found for you to stay has its own school, and it's too far to walk here."

"I don't want to move again, Pa. Why can't I stay with you at the wrecking yard? I won't be any trouble. I promise. I'll stay out of your way."

Bill bounded down the stairs, popped open the rear door, and scooted in beside Aaron and Lynch. "Pa, Charles gets to be in a play!"

"I heard," Will said.

"It ain't fair, Pa," Charles said through tears.

"Charles, if I've told you once, I've told you twenty times not to say 'ain't.' It isn't fair. You're right. It isn't fair, but I'm out of options here."

"What's options, Pa?" Bill asked. "Why does Charles need options?"

"I found a place for you boys to live for a while, and it comes with its own school. It's too far to walk here every day, so I'm taking you out of this school and putting you in a new one."

"Where is it, Pa? Can we go see it?"

"Yes. We're going back to the yard to get your things, and then we're going there for supper and to get you settled."

"I need to go tell my teacher I can't be in the play," Charles said, wiping tears with his shirtsleeve.

It's hard being a mother when you can't put your arms around your child to comfort them. I'd never heard my son sound so sad, so defeated, so heartbroken. Charles pushed the car door open and slipped to the ground. He ran for the building. I knew he hoped once he was inside, he'd be able to get the teacher to intervene on his behalf, but that was not to be. She listened and offered a sympathetic expression, but she declined to "go talk to my pa."

"I never interfere with a parent's decision," she said. "I'm very sorry, Charles. You would have been wonderful in the part. Maybe you will get to be in a play at your new school."

A dejected Charles, head down and shoulders slumped, slowly walked back to the car.

Hovering over the scene like a mother hen, I watched the boys scramble out of the car and get their boxes of belongings, piling dirty clothes on top of clean, stuffing instead of folding, and squabbling over what belonged to whom. To say Charles was morose would be putting it mildly. I knew Will wouldn't have an easy time with this move. He hoped that Charles, often described as "the most saintlike child I've ever known," would win over the sisters and staff in the new school and children's home to ease the transition for a more truculent Bill, rambunctious Aaron, and nearly blind Lynch.

On the drive back to the Arizona Children's Home, Will explained that this was a nice place where kids could stay, have good meals, and make lots of new friends who were missing a mother, father, or both, just like our boys. When he finished, a quiet settled over the car as each of my sons pondered the parts they could understand.

Charles and Bill exchanged looks that told me they understood far beyond their years.

Aaron and Lynch picked up on the dour mood of their older brothers and sat quietly, waiting to see this new home their pa had found.

"Will you be staying here too?" Charles asked.

"No. This is a home for children, and the only adults are the schoolteachers and the staff who run the place. It isn't for whole families."

"Is it an orphans' home?" Bill asked.

"I guess some people would call it that. But lots of the kids there are like you boys. They have a parent or even two parents, but the parents can't take care of them for one reason or another."

"Will we get adopted?" Charles asked. "Aunt Julia said she and Uncle Sam might adopt me."

Oh, how my heart ached then. I wanted to fold them in my arms and squeeze until their eyes popped. Where had they learned about adoption and orphans' homes?

"No," Will said, putting a definite note on it. "I'll never let any of you be adopted out of our family. If Aunt Eula wanted to adopt one or two of you, I might consider it, but not unless they're blood."

"What's blood mean?" Bill asked.

"Blood is someone in your family. Your ma and me weren't blood, but we were married, so you kids are our blood. Aunt Julia's your ma's blood, and Aunt Eula is mine. I'd never let someone who wasn't blood take any of you."

"If Aunt Julia's ma's blood, she could adopt me, right?"

"Yes, Charles, that's right. But I want you boys to stay together. We've already lost Maisie, and your brothers need you."

They drove through the gates of the impressive yellow home, and Will pulled to a stop right in front. It was still thirty minutes until suppertime, but Will figured there would be papers to sign, so he went straight to Mrs. Bailey's office, trailing four anxious boys behind. Mrs. Bailey asked the boys to sit in the waiting room outside her office, and she told Will to come inside.

"I need to be clear about one thing right up front," he said. "I'm not giving up my rights to these boys, and I won't allow any of them to be adopted."

"I understand, Mr. Jones, but you must be prepared for that if you aren't able to keep abreast of the board arrangements. Of course, we would notify you and allow you the opportunity to come for the children."

"I brought a telephone number so you can reach me at work. I don't know where I'll be living. I haven't found a room yet. I'll let you know as soon as I do. Can I visit them on weekends?"

"Yes, we can arrange that. You can't take them off the grounds, but you may visit and spend time with them on any non-school day."

"I want to see where they will be sleeping before I go tonight. I need to be able to picture them."

"Of course. After supper, I will show them their beds in the dorm. The three eldest will be in the primary dorm and the youngest in the pre-school dorm."

"They won't be together? I didn't know that. I'm not sure I can leave them if they can't sleep in the same room. They've always slept in the same room. It might scare them to be separated." Will was talking more to himself than Mrs. Bailey. It never occurred to him the boys wouldn't remain together. This place had pluses and minuses, and this was a giant minus.

Mrs. Bailey did her best to settle Will's nerves. She had him sign papers stating the monthly board would be twenty-five dollars for four boys, ages five, seven, eight, and nine. He was earning forty cents an hour, which gave him sixteen dollars a week before deductions and left him with about fourteen dollars a week to live on. He did a quick calculation in his head and realized the board would take almost half of his wages. He wasn't sure he would have enough to rent a room for himself and eat.

"Would it be possible to make the payments weekly? Say six and a quarter every Friday when I get paid?"

"Yes, that would be satisfactory. I do hope you can keep up. I know it's hard. We have so many children who started as boarders but are now up for adoption."

"Well, that won't be any of mine," Will said, affixing his signature to the last of the papers and turning the pile back to Mrs. Bailey.

"Excellent," she said. "Shall we go in for supper then?" She led the way to the dining room, where a special table had been set for Will and the boys. Mrs. Bailey joined them.

The boys hadn't had a square meal since they left the Richey house, and they ate with gusto. Will was pleased that the food was so tasty and was satisfied that the children would be well-fed. He noticed that at each dining table, one adult sat with the six to seven children and guided the youngsters with proper table manners.

Mrs. Bailey did so at his table without ever raising her voice and without ever making Will or the boys feel embarrassed. She would pick up a fork from the array to the left of her plate and say something like, "I'm always so thankful we have both a proper fork for our salad and a larger fork for our main course," or, "passing dishes from the right to the left keeps everyone from being confused as to who has been served and who has not." She said, "I see your boys know how to sit up straight at the table. So often, we find youngsters have wobbly backbones." She helped Aaron with his napkin, tucking an edge into the neck of his shirt and spreading it down his front. As she did so, she said, "Remember, your napkin is always on the left under your forks. Just slide it out and tuck it under your chin like this." Her instructions were gentle and informative, and the boys followed along, mesmerized.

Will observed that all the children in the dining room were attentive to the staff person at their table, followed instructions he couldn't hear, ate with proper manners, and sat very straight in their chairs. The atmosphere in the room was calm, as opposed to subdued. It wasn't as if the children were being forced to do something they didn't want to do, but rather that they were comfortable and confident with their learned skills. It eased his mind.

When dinner was finished and all the plates were slicked clean, Mrs. Bailey said, "Now, in gratitude for our cooks preparing such a fine meal, we each take our dishes to the kitchen, wait in line for the sink, rinse and stack the plates, and put our flatware in the bin to soak."

"What's flatware?" Charles asked.

"That's an excellent question, Charles. Flatware is also known as silverware or eating utensils. It is the forks, knives, and spoons you have been using." She stood and said, "Now gather your flatware and plates and follow me. Mr. Jones, you may wish to help Lynch. I'm afraid he might trip and drop something without a guide to help him find the kitchen."

The boys gazed wide-eyed as Will gathered both his implements and his youngest son's and nodded to them to follow this kindly woman. I watched with pride as they waited their turn in line at the sink and watched other children rinse their plates and stack them on the growing pile next to the dishpan full of sudsy water.

"Now, boys," Mrs. Bailey said, "I promised your father I'd show you where you will be sleeping and let him tuck you in before prayers. Follow me, please."

The troop trailed behind Mrs. Bailey until they reached the door marked Dormitory B. Inside, the smell of many children, fresh linens, old pillows, and oiled wood floors rose to wrap them in a new reality; this was where they would sleep.

Mrs. Bailey showed the boys to three beds at the end of a long row. "These will be for the older boys. We'll put the youngest in Dormitory A through here." She indicated a set of doors with glass windows at the end of the hall closest to their beds.

Charles looked at Will with a question in his eyes.

"What?" Will asked.

"Pa, can't Lyn sleep in my bed with me? He'll be afraid if he's by himself in there."

"I'm sorry, Charles," Mrs. Bailey said, "the younger children require more nighttime attention, and we only have night attendants in Dormitory A. If he's frightened at first, the attendant will hold him and sing to him until he falls asleep. You'll be close by if she needs your help. You will have enough on your hands helping your other two brothers feel comfortable in their new home."

Will helped the boys get into their pajamas and took them next door to watch as he got Lynch ready for bed and settled. They gathered around Will while Mrs. Bailey said the bedtime prayer with which they were all well acquainted. When she finished, she took Will by the elbow and guided him toward Dormitory B, the boys in tow.

As soon as the doors closed, Lynch erupted with a wail of misery that stopped Will cold. He looked at the matron and said, "I can't leave him in a strange place like that all by himself. Please let him sleep with Charles the first few nights until he gets used to this place."

Lynch screamed, "Daddy, Char'es, Daddy, Char'es," until Will simply pushed his way into the other dormitory and snatched him from the bed.

Mrs. Bailey attempted to extract him from Will's arms, but he wasn't having it. He clung to his daddy. Will stroked his head, wiped his tears, jostled him up and down, and shushed. Once he had Lynch calmed, he turned to her and said, "I don't mean to tell you how to run your facility, but this child has already had enough upset in his life for me to leave him in this condition. If you can't bring yourself to let him sleep with his brother, I'm taking all of them back to live in the wrecking yard."

"Well, I don't know," she said, "I…"

"Let me help you out here then," Will said, "Lynch Davidson Jones is sleeping in the bed with his brother tonight and every night until I can bring them back to live with me."

A little thrill ran through me. I was so proud of Will. He stood his ground, and Lynch slept with Charles for as long as they were in the

Arizona Children's Home. It didn't stop him from crying himself to sleep any more than it stopped Bill and Aaron from doing the same every night that followed for a year.

CHAPTER TWENTY-ONE

So much that was good happened at the Arizona Children's Home. The boys learned comportment, table manners suitable for "refined company," housekeeping skills that would serve them well wherever they lived, and a school curriculum that was both rigorous and engaging. All three were enrolled in the school, even though Aaron had not met the first-grade age requirement. The nuns who taught my boys were fair, pleasant, and stern disciplinarians. I was never sure if the boys were so traumatized by the continual upsets in their lives, or fear of some unknown punishment from the frightening lady robed in black, that they settled in so easily. Whatever it was, all three of them knuckled down to business in the classroom.

Bill received high praise for his longhand exercises and had his work displayed as an example to the other children. He was meticulous in his concentration on making the loops, curls, and lines as precisely as the examples in his penmanship book.

Aaron was judged "exceptionally bright" by Sister Mary Frances and learned to read and make his letters within the first month. She moved him to a chair in the advanced section of first graders, and he reveled in his glory. In the evenings, he insisted on reading to Lynch, getting quiet assistance from Charles when he got stuck on a new word.

Charles was a favorite of everyone—students, teachers, and staff alike. His scores in "comportment" were as high as possible. He was a solid student and stayed near the head of his fifth-grade class. From the outside, it didn't look like they had suffered greatly from my death or the constant upheaval of moving every other whipstitch. Only I heard them cry themselves to sleep every night. Only I realized how they suffered for the soft arms of a mother or a squishy lap to sit on.

Will visited every weekend. He couldn't take the boys off the grounds, but he taught them to throw a baseball, took turns racing them around the sprawling building, even brought his cribbage board and taught Charles and Bill how to play. He held Lynch in his lap and nuzzled his snow-white hair; then, he went home and drank himself to sleep.

Hooch was hard to come by and more expensive than it had ever been before prohibition. Unfortunately, he discovered that his boss, Mr. Blake, had an illegal still deep in the bowels of the wrecking yard and sold liquor out the back door. That, and the fact that he took the cost of the hooch right out of Will's pay, made it both available and convenient.

I knew Will was lonely, and I knew alcohol had a strong pull on him. To his credit, he never showed up drunk to visit the boys—hung over a time or two—but never drunk. I couldn't fault him for drinking. It dulled the deep ache inside. No matter how hard I tried to comfort him—be there for him—show him how much I still loved him, he couldn't feel me or sense my presence when he was drinking.

It was nearing a year since the boys were boarded at the Arizona Children's Home. So far, Will had kept abreast of the payments. He lost even more weight off his lanky frame by using his food money to buy booze, but Mrs. Bailey invited him to supper with his boys every Sunday. It was often the only meal he had all week.

One Sunday in late May, a large, luxurious car pulled up to the home's front steps. A well-heeled couple stepped out and made their way inside. Mrs. Bailey greeted them at the door. Clearly, she was expecting them, as they followed her to her office without delay or conversation. Once they were seated, she said, "I understand you're looking to adopt a child around the age of eight. Is that correct?"

"Yes," the man said, "but it has to be a boy."

"Oh?" Mrs. Bailey said. "Any particular reason you want a boy?"

"Yes," the man said, leaning forward as if to share a confidence, "our son was that age when he died from diphtheria. That was in twenty-one. We would like to continue raising a boy from that age."

"We have several youngsters that might appeal to you. Would you like to meet some of them?"

"Yes," the woman said. "I want a boy who is attractive and smart. We want to offer a good home and a superior education. He must be white, though. No Mexican children, please."

"Of course," Mrs. Bailey said, sorting through a small stack of cards on her desk and slipping three from the pile. "I have three boys in mind. I'll send someone for them one at a time. They're all in class just now, but it shouldn't be any trouble to excuse them."

And with that, she set in motion the most awful scenario imaginable. Aaron was one of her chosen, the first to meet the couple. He was on his best behavior, which, of course, was the worst possible time. His hair was combed, his clothes were clean, and he looked like an angel. He met all their criteria.

I used every power I had to intervene. I shouted, "No!" but no one heard me. I cried and reached for my boy but couldn't hold on. A teardrop landed on his shirt front, and he glanced up, startled. It was all to no avail. Aaron charmed the couple, answered their questions clearly and confidently, smiled sweetly, and wasn't shy or reticent. He had no idea why he had been called to meet them.

When the three interviews concluded, the couple told Mrs. Bailey they wanted Aaron.

"I was afraid of that," she said, frowning.

"Why?" the man asked. "Is there something you haven't told us about him?"

"Oh no, nothing like that. It's just that he's what we call a boarder, meaning his family pays us to keep him. His father has been quite regular about the payments, and technically, I can't proceed with adoption unless his father agrees to waive his parental rights. I will need a few days to make contact and determine if he has changed his mind about letting the boy go. Aaron has been with us for almost a year, and it's time for the father to take him back or let him go to a good family. I'll see what I can do."

I immediately flew to Will, knocked over things he was taking off cars, pushed parts from their perch onto his feet, and did everything possible to attract his attention. Exertion like this exhausted me. I didn't have the normal energy of a human being, and my frustration was at fever pitch.

Mr. Blake wandered out of the office hut and meandered among the cars and equipment, looking for Will. He had a message. Will had received a phone call. Mr. Blake wasn't in any hurry, and once he found Will, he had forgotten why he was looking for him. They jawboned for ten minutes before Mr. Blake suddenly remembered why he wanted Will. He reached into the pocket of his overalls and pulled out a crumpled note with the number of the orphanage.

Will took the note and said, "I need to use the phone in the office. That okay?"

"Sure. Yeah. I guess," Mr. Blake said. "I'll walk back that way with you then."

"I need to hurry. This is the number of the home. Something might have happened to one of my boys." And with that, he was off. He sprinted to the office hut, hoping to outpace Mr. Blake and have some privacy when he made the call.

Mrs. Bailey picked up on the first ring. "Oh, Mr. Jones. I'm glad you called right away."

"Has something happened to one of my boys?" Will shouted into the receiver.

"No need to shout, Mr. Jones. I can hear you quite well."

"What's happened? Is something wrong with one of the kids?"

"No, nothing like that," Mrs. Bailey said. "I'm going to need you to come in and discuss something with me. Could you come this evening?"

"I'll come right now," Will shouted again. "Tell me what it's about."

"I'd prefer not to over the telephone; this is a sensitive matter."

"I'll be there in a half-hour," Will said, only slightly more controlled, and slammed the receiver back onto the hook.

Mr. Blake wandered into the hut as Will finished the conversation. "I have to leave right now," Will said. "Can't say if I'll see you in the morning since I don't know what's happened."

Mr. Blake nodded. "Take whatever time you need. I ain't goin' nowhere."

Will raced to his car and drove as fast as he could push it to the looming yellow building that housed our boys. I floated along, weary from my effort to gain Will's attention. We went up the stairs together, and I hovered over him as he hastened down the hall to Mrs. Bailey's office.

He pounded on the door, and Mrs. Bailey called, "Come in," so he went, and I joined him.

"What's happened?" Will said, louder than necessary.

"Please, Mr. Jones. Calm yourself. All your boys are just fine. Please, take a seat."

Once Will was seated, Mrs. Bailey came out from behind the desk and sat across from him in the second guest chair. "Mr. Jones, you realize it has been nearly a year since we entered into our agreement to board the children until you found a place to live."

"Yes, but I've only been able to afford a single room in a boarding house for adult males. I don't make enough to rent a house and hire a lady to look after the boys. I've held up my end. I've paid the board every week like we said."

"Indeed, you have. That isn't the point. We were never meant to be a permanent solution to your problem. We are an orphanage. Children in our care are normally adopted into a welcoming family within a few months. I've looked the other way on several occasions, waiting for you to let me know when you planned to take them back. I'm sorry, but I am no longer able to do that. A lovely, well-situated couple has requested to adopt Aaron. I'm obligated to place him unless you are prepared to take all the boys within the next three days."

Will felt cornered, and he erupted, "Three days? How am I supposed to find a place for them in three days? Besides, school won't be out for another week. Are you booting them out of school before the end of the year?" He jumped to his feet and paced. "Are you nuts?"

"No, Mr. Jones, I'm not 'nuts,' as you put it, but I am under pressure from my board of supervisors to initiate placements as quickly as possible for all children who have been with us six months or longer. I'm afraid it's out of my hands."

"What about school? Can't they at least finish the school year here? They love this school, and they're all doing well from all accounts."

"Yes, they are doing well in school and seem to have adjusted to group living quite easily. You have been prompt with the payments and visited much more often than any other parent in my experience. It's clear you care deeply for your boys. I wish I had better news for you today, but unless you sign the papers releasing the children for adoption, I am going to have to insist that you remove them in three days."

"Are you serious? You won't let them stay one more week to finish the school year?"

"That is something I hadn't considered. I don't suppose it will do any harm for them to remain until school lets out. But if I agree, you must come for them before Decoration Day. I will spare Aaron from being adopted, but I'd like you to consider the placement he has been offered. Perhaps it will change your mind."

"No. Nothing will change my mind. I promised his mother I'd take care of him, and that means keeping the boys together unless they're with relatives in the same town."

"This couple has a dry goods business that has prospered. Their eight-year-old son died in the diphtheria scare of 1921. They feel they are ready to raise a son from that age and provide him with an exceptional education—even a university education if he wants that. Their request was for a bright child, and Aaron's was the first name that came to mind."

"No. I don't care if they live in a castle and eat off solid gold plates. No son of mine is going to be adopted outside the family."

Then, the strangest thing happened. It was as if someone had poked a hole in Will and let all his air out. He slumped down onto the chair and broke into sobs. His body shook, and his hands trembled. I was at a loss, but Mrs. Bailey, bless her heart, went to him, wrapped his quaking body in her ample arms, and pressed his head against her soft bosom. She patted his back and said, "There, there. You'll figure it out. I won't press you to remove the boys until school is over. I'll do what I can to help you find a decent place for them."

Will snuffled and found his handkerchief to tidy up his face and blow his nose. He mumbled, "I'm sorry. I don't know what got into me."

"I know," she said. "I know exactly what got into you. The pressure you're under to care for these four wonderful children is more than any man could handle alone. I had hoped you would find a suitable woman to marry to help with the effort, but I know you were spending all your courting hours visiting the boys. That didn't leave much time to give attention elsewhere. You and your boys have my sympathy. I've grown very fond of all of you."

Will asked to see the boys, and Mrs. Bailey said, "Why don't you join us for supper tonight? It will please the children immensely, and I always enjoy your company."

A grateful Will collected himself and agreed. He went to stand outside the classroom to greet the boys when they emerged.

CHAPTER TWENTY-TWO

Will worked hard to find a house suitable for him and the boys, but he was so low on money that he had to ask Mr. Blake to advance his wages so he could rent something.

I was delighted as the boys spilled out of the car, excited to be with Will again. I watched their faces fall as they stepped inside the shack that was their new home. They were now used to clean beds and clean spaces. They had grown accustomed to regular meals. They practiced good table manners. This run-down place didn't even have a table.

Charles and Bill took in the dirty mattresses on the floor and looked at each other with mouths turned down at the corners and eyes scrunched together in a frown. Disappointment spread ear to ear. No one spoke.

"Well," Will said, sensing their let-down, "It's not much, but it was all I could find that I could afford. We'll just have to make do."

"It's okay, Pa," Charles said, "at least we'll be with you every day." Our young optimist always found the sunny side of every situation. Once he spoke up, the others chimed in—excited and all talking at once.

"Daddy, can I go outside?"

"Pa, where's the kitchen?"

"Daddy, pee." That from Lynch brought all conversation to a halt.

Will scrambled to lift Lynch and carry him to the toilet built into a cubby on the back porch. The others all followed. "Now, Lyn, let's pull your trousers down, and I'll help you. This toilet is high off the ground, so I don't think you can aim high enough to get over the rim."

Will was right. The toilet was built on a pedestal so it would drain into an old washtub underneath the floor. There was a door on the outside so Will could extract the pan to empty it—at least it had handles. The boys were used to flush toilets now, so this was a new adventure.

"I'll show you how to empty it, Charles. We'll need to do it at least once a day, maybe more. We'll see." He lifted Lynch and helped him point in the general direction of the toilet. Once they succeeded, he set Lynch down and asked if anyone else needed help reaching the pot.

Thinking this looked like fun, Aaron said, "I do, Daddy," and Bill said, "I do, Pa."

Will helped them and said," I think we should find a box or a piece of wood for you to stand on."

Charles was the only one tall enough to reach and aim by himself. Duty done, Will poured a full bucket of water into the toilet bowl to flush the waste. "Charles, you should make sure everyone goes at the same time so we don't use more water than necessary. If we use too much, the pan will overfill and be harder to empty. And don't pour water in if all they do is pee. Save it for number two."

This contraption wasn't as efficient as a privy, but it looked modern. When they were done with this new adventure, Will said, "Let's go find the kitchen and rustle up something to eat."

A chorus of agreement filled the air, and they eagerly trooped after Will.

Finding the kitchen was easy. Finding something to eat in the kitchen was another matter. There was no icebox, so once again, all Will had purchased was bread and peanut butter.

Charles couldn't hide his disappointment. Of all the boys, he was the one who would most miss the tasty, solid meals from the orphanage. He loved working with Cook and learning how to prepare simple dishes. "Pa," he whispered, "if you take me to the grocery, I can find a few things to cook for us."

"Sure thing," Will said. "We'll go tomorrow. I want to stop over to Rosemary and Favel's tonight to see if Mrs. Richey will loan us some covers for the mattresses."

Charles nodded with his eyes downcast. "Are you still married to Mrs. Richey?"

"Yes…I am…I guess. She never did have papers served, so I suppose we're still married."

Bill and Aaron jumped up and down, excited to see Favel and Rosemary. "Can we go right now?" Bill asked.

"You bet," Will said. "Jump in the car, and let's find some bedding so we can sleep tonight."

It wasn't the first time Will had seen Faye since they split the sheets. He'd been by the house a time or two to check on how she was doing and collect any mail that might have come. He always went with the thought that maybe they might patch things up, and he could take the boys back to live in comfort. But they always ended up in, at best, a tense conversation and, at worst, an argument. He didn't have the kind of feelings for her she wanted him to have, and his visits let her down all over. Her spirits always soared when she saw him again, only for them to collapse in a heap of disappointment after a few minutes of conversation.

Faye wasn't surprised to see Will, but she never expected him to bring the boys with him. She knew he had put them in the children's home, so she was taken aback when they bounded up the walk, calling to Favel and Rosemary. The children, however, were thrilled to see one another and squealed with delight at seeing their stepsiblings again.

The only one who held back was Charles. He was old enough to guess the situation would be awkward for his pa and Faye and curious enough about their arrangement to want to be privy to the conversation. So, he eavesdropped right along with me.

"Faye." Will stuck out his hand to shake hers.

"Will," she said, her voice hesitating with suspicion, "what brings you to our doorstep?"

"I need a favor, and I don't have many options this late in the day."

"Oh? Do you want the boys to spend the night here?"

She hadn't included Will in the idea, but the air was thick with implication.

"No." Will's voice was flat, and that put the answer in clear perspective for Faye.

She tensed. "What favor then?"

"I rented a place on the outskirts of town, and it has mattresses but no bedding. I wondered if you would loan us those blankets we had when we went to the wrecking yard to live?"

"Is that all?"

"Well, if you have any victuals to spare, we could make good use of some of your home-canned fruits and vegetables. I'm flat broke after paying rent, and all we have is bread and peanut butter."

Faye softened and took pity on Will. "I think I can manage that. Let me round up some bed linens and I'll pack a box of food for you. I'm happy you finally found a place. I'll bet the boys were glad to be back home with you."

"So far, but I think they'll miss the regular meals. School's out now, so I needed to put them up for adoption or take them back. No way am I letting anyone adopt one of them."

My four and Faye's two ran into the house, and Bill shouted, "Pa, can we spend the night here?"

Rosemary and Favel bounced in place, shouting, "Can they, Mama? Please."

Will put his arm across Bill's shoulders and pulled him close, "Another time, son. Not tonight. We need to make our beds and put our place together before morning. I'm going to need all of you to help."

All the children pulled glum faces, but none of them argued. Faye removed herself to find the items Will needed, and Charles slipped quietly out the door and into the car's front seat.

When Faye returned with an armload of bedding, Will called Charles to take it. He followed Faye into the larder while she loaded up a large box with green beans, okra, peaches, pears, and corn neatly preserved in Mason jars with little gingham caps under the lids.

"I'll pay you for this as soon as I get paid again," he said.

"No, you won't," Faye said. "In case you've forgotten, I'm still your wife. It's the least I can do. If you run out and need more, just ask." She straightened and put her arms around Will's neck, pulling him in for a kiss. "This is all the payment I need."

Will didn't resist her advance and returned the kiss she offered. Then he stepped back, lifted the box, and carried it to the car.

It was clear to me that Faye wanted to reconcile with Will. It would have given him a place for the boys, as well as someone to look after them when he wasn't home, but he was a stubborn man, and her attitude that he should paddle or strap the boys to make them behave went against everything he and I had agreed to before Charles was born. Will rounded up Bill, Aaron, and Lynch and headed back to the little shack in the desert.

CHAPTER TWENTY-THREE

Will opened a jar of pears to go with the peanut butter and bread for supper. The boys ate without complaint. Then Charles helped him put the bed linens on the mattresses and one blanket on each bed. He put Charles and Aaron pointed feet down on the larger mattress, and Bill at the bottom with feet pointed up between his brother's legs. When the boys were situated, Will gave firm instructions about not kicking the legs of the person beside them. He took Lynch into the bedroom to sleep with him, then thought better of it and carried Lynch back to the main room and plopped him down on the floor next to the big mattress. "We better start the habit of saying our prayers together before we go off to sleep," he said.

They recited in unison, "Now I lay me down to sleep, I pray the Lord my soul to keep, please keep me safe throughout the night, and wake me with the morning light. Bless Maisie, bless Aunt Eula, bless Aunt Julia, bless Aunt Edelene, Bless Pa, and bless everyone in the whole wide world. Amen."

"Pa, can we bless Mrs. Bailey?" Bill asked.

"And Sister Mary Frances?" Aaron said.

"And we forgot Granmama and Granpapa," Charles said.

"Yes, let's say the whole prayer together one more time, and when we come to the blessings, each of you chooses the one you want to bless," Will said.

They repeated the prayer, and each boy, except Lynch, had one new person to add to the blessing. I was overjoyed to watch this scene. Will hadn't had a drink in days. The boys were happy to be with him even though their surroundings were less than desirable, and the jubilant mood I detected in Will earlier was evident in every look, every word, and every action he took. Just hearing him recite their bedtime prayer with them calmed me in a way I hadn't felt in a long time.

Excitement, exhaustion, and a welcome end to the day let them all sleep soundly on their lumpy mattresses that reeked of other unfortunate people, mouse droppings, and stale air. They were together. That was all that mattered.

Will knew he had to return to work. Every hour he spent searching for housing and figuring out how to provide for the boys was fifty cents he wouldn't have in his pocket next payday. That, and the matter of his hooch account and the loan from Mr. Blake, didn't make for a promising outlook.

He had missed three full days of work. That meant his pay would only be eight dollars this week. Mr. Blake took out a dollar for the loan and a dollar for his hooch bill and Will pocketed the other six without taking time to count it.

Whatever it was, it would be three dollars less when the landlord came around, and it would need to last another week. If Faye hadn't been so generous with her larder he wouldn't have had anything to feed the boys. She said to come back if he needed more, but he didn't want to because he knew it got her hopes up, and he didn't want to stay married. He hurried home to face whatever trouble the boys had managed to get into while he was gone.

Will gave Charles strict instructions to keep the other boys inside the house when he wasn't home. He told him not to answer the door if any adults came by. Will worried that the state welfare would discover the arrangement and take the kids into custody. Most of all, he worried that these four active boys would find some dangerous activity outside that would leave them injured or dead. Nothing inside the house could hurt them unless they decided to climb into that toilet or some such thing. Boredom was the biggest worry. In Will's experience, when kids are bored, they find trouble. He dreaded what might greet him as much as he relished the thought that he was going home to his boys.

I hovered over the boys all day that first day. They did as they were told and stayed inside, although the temperature outside made staying indoors uncomfortable. And Will was right. They were bored. He had no money to buy them toys, books, or coloring crayons.

They each had a storybook given to them by Mrs. Bailey when they left the orphanage, and they took turns reading each other's books. That took them most of the morning. By afternoon, they were hungry, hot, and disgruntled.

Bill said he was going outside to "explore." Charles threatened the wrath of God if he stepped one foot outside the door. Bill tried to pull the door open, and Charles slugged him. That started the melee that evolved into a free-for-all wrestling match that left Aaron with a bloody nose, Lynch in the corner covering his eyes, stomping up and down and screaming, and Bill and Charles exhausted.

Charles attempted to staunch the blood flow from Aaron's nose and eventually settled for having him lie on the mattress holding a water-soaked sock under it.

Will wanted to come home for lunch, but he couldn't afford petrol for the car to make more than one trip in and one return trip each day. He had told Charles to fix peanut butter sandwiches and open a jar of peaches.

Charles wrestled with the lid on the fruit jar for several minutes before Bill said, "Give it to me," and roundly banged it against the wood counter, breaking the seal. He'd seen me open jars that way and remembered. The jar didn't break, the lid promptly came free, and each boy enjoyed half a peach with their slice of bread folded in half to make a peanut butter sandwich. They drank warm water from the kitchen faucet to wash things down.

After lunch, they all lay down on the well-used mattress and took a long nap. When Will got home, they were still asleep. He woke them and asked what they had done all day that made them so tired.

Charles said, "We read, we wrestled, and we ate. There isn't much to do here, Pa. Tomorrow, we want to go outside and explore."

Will said, "We'll go outside after it cools off. I'll explore with you and tell you where you can and can't go. I need to show you how to empty that piss can under the toilet, too. It's a two-man job."

Will helped Charles fix green beans, okra, and bread for dinner. Faye cooked the okra before she canned it and seasoned it with garlic and salt. Four hungry boys and one hungry man devoured their meager dinner. Aaron said, "Pa, can we have pears again?"

"No, Aaron, not tonight. We don't have much food, and it needs to last us the rest of the week until I get paid again."

Aaron stuck out his lower lip and turned away.

"Don't pout, Aaron. I'm doing the best I can. If we eat pears tonight, we won't have anything to eat for breakfast tomorrow."

"Will too," Aaron said. "We have four more jars of pears."

"It's nice to know you can count and that you took inventory. You'll just have to trust me on this. We can't have pears tonight."

After they ate their room-temperature meal, Will said, "Okay, men, let's go explore around here and find a safe place for you to play."

The boys all scrambled off the wood boxes Will had salvaged from the wrecking yard to use for chairs. The boxes fell over and clattered to the floor as they rushed for the door.

Will followed at an amble, trying to roll a smoke. There wasn't a lot to see outside. I'd already scoped out the surroundings. There didn't appear to be anything too dangerous, but there was nothing very interesting either. It wasn't anything like the playground they had enjoyed at the children's home and not at all like our place in the Texas Hill Country.

Around the back of the house, and some distance away, was a large hole covered with a sheet of tin roofing. Will called to the boys, "Hey, guys, come here. I want to show you the one thing you can't do here."

When the boys gathered around him, he slid the tin back and exposed the sewage dump. A rank and rancid odor struck all of them at the same instant, and shouts of, "Ick," "puke," "gross," "pew," and a few other choice epithets assaulted Will, along with the horrid stench. He threw his head back and laughed. He laughed so heartily that it stopped the boys cold as they tried to absorb both this gross pit in the ground and the uncharacteristic mirth exhibited by their stoic pa.

"What, Pa? What's so funny?" Charles asked.

"You. You're what's so funny," Will said through his laughter. "Never in my life have I heard four boys curse something so hard. I guess I won't have to worry too much about you getting near this pit."

"I ain't never goin' near that pit, Pa," Charles said, and Bill and Aaron echoed his sentiment.

"I'm not ever going, Charles. How many times do I need to tell you 'ain't' isn't a word?' Men who don't use proper English don't go far in life. If you want to end up working in a pit mine, you just keep talking like that."

"Granpapa says 'ain't,'" Charles said.

"I don't give a frog's leap what Granpapa says. We don't say 'ain't' in this family."

The moment of levity was over, and Will got right down to business. "Okay, let's go pull that piss pan from under the shed, and I'll show you how to empty it."

"Paaaa," Charles wailed. "I don't want to empty that thing. It stinks. Can't you do it?"

"I can, Charles, and I will. But I want you to learn how to do it in case you ever need to. We can't let it get so full it runs over underneath the shed, or we'll be smellin' sewage all day and all night, too."

"We can just pee out the back door on the ground, Pa. We don't need to use that toilet. It's too high up for Lyn anyway. I have to lift him every time."

"Well, you need it for number two. Now, come on and help me." Will had Charles slide the metal back from the edge of the pit, and he tipped the washtub so the waste spilled down the side of the hole. The other three boys stared in fascination, completely forgetting the horrible odor.

Once that task was behind them, Will took them into the desert behind the house. He cautioned them about touching the cactus and told them how to listen for the tell-tale rattle of the diamondback and brown rattlesnakes that might be in the area. He said, "Charles. Bill. Always bring that flat-bladed shovel when you come out in the desert like this. It's got a sharp edge on the bottom for cutting off a rattler's head. It's leaning up against the house by the back door. And don't any of you ever come out here alone. Charles, you're responsible for Lyn. If he wanders off by himself, no telling what might happen to him. Bill, you're responsible for Aaron..."

"Pa!" Aaron said, "I'm big enough to take care of myself. I don't need Bill!"

"I know you think you're big enough, but I'm putting Bill in charge of you. I hope you'll keep each other out of trouble, but somebody has to be boss."

Aaron slugged Bill in the arm and said, "You're not the boss of me."

Bill hit Aaron back, and the two of them ended up in a dusty tussle on the ground until Will grabbed each boy by an arm and jerked him upright. "Now, that's enough! I'm the one making the rules, Aaron. You had no cause to hit Bill. And Bill, you're bigger than Aaron, and I expect you to control yourself and not hit him back."

"But, Pa, if I can't hit him back, he'll just keep hitting me. It's not fair."

"Lots of things in life aren't fair, Bill. A good boss uses words, not fists. If you can't learn to manage yourself, I'll have to put Charles in charge of all of you."

Will pointed out the two other houses nearby and told the boys if they ever had an emergency when he wasn't home, they should go to one of those houses and ask for help.

"It's walking distance to your new school from here. Want to walk over and take a gander?"

"What's a gander, Pa?" Bill said, his lips in a pout.

"It just means check it out and see for ourselves what it's like."

A glum Bill, smug Aaron, and self-important Charles, with Lynch by the hand, fell in beside Will for the half-mile walk to the school.

CHAPTER TWENTY-FOUR

The school was a godsend. It was easy walking distance from the shack, and it had a fenced playground with swings, a teeter-totter, monkey bars, and a merry-go-round. The boys were thrilled to find such entertainment so close to home. Will was comforted by the thought that there would be something for them to do during the day besides getting impaled on a cactus or bitten by a rattlesnake. He thought they might even make friends with other kids around the area. It would make starting over in a new school—in Charles's case, for the fifth time—a little easier to swallow.

"Daddy, can we play on these?"

"Pa, can I push Lyn on the swings?"

"Swing! Swing!" Lynch said.

"Can I climb on the monkey bars?"

They all talked at once. Poor Will. He scrambled to answer each of them before they ran ahead and pushed open the unlocked gate, making their way to every piece of equipment on the playground.

Aaron sat on one end of the teeter-totter and shouted, "Bill, come teeter with me!"

Bill jumped onto the merry-go-round and spun it as fast as he could make it go. He hollered, "No. Come get on this. I'll spin it real fast for you."

Aaron abandoned the teeter-totter, and Bill dragged his shoes in the dirt to stop the merry-go-round so his brother could climb aboard. "Hang on! I'm going to get us going real fast."

"Not too hard," Will hollered. "I don't want him falling off that thing and cracking his head open."

"I won't fall," Aaron said. "I'll hold on tight!"

Charles lifted Lynch onto a heavy board swing and wrapped his hands around the ropes. "Don't let go, Lyn," he cautioned. "I won't push too hard."

It all looked harmless enough, and the boys were certainly having fun. As for me, I knew Aaron would lose his grip and tumble off the whirling platform. Will would get mad at Bill for making the merry-go-round spin so fast. Lynch would tell his brother to push the swing harder and fall out on his head, screaming bloody murder, and Charles would blame himself for whatever happened. But there was nothing I could do.

The first accident was as I predicted. Aaron tried to get off the fast-spinning merry-go-round and fell to the ground, skinning his elbows and knees. "Daddy, he wouldn't stop it so I could get off," he said through tears.

Will dusted him off and said, "Go play on the monkey bars. At least they stay in one place."

No sooner had he rescued one son than our youngest slipped out of the swing and cracked his head so hard Will heard it and turned. A stunned Lynch took a few seconds to inhale a lungful and let loose his scream of indignation at being dumped.

"I'm sorry, Pa. I didn't push him hard. He let go. I told him to hold on tight."

He wasn't bleeding, and Charles and Will ran to his rescue. Will sat on the heavy wooden board and lifted Lynch onto his lap. Charles's barrage of defensive statements continued nonstop until Will said, "It's okay. It's not your fault. He's just too little to hold on to those fat ropes. You'll need to make sure Bill is here to swing with him. He can put him on his lap like this, and Lyn can hang on to Bill's overall straps. Just swing them real gentle like."

"I did," Charles said, his eyes brimming.

"I know you thought you were pushing easy, but it's hard to tell when you're behind the swing. Just be careful. You wouldn't know what to do if he cracks his head open when I'm not here."

Charles leaned down and hugged Lynch as he stopped crying. "Sorry, Lyn. I didn't mean to hurt you."

I ached with pity. He had such a tender heart. He was the one son I knew would never harm another on purpose.

"I think we've done enough playing for tonight," Will said, "What say we head home and try out our beds?"

The boys were now satisfied that they would have something entertaining to do in the morning, so they fell into step alongside their pa. I wasn't sure this playground was a good idea without adult supervision, but it came out on top when I weighed it against the cactus and the snakes. I could always hope there would be other children and even a mother or two during the day.

It had occurred to me that Will would not be able to go to San Antonio to see Maisie now that the boys were under his care again, and I decided I should make a visit. I knew Will missed her, and when her brothers said their prayers, they never failed to ask for a blessing for their baby sister. They missed her, too.

Will called his sister at least once a month from the office phone at the wrecking yard. Mr. Blake was accommodating in that regard but always took the charge out of Will's meager pay. A telephone was an expensive luxury Will couldn't afford.

Fred made a slow recovery from his heart attack, and Eula now had a retired invalid and a four-year-old to care for full-time. She lamented that it was difficult to tell which one was the four-year-old. Will's sister was a saint on earth. She adored Maisie and gave her all the loving attention a little girl could want or hope for. She and Fred read to our daughter so often that she memorized every nursery rhyme in the Mother Goose book. She prattled a blue streak and charmed everyone with her precocious ways. There was even talk of starting her in school at age five since her birthday was December twenty-seventh. If they waited until she was six, she would be older than most of her classmates, and Will's sister thought Maisie could easily learn to read and write with six-year-olds.

I longed to hold that little curly-headed doll against my breast, but she slipped right through my arms. She sensed my presence when I reached for her and giggled with delight. Then she called out, "Mama, Mama," and I thought she was aware it was me, but Eula responded, and Maisie flew to her and wrapped her pudgy arms around her new mama's legs.

Eula patted her head of dark curls and tipped her cherubic face up with her fingertips. "What is it, buttercup?" she asked, acknowledging Maisie with the most adoring look.

"I tickle!" my daughter exclaimed.

"You tickle?"

"Yeth. I tickle."

Eula reached for my daughter, plucked her off the ground, and into her arms. "Well, that must mean it's story time," she said. "Would you like Mama to read you Peter Rabbit?"

"Yeth, Yeth!" Maisie said, "Read Peter."

I kept my visit brief and decided to return to Tucson to keep a keen eye on the boys. Our daughter was clearly well cared-for, was well loved, and would grow up in a safe and happy home. I wanted to tell Will how smoothly things were going for Maisie. I knew he worried about her more than he needed to, but I couldn't find a way.

As unbelievable as it sounds, even to my ear, the summer passed without any major mishaps or incidents. The kids encountered a rattlesnake, and Charles sliced its head clean off with the sharpened shovel. He couldn't wait to tell Will about his skillful act of courage saving Lynch.

When Will got home that night, all the boys crowded around, talking over each other. Will said, "Whoa, there. One at a time. What are y'all so worked up about?"

"Charles killed a snake, Pa," Bill shouted over the others. "He cut its head clean off, like you said."

Will looked for Charles, and when he spotted him, he grinned. "That true, son? You killed a snake?"

Charles met his pa's grin with a nod and a bit of uncertainty in his eyes.

"What kind was it?" Will asked.

"Rattler," Charles said. "Lyn was getting ready to pick it up, and I was behind it a little. I brought the blade down hard, like you said, and cut its head off. Want to see?"

"'Course I want to see," Will said. "Good job! I guess I left the right man in charge."

Charles's chest swelled, and he beamed from ear to ear. The boys all turned at once and ran out the back door to show Will what had caused the greatest excitement in all their days so far.

Will declared the kill a "brown diamondback rattler and a damned big one at that.'" He measured the dead snake at three feet, including four rattles. "Not as long as some I've seen," he said. "But long enough to be mighty dangerous. You did a fine job here, son. I'm real proud of you."

Charles wasn't used to much praise from his pa, and he lapped it up like a hungry pup. Aaron, Bill, and Lynch would all now look to him as their hero and protector. "This should be a lesson to us all," Will said. "It isn't a good idea for you kids to play out here."

Four blond heads with wide eyes bobbed in agreement.

"We'll go up to the school tomorrow," Bill offered. "There aren't any snakes up there."

"Well, now, that might not exactly be the case," Will said. "Out here in the desert, you can run across a snake 'most anyplace. The thing is, they're shy, and if you stand still, they'll probably move on. Keep your eyes open, and never poke at them."

CHAPTER TWENTY-FIVE

September rolled in like a curse in a church. It was hotter than anything Will had experienced in the Texas Hill Country. It was time to enroll in the school they had enjoyed playing around all summer. They were excited. Will was nervous because he knew there would be questions as to why their previous school had been at the Arizona Children's Home. He worried about the authorities challenging his right to raise his boys alone. His defensiveness made him appear uncooperative, raising suspicions where he least needed them.

Will took the morning off on enrollment day. He piled the kids into the car and drove to the school. He walked them inside to register.

The woman staffing the registration desk for new students looked up and smiled. "Well, hello there," she said, "this looks like a whole new family for us."

"I need to register all four of them," Will said.

"Let's take them one at a time, eldest first," the lady said in a pleasant tone.

Charles stepped up, and the registrar handed him a clipboard with a form to complete. "It looks like you're old enough to fill this out by yourself. It will save time if you do it while I do one of your brothers."

Charles hesitated and searched Will's face for approval.

"Go on, then," Will said, giving Charles a nod.

"You can sit on that bench against the wall over there by the office," the lady said, nodding in that direction, and Charles promptly complied.

Some questions were hard for him. "Mother's name," for example, stopped him. "Pa," he said, "what should I put here?"

Will stepped over and read the questionnaire. "I'll do it, Charles," he said, taking the clipboard and pencil. He returned to the desk and said to the woman, "I'll put the answers on one questionnaire, and you can fill them in on the others. They're all the same except for name and age."

"I'm sorry—" she glanced down at the paper "—Mr. Jones, is it? I just thought the boy could help us along."

"No need," Will said, handing the completed form to her. "I have four boys for you today. Charles is ready for sixth grade. William—he goes by Bill—age ten, ready for fifth. Aaron will be nine on the twenty-fifth of this month, in fourth, and Lynch, seven, for second grade. They all have the same mother and the same father."

"Will we be receiving records from their previous school...where did you say they were transferring from?"

"I didn't. They've been in the Arizona Children's Home and St. Mary's School due to the death of their mother."

"Oh." She glanced up, startled. "I'm so sorry. I'll send right over for their records. Now, let me give you a map with their rooms marked and you can walk them to their class this first day. Changing schools can be a frightening experience under the best of circumstances. It won't hurt for you to stay and help them adjust."

"I have to work. Charles can walk them to their rooms—the ones that need it anyway." Will sounded stern and dismissive.

I knew the woman was trying to be friendly and helpful, but I'll admit I enjoyed her discomfort when she found out the boys didn't have a mother.

Charles took the map with the rooms marked in red and headed off down the hall with Lynch by the hand, his brothers trailing close behind. Charles pulled his hand free of Lynch's grip and put his handkerchief over his mouth to cough. He had developed a lingering and irritating hack in the last days of summer. It worried me, but Will didn't take much notice, and Charles never complained.

Once each boy was firmly planted in their new classroom and introductions made to each teacher, Charles made his way to the room marked on the map for his class.

Charles loved school, and he slipped into the desk chair the teacher indicated with eager anticipation. He coughed again and dipped into his pant pocket for his handkerchief.

This time the coughing lingered, and the teacher asked, "Are you alright? Do you need to get a drink of water?"

"I don't think so," he answered, turning his attention to the book on his desktop.

The boys had been in the new school a mere five days when the lady from social welfare made a call at the house. Newly armed with an address, a report from the school registrar querying about proper supervision in the home, and an additional health-related concern from Charles's teacher, she tapped lightly on the rickety front door.

The boys froze. Will had impressed on them never to answer the door when he wasn't home. The knocking continued, and a woman called, "Please open the door. I need to speak to you."

Probably because it was a lady's voice, and because children are curious, a quick discussion inside the house resulted in Bill going to the door. "Who is it?" he asked.

"Miss Van Acker, from social welfare," came the reply.

"What do you want?" Bill asked.

"I need to check to ensure the children living in this house are safe and properly cared for. Is your mother here?"

Bill looked at Charles.

Charles shook his head.

Aaron shouted, "She's dead."

Silence greeted his outburst until the woman recovered her bearings and said, "Oh, I'm terribly sorry to hear that. Won't you please open the door so I can see who I'm talking to?"

"We aren't supposed to open the door when Pa's not here," Bill said. "You should come back when he gets home from work."

The woman gave up and walked away from the door. Charles watched through a tear in the curtain on the front window, and they all heaved a sigh of relief.

When Will arrived, the boys accosted him with a barrage of information. Once he sorted it out, he knew trouble would soon come knocking.

"Get your things together," he said. "I'm taking you to Faye's for the night."

The boys moved fast, and Will had them in the car less than twenty minutes after he got home.

Faye answered her door on the first knock. "Will, what a surprise... and you've got the boys with you again."

"Yeah. Faye, I need a favor. Social welfare sent someone to the house today. I'm afraid they will try to take the boys away from me. Can they stay here tonight?"

"I suppose so," Faye said with a voice full of doubt and misgiving.

"It won't be for long. I just need a couple of days to get a plan in place."

"Will you be staying too?" she asked, looking hopefully at Will.

"No." Will said, "I need to get back to find out what this is all about in case she comes around again. If the kids aren't there when she comes, she can't very well take them. I'll come back in the morning and pick them up in time for school."

The boys stood behind Will, looking shamefaced. They didn't like the sound of what their pa was telling Faye, and they didn't like thinking about being uprooted again.

Will and Faye stared at each other until she finally stepped aside and said, "Come on in."

When Will returned to his house, a car was parked in the front yard with a woman and a man inside. Will and I both knew this man was there to take the boys, and the anger that rose in him scared me. He clenched his jaw, and the cords in his neck tightened and pulsed with every breath he drew. He got out and walked past the other car without a sideways glance.

Miss Van Acker and the man with her got out and followed him to the door. "Mr. Jones?" she called to Will. "Might we have a few minutes of your time?"

"What about?" Will said over his shoulder.

"About the welfare of your children," she said. "I'm Miss Van Acker with the Arizona Department of Social Welfare, and we've had a report of concern."

"What children?" Will said. "Do you see any children here?"

"Well, no, not right now, I don't, but they were inside the house earlier. Perhaps they are inside?"

Will threw open the door and stood aside. "Look for yourself," he said, "If you find any in there, let me know."

But of course the boys weren't there, and Miss Van Acker was left with nothing but empty threats about the consequences of unsupervised children and children whose health was not being properly monitored.

"I don't know what you're talking about," Will said.

"Mr. Jones," she said, "we have received a report from the school that you have four boys living here and no one home to supervise them when they aren't in school. One of them has a concerning cough and needs medical attention. I don't know what you've done with them this evening, but I am inclined to recommend removing them from your custody based on the unsanitary conditions of this dwelling."

"Well, if you can find them, you can remove them. Until then, I'd suggest you leave me in peace."

Once the welfare worker and her cohort had gone, Will got into the car and drove straight to the Arizona Children's Home. He took the front steps three at a time and marched down the hall to Mrs. Bailey's office. The door was closed, and the light was out. He hunted around for someone to help him find her and noticed that the light was still on in Cook's kitchen. Cook greeted Will like an old friend and offered to go to Mrs. Bailey's private quarters and bring her back to talk to him.

Mrs. Bailey, already retired for the night, shuffled down the long hallway in her robe and slippers with her nightcap on. "Mr. Jones," she exclaimed with alarm, "has something happened?"

"Yes," Will said, "the social welfare people are trying to take the boys away from me. I need a place they can stay for a month or so. I want to go to Oregon to see my brother and his wife and find out if they'll help me. I'm pretty sure they'll take the boys, and if they will, I can move up that way and get a job working in the woods or a mill or something."

"But what about your daughter? Isn't she still in San Antonio?"

"Yes. But my sister Eula has her, and she's happy. Eula doesn't have children, and Maisie's like her own. I hate to leave and be so far away, but I can't take care of a little girl. She needs a mother."

"What do you want of me?" Mrs. Bailey asked.

"I want you to agree to let the boys stay here for a month while I make arrangements in Oregon. I want you to let them stay without fear of adoption. I trust you. I can't say that about many folks."

"I see," Mrs. Bailey said. "May I think about this over the weekend? You could come back on Sunday evening for my answer. I can't decide this on my own. I need to discuss it with my board of supervisors. Your request is very unusual."

"Please, ma'am. The boys were happy here. They felt at home with you. I can't go to Oregon and leave them with strangers. I'll pay board."

"Let me think on it, Mr. Jones. Come back on Sunday."

"Can I bring the boys with me?"

The matron hesitated, and then she met Will's eyes and saw what I could see—pure desperation.

"I suppose that would be alright," she said.

And that's how the boys ended up at the orphanage for the second time. Will brought them, and they stayed. They were pretty happy with the arrangement, although upset that they wouldn't see Will for several weeks. He explained that he was going north to find a permanent home for them—a place where they would be loved and provided for with a mother, father, and cousins who would be like having more brothers.

During that month at the Arizona Children's Home, Charles's cough worsened, and nothing the doctor prescribed helped. He began to lose weight and felt poorly much of the time. He was anxious to move to Oregon.

CHAPTER TWENTY-SIX

But that was not to be. When Will returned from Oregon he had an agreement with his oldest brother, Irv Junior, and his wife, Beulah. They had agreed to take three of the boys. I assumed it would be Charles, Bill, and Aaron. What he would do with Lynch, he didn't know. Beulah thought caring for a nearly blind child would be more than she could manage.

She said, "My heart aches for you, Will. Truly, it does, but I just can't see how I'd manage two of my own and four of yours when one needs extra minding."

Will told her the older boys would do most of the minding, but she didn't relent.

"I think three more is enough, Will. You might want to look into the blind school for him. Maybe they'd take your boy."

Will barely registered her suggestion. He wanted the boys together, but fate had other plans. When he returned to the orphanage to collect our sons, Mrs. Bailey called him into her office for a private conversation.

"Mr. Jones," she began, assuming a more formal tone than their recent conversations had taken, "Charles must see a specialist about his cough. His lungs hurt, and he is losing weight. Our doctor hasn't been able to pinpoint a cause, and nothing he has prescribed is making a difference. He recommends a test for tuberculosis, but they don't have any way to perform it here in Tucson. You will need to take him to San Antonio."

Will sputtered, "B-b-but I wasn't going to go to San Antonio again. I was going to head straight up to Oregon with all the boys."

"I'm sorry, Mr. Jones, I know your burden is great and you are doing your best, but I don't think it would be wise for him to leave a warm, dry climate for a cold, damp one right now."

"I can't afford train tickets to San Antonio for all of us."

"I thought that might be the case. I've arranged with my board to allow the other three to remain here, at no further cost to you, until you are able to return for them. I'm sorry, but it's the best I can do."

"No adopting them out?"

"No. I've been clear with the board on that issue. This is an exception, but they have agreed. I hope you won't be gone long."

"I can't be gone long. I need to work, and to work I need to get to Oregon. My job at the wrecking yard is over. This depression we're in hurt automobile manufacturers somethin' fierce. When people aren't buying new cars, they aren't wrecking old cars, and that's where we get our business."

"I'm sorry to hear that. I expect we will be seeing quite a jump in enrollment as well, with even fewer resources to care for the children. I want you to know how much I appreciate how you always paid your board on time. If we can give a little back to you by letting the younger boys stay for a few days or weeks, we are happy to do it."

Will left Mrs. Bailey's office with an added burden. Now, he had to explain to the boys why he was taking Charles to see Maisie, Aunt Julia, Aunt Eula, and Uncle Fred, and leaving them behind. Mrs. Bailey's suggestion that Charles might have something serious, like tuberculosis, stunned him. Kids coughed all the time. It was part of growing up to get a sore throat, have the sniffles, and cough. He'd heard Charles sometimes hacking in the night all through the summer. It never occurred to him it might be anything more than a childhood cold.

The boys were excited to see their pa again. He shook hands with Charles and gave Bill and Aaron each a hug. Lynch he plucked off the floor and swung around like a whirligig. Everyone laughed, and Lynch shrieked with delight at a few seconds of special attention. Will set Lynch down and herded the boys outside to the front stoop. He sat down and pulled Lynch onto his lap.

A confused Bill asked, "Why are we stopping here? Why aren't we getting in the car?"

He was just old enough to have picked up that something wasn't right. They were leaving the orphanage, weren't they? Then why stop on the front steps?

Will looked up at Charles and said, "Sit."

Charles, as always, did as he was told.

Bill said, "Pa, aren't we leaving?"

"Sit," Will said, and Bill reluctantly perched on the step below Will. Aaron didn't need to be told and plunked down next to Bill.

"Something's come up. I need to go to San Antonio. I want to see Maisie before we leave for Oregon, and I can't afford to take you all with me. Train tickets are too expensive for all of us to go. I'm taking Charles."

"Why, Pa?" Bill asked. "Why Charles and not me?"

"Charles is the oldest. I want him to see his sister again, and Aunt Julia has asked him to visit her before we leave. I know it's disappointing, but that's the way it has to be this time."

"It's not fair," Aaron said, his tears gathering. "I want to see Maisie too."

"I know you do, son. I know you all miss her and want to see her, but it isn't going to be this time."

How long will you be gone?" Bill asked.

"I hope it's just a few days. I want to get you out of here and on our way to Oregon just as much as you do. The farm Uncle Irvin and Aunt Beulah have is real nice. Lots of land and woods for you to hunt in, and a river right through the middle so you can fish." He patted Bill's head and ruffled his hair.

"Don't!" Bill shouted. "I don't care! I want to go see Maisie with you."

"Not this trip. Charles, get your things. We have a train to catch. I'll be back for the rest of you as soon as I can. Behave and make me proud."

With that, he stood Lynch on the step with Bill and Aaron and headed for the car. He didn't turn around to see the three glum faces with tears in their eyes watching him walk away.

Charles followed Will but stopped at the bottom of the steps and turned to his brothers. "It won't be long, Bill. I'll visit quick so Pa can get right back. See you in a few days."

It wasn't until the car pulled out of the long drive that Bill stood and tugged his brothers to their feet. "Let's go," he said and climbed to the porch to open the door.

"Are you the boss of us now?" Aaron asked.

"I guess so," Bill said, with a pout in his voice. "I'm the oldest, so I think that means I'm in charge."

CHAPTER TWENTY-SEVEN

Will waited until he and Charles were settled on the train to tell him the real reason they were going to San Antone. Words like consumption and tuberculosis weren't words Charles was familiar with, and Will was afraid it would scare poor Charles to hear them.

"Charles," he began, "Mrs. Bailey tells me you've been seeing the doctor at the home."

"Yeah. He wanted to see if he could get my cough to go away."

"Did he explain to you what he thought might be going on? You've had the cough since before school let out last spring."

"No. He just told me to drink lots of water and get lots of rest. I've been tryin', Pa, but it's hard when the other kids want me to play with them all the time. Besides, I knew you wanted me to keep an eye on Lyn. Bill and Aaron forget he can't see very well sometimes."

"You've taken on a lot of responsibility for your brothers since your ma died. I'm proud of you."

"Thanks."

"Charles, the doctor thinks you might have tuberculosis. When we get to San Antonio, we go straight to the hospital, where they have a new test. Once we know the result, we will see Maisie and your aunties."

"What is it, Pa?"

"It's a disease that strikes the lungs and makes it hard to breathe. I don't think there's any treatment for it—only rest, like the doctor already told you. The trouble is, you aren't supposed to be around other people for a while. It's very catching."

"So, if I have it, what will happen to me?"

"I don't know, son. We'll need to let the doctor help us figure that out. The thing is, I don't think I should take you to Oregon. It rains a lot up north, and it could be worse for your cough."

"But I don't want to stay if the others are going."

"I know. Let's wait to see what the doc says before we decide."

Will let Eula know when they arrived. He and Charles took a taxi to the hospital the doctor in Tucson had written down. Our son was hurried into a private room, where the doctor explained he would inject a small amount of the bacillus under the skin of Charles's left forearm.

He told Will, "I want you to come back in two days, and we will see if there is a reaction. You realize that all the members of your family who have had contact with this young man should also be tested, don't you? You should be tested, too. Would you like to take the test today?"

"No, thank you," Will said, "I'll wait until we get Charles's results. I don't have a cough."

"No, but that isn't the only indicator," the doctor said. "Have you been having difficulty sleeping? You're very thin. Have you lost weight recently? Those are also symptoms of the disease."

"I'll wait," Will said, not acknowledging that he'd had trouble sleeping every night for the past four years and not enough to eat in almost as long. He'd always been thin, but he did look thinner to me now than before he left for Oregon.

Will called Eula from the hospital and told her he thought he should get a room for himself and Charles for the next two nights, or until they had the test results.

When Will and Charles returned for the results, the doctor said they were "inconclusive." He said, "You take care of that cough now, young man. If it gets any worse, you need to come back and have the test again. You are staying in the area, aren't you?"

"Well, me and my dad were going to Oregon as soon as we knew I was okay."

"I need to talk to your father then," the doctor said. "You wait right here." He left Charles perched on the edge of an examination table and went to find Will, who waited close to the door he figured the doctor and his son had disappeared through.

"Ahh. There you are," the doctor said.

"I stepped out for a smoke, and you took my boy before I got back."

"Come with me, Mr. Jones. There are a couple of things we need to discuss."

Will followed the doctor, peering through the openings to each door he passed, looking for Charles. The doctor stopped suddenly, and Will bumped into him. "Sorry," he mumbled. "I was hoping to spot Charles and wasn't paying attention."

"Oh, you'll see him soon enough. We need to go over a couple of things first. Your boy tells me you plan to take him to Oregon. Is that right?"

"Yes. I have four boys; my older brother and his wife have agreed to take three of them and raise them. Don't know what I'm going to do with the youngest one yet."

"How old are the others?"

"Ten, almost nine, and almost seven."

"And Charles is?"

"Eleven, almost twelve. They have a sister too, but she's only five and a half and is staying in San Antonio."

"No mother?"

"No mother. She died in twenty-six."

"I'm sorry to hear that. Well, Mr. Jones, the test we did on Charles was inconclusive. It showed what we think was a reaction but not enough of one to say one way or the other. If the cough persists, I advise you to bring him back every three months for a retest. TB is a troublesome disease. It can lie dormant for many years. In Charles's case, he shouldn't be around other children as long as he has a cough. If nothing more dramatic shows up within the year, I will clear him to travel."

Poor Will. He looked like someone had hit him in the face with a wet towel. This was not the news he hoped for, and it put him in an even bigger bind than the one at the Arizona Children's Home. His mind was spinning faster than a playground merry-go-round. Where could he leave Charles? If he only had Bill, Aaron, and Lynch, would Beulah agree to take Lynch? Could he take Charles to see Maisie? Which of his sisters could he count on to take Charles? Should he call Julia and see if she would take him?

Once the initial shock wore off, Will stood and thanked the doctor for his advice. "I don't know what to do next," he said. "I left the other three at an orphanage in Tucson, and I have to go back and get them. I don't have a job. I'm almost out of money. If Charles can't be around other kids, I don't know where to put him. Everybody I know here has kids."

The words fell out in a stream. It sounded like he was talking to himself, but the doctor was listening. "It isn't that he can't be around other children. He just needs to keep his face covered. He can go to school. He just can't play sports or other exerting activities until we know. He needs a quiet place to rest and get his health back."

Will shook his head. The bewilderment on his face made my heart ache. He needed me to tell him how to solve this problem, and I couldn't. I thought very hard about Julia. I wanted Will to land on her as the solution. Charles loved her, and she loved him. She didn't have children. It could be a good thing for both of them.

The doctor led Will to the room where Charles sat, clad in an examination garment, his shoes, and socks. A tiny patch covered the test on his forearm.

"Why you in that get-up?" Will asked.

Charles shrugged and said, "The nurse told me to take off my pants and shirt and put this on. I don't know why."

"Time to go, Tiger. We have places to go and people to see. Ready?"

Charles slid off the table and grabbed his clothes off a chair. Once dressed, he looked up at his pa and said, "Am I going to be all right?"

"Sure, you are. We have some things to decide, but I'm sure your ma is watching over you, and she'll see to it you're all right."

"Pa, do I have that word the doctor said? Tubber-something."

"Tuberculosis, and no, you don't have it yet, but the next year will tell the story."

He took Charles by the hand and led him out of the hospital. He handed Charles his handkerchief and said, "Make this into a bandit mask and tie it over your nose and mouth. The doc says you need to keep your face covered when you're around other kids, and I want to go see Maisie."

"Me too!" Charles skipped along the hallway and pushed through the big door at the end. "I'll race you to the car," he called back at Will.

"No, Charles, no racing. That's the other thing the doc said, no rambunctious activities."

Charles pulled up and stopped. "No running?"

"No running. No jumping. No playing catch. No roughhousing with your brothers. I think you've been sentenced to a year of no fun."

"So, I'm not really okay, am I?" he said as another coughing fit struck.

"The doctor says you need to stay in San Antone for a year and come in for tests every three months. No travel to Oregon until we know this isn't something serious."

I watched with a broken heart as tears filled Charles's eyes. "Where will I stay? Are you going to take the others and go without me?"

"I don't have much of a choice, son. I don't want to leave you, but I thought we might ask your aunt Julia if her invitation for you to live with them and go to school here is still good."

Charles's face brightened at the mention of Julia, and he bravely fought back the tears. After a long pause, he said, "Okay. If I can stay with Aunt Julia. But you'll come back for me as soon as they know I'm not sick, right?"

"You better believe it. You're my boy. Nobody's going to take you away and keep you if I can help it. Now, let's go see Maisie and Aunt Eula."

The visit to Eula and Fred was awkward. Maisie hardly remembered Will and shied away from Charles with his face covered like a robber. Will explained to Eula what the doctor said, and she was reluctant to encourage Maisie to go to him or be near Charles.

"Do you still have your room?" she asked. "I think it would be best for everyone if you stayed there again tonight."

The fear of consumption was strong in everyone. Eula knew how contagious it was and how little there was to be done for its victims. Fred was in fragile health, and Eula's first consideration had to be her husband and our daughter. Will's only hope was Julia. Will and Charles ate a hearty dinner at Eula's table before they left to see my sister. Eula sat Charles at the far end of the table and put herself and Will between him and Fred.

Will and Charles drove to Julia and Sam's place first thing the next morning.

Julia greeted them on the front porch with a wide grin and arms open to Charles.

Will leaned toward her and planted a brief kiss on her cheek as she engulfed Charles. His gesture surprised my sister and me. I think it was the first time I'd ever seen Will show Julia the slightest affection. "You might not want to get too familiar with Charles," he said, surprising Julia even more.

"Whyever not?" she asked, taking a step back and dropping her arms.

"The doc told us he shouldn't have close personal contact with people until they know one way or the other if he has TB."

"Oh," Julia said, with a stricken look.

"It's okay, Aunt Julia," Charles said. "I held my breath so I wouldn't breathe any germs on you."

"Bless your heart," she said, making sad eyes and dipping her head to the side. She squared herself and said, "What exactly did the doctor say, Will? You know how hard it is for me to keep my hands off this boy."

"Yeah," Will said, "I do. But the news wasn't what we hoped it would be. The test was inconclusive, and the doc says he shouldn't come to Oregon with the rest of us. That, and the fact he can't be around other kids unless his face is covered."

"Oh my," Julia said, "so he can't go to school?"

"No, that's not the case. He can go to school, but he has to keep his face covered when he's around other kids. And hugging and kissing him isn't recommended until we have a clean test."

"I'm so sorry, Charles," Julia said. "I have been looking forward to giving that handsome face lots of smooches and you a bear hug." She smiled and made it seem like a tease.

Charles grinned in return and said, "When the doctor says it's okay again, you'll be the first person I hug."

Julia's lilting laughter sifted into the air, and she said, "Come on inside, Will, and tell me what your plans are."

They sat at the kitchen table, and Julia made tea. As soon as she sat down with them, Will said, "Julia, I need to know if your invitation for Charles to live with you and Sam and go to school here is still open. I'd understand if you said no, him bein' sick and all, but I'm sure hopin' otherwise."

Julia peered down at her cup as if the tea leaves would tell her what to say. I could tell she struggled with the answer Will hoped for. After what seemed like an eternity, during which Will, Charles, and I held our breath, she raised her eyes.

"I want to say yes, Will, truly I do. But I have to talk to Sam about something as important as this. He wasn't happy with you when you took Charles away from us the last time. If you leave Charles with us, I need your commitment that he can stay until he graduates high school."

"But I want to go to Oregon with Pa and my brothers," Charles said.

"I'm sure you do," Julia said, "but Uncle Sam is unlikely to agree unless you stay until you're eighteen. He doesn't think it's right to keep bouncing you around from one place to another, and he knows how heartbroken I was the last time I had to give you up."

"I'm sorry, Aunt Julia, but Pa needed my help with the others."

"I understand, Charles, but if Sam and I take you again, it has to be for real."

Will looked from one to the other, not knowing what to say. Charles looked at Will with a sorrowful face. Julia looked into her teacup. But I recognized the determination in her eyes and knew she would not relent.

"Pa, if I stay with Aunt Julia, will I ever get to see Aaron and Dubbya'E and Lyn again?"

"Of course, you'll get to see them again. It won't be very often because it costs a lot to travel so far, but I'll make sure they write to you, and we will all come to see you as soon as we can."

I could tell the answer wasn't as satisfying as Charles had hoped. I also knew that in his heart, he longed to stay with Julia. Their bond formed before he could write; she was the closest thing to me in his world. Waiting out the results of his tests would best be done with a mother.

"Okay," he said, "if you promise."

"I promise," Will said, looking Julia in the eye.

"I'll talk to Sam tonight and let you know in the morning," Julia said.

"Julia, I need to get back to Tucson and pick the boys up from the children's home. Mrs. Bailey has a kind heart, but she doesn't bend rules very far. Would it be possible for you to call Sam now?"

"I suppose I could do that," Julia said as she stood to go to the hallway where the phone was mounted on the wall.

"Charles and I will step outside for a breath of air," Will said.

When Julia joined them on the front steps, her face bore a satisfied smile. "The answer is yes, Will! Sam agrees if you promise you won't try to claim him again before he graduates."

"I already promised, Julia. I may not be worth much in your eyes, but I am a man of my word."

CHAPTER TWENTY-EIGHT

Will picked up the boys and thanked Mrs. Bailey for letting them stay. He loaded their meager belongings into the car and drove straight to Faye's. He had called her from the train station and asked if they could all stay with her that night, and she agreed. He had some housekeeping to tend to with Faye before he left Tucson.

The first thing he noticed was the For Sale sign. The next thing was how thin she was, standing on the stoop waiting for them. Rosemary and Favel stood next to her, looking forlorn. The depression that gripped the country put too many men out of work for Faye to keep her boarding house full enough to support them. Earlier, when Will told her he was leaving for Oregon, she decided to sell and follow him. He may not have wanted her to follow, but they were still married. If she had made up her mind, he wouldn't argue.

The boys tumbled out of the car and raced to greet Rosemary and Favel. Once the kids were inside, Faye and Will sat on the porch swing.

"So, it looks like you've decided to follow," Will said, pushing his hat back to cool his forehead.

"I have," Faye said. "I know you don't want to hear it, but I still love you and the boys. If you're going to make this move, I want to be there too."

"Faye, it's never going to be right between us. I can't forget Maidee, and I don't want to. I was lonely and desperate, and I took advantage of your kind heart. I'm sorry. Following me isn't going to change anything."

"I don't expect it to. But if we aren't even in the same state, I won't have any more chance than a snowball in hell. If I follow you, maybe you'll visit from time to time, and I can help some with the boys."

"It's no good, Faye. I don't love you. You've been more than kind, and you've done enough for us. We need to do this on our own. Anyway, that's not what I wanted to talk about. Charles might have TB. The test didn't tell us one way or the other, and I had to leave him in San Antonio with Maidee's sister. He isn't supposed to be in close contact with other children for the next year. Maybe you could ride up to Oregon with me when I come back for him."

"I hope it doesn't take a year to sell this place. What will you do if he does have TB? Rosemary and Favel shouldn't be exposed either."

"I know. It was just a suggestion. The least I could do to repay you for all you've done. If it hadn't been for your preserves, I think the boys and I would have starved to death last summer."

"I was glad to help."

"Anyway, thank you. You have any whiskey? I could sure use a drink."

Faye stood and went inside to get two glasses and a bottle of hooch. Will had been so good about not drinking recently, I was almost surprised he asked. But then, I knew better than anyone how he dealt with troubles.

Will took the glass she offered and gulped the whiskey down in one swallow.

"There's more here, Will. You don't need to inhale it."

"I need to borrow money for gas. I can't make it to Oregon on what I have. We can sleep in the car, but we could use a few sandwiches and some fruit if you can spare it. I'll pay you back as soon as I get a paycheck. I need to find a job first, but I swear I'll pay you back before anything else."

Will's words spilled out faster than he had gulped the whiskey. I knew it was hard for him to ask. It seemed like Faye was the only person who never made him feel small when he was on his uppers.

"How much do you need?"

"If you can go twenty, I think we can make it. That will buy us a hundred gallons, and with what I have, I think it will get us there."

"Will you promise to write to me? Do you have your brother's address so I can reach you if necessary? I want to know you got there okay, and I want you to let me know how Charles is as soon as you hear."

"Yeah. They have a telephone, too. I'll leave you the number. Please don't start out without letting me know you're on the way."

"I promise."

"I need to turn in so we can get an early start."

"I'll get the money and meet you inside. Where are you going to sleep?

"Would you like me to sleep with you?"

"Very much."

"I'll have one more drink and see you soon."

Faye packed sandwiches, lemonade, and apples for Will and the boys and put the food box near the front door so Will could carry it to the car in the morning. Once all the kids were settled in their beds, she hurried down the hall to change her sheets. I could tell she was nervous about inviting Will to her bed. She had pinned her hopes on reconciliation, and Will had pulled the rug out from under her. Now, she would have one more chance to tempt him to reconsider.

Will walked into the bedroom he and Faye had shared for the last time almost two years ago. He stripped to his skivvies and crawled between the sheets.

Faye turned her body and reached for him. He stiffened at her touch, and she almost lost her nerve. "Faye, we need to think about getting a divorce."

"I don't want a divorce, and you can't afford one," she said, rolling onto her back. It was the first time in my observation she had ever said anything that could make Will feel less than.

"Not now, I can't," he said. "As soon as I get a job up north, I'll file the papers. That is after I send you the twenty dollars I owe you."

"Make love to me and keep the twenty dollars." She rolled toward him again and caressed him, slipping her hand inside his shorts.

Will's body responded of its own accord. He groaned and raised his hips to meet her touch. "It won't change anything between us," he mumbled between moans and feeble attempts to get her to remove her hand.

"You've made that clear," she whispered next to his ear. "I'm your wife, like it or not, and I have needs, just the same as you do."

"If I drink enough whiskey, I forget about my needs. You might want to try it sometime."

"No thanks. I'll keep it in mind for another time, though. Right now, the sexiest man I know is in bed with me, and I intend to have my needs met."

And they made love. It was the most successful coupling they had ever experienced. If Faye was bent on turning Will's head, she was mighty close to succeeding. I felt guilty watching them and moved my oversight down the hall to my sleeping sons.

CHAPTER TWENTY-NINE

Packed to the ceiling, our trusty Lizzie rolled out of Tucson early that late fall morning in 1930. The boys shouted out the windows to everyone they passed, "Oregon, here we come!"

Will explained Charles's absence by saying he wanted to stay with Aunt Julia and attend school in San Antonio. He never mentioned the doctor or the test that didn't tell them anything. He never told them Charles couldn't be around other children. He let them believe Charles had chosen a life with Julia over his life with them. Of course, it was a terrible mistake that would have unforeseen consequences as the boys attempted to adapt to yet another living situation.

Will tried to make the trip an adventure, and he succeeded for the most part. He told them stories about the great hunting on Irvin's farm and the steelhead they could catch from the Siletz River that ran through the property. He spun yarns long enough to knit an Afghan, and the boys ate it up.

None of them knew what awaited them, but I had seen enough of the goings-on in that family to know it wouldn't be a picnic. Irvin Junior was just like his pa. Unforgiving, mean as a rattlesnake, and utterly unaware of the feelings and sensitivities of his wife and children. A strap to him was just a necessary tool of discipline. Will hadn't been with them long enough to see his older brother in action, but I had. I watched them day and night from the moment Will decided to take our boys to live with them.

I knew this was a big mistake, but I was powerless to change Will's mind. I tried everything I knew to impress upon him the foolhardiness of this plan. He was so anxious and frustrated and beaten down that he couldn't feel me. At night, when they stopped to rest so Will could get a couple of hours of shut-eye, I pressed on his mind and his heart. I was sorry for the promise I had extracted before I died. I could now see how hard it was for a single man to raise children alone. I never expected Will to leave Utopia. Neighbors would have helped him. Elizabeth and Emma were there. His uncle Robert stood tall in his life and wouldn't have let Will fail. He had the Masons and the Eastern Star. He left to outrun his grief, and still, my death dogged him at every turn. I felt ashamed for doubting he could still love me if he learned that Jimmy had ravaged me. If I'd told him, none of this would be happening.

Highway 80 out of Tucson led northwest toward Phoenix. It was a mix of compacted desert and gravel. If Will thought the road from Utopia to San Antone was potholed and rutted, he had yet to experience one like this.

The going was slow, and the kids were jostled about. I thought one might accidentally open a door and fall out. At first, Will tried to make them keep the windows rolled up, but he soon gave up due to the oppressive heat. They stopped every twenty miles or so to refill the radiator. Will knew if he let Lizzie overheat, they would all wish they were dead instead of just "dyin' from the heat," as Bill put it.

"You may think you're dyin' from the heat, but you'd best get used to it," Will admonished. "We have a long way to go before you'll feel the cool air of the Northwest. It's worth it, though."

The boys groaned and stuck their heads out the open windows to let the breeze cool them. The first leg of this journey was one hundred and sixteen miles. At a top speed of twenty miles an hour, Will expected to make it the first day on the road. The drive time was around six hours, but he had to factor in the radiator stops and let the boys stretch their legs and pee. They left at daybreak and arrived at their first overnight stop at nine that evening, hot, tired, dusty, and smelly.

Will would have preferred driving at night when it was cooler. The next leg of the journey from Phoenix to Kingman was one hundred ninety-four miles, part hard surface, and part compacted desert and gravel. Will figured it would be a two-day trip.

The second night he planned to find a river or creek to camp next to so they could bathe and cool down. The three hundred and nineteen-mile leg between Kingman and Los Angeles on Route 66 would be easier, as it was all paved surface. It was still desert terrain, but there were supposedly oases where you could stop, refill water jugs, and even sleep if necessary. Will thought he could cover that last remote stretch in two long days at the increased speed of thirty-five to forty miles per hour. But the road was rough as a cob, and he couldn't push the automobile past thirty-five without it shimmying so hard it made their teeth rattle. They camped under the stars for two nights and didn't make it to Los Angeles until afternoon on the third day.

The real test of Lizzie and the boys' endurance would come on the nine hundred-mile Highway 99 between Los Angeles and Corvallis, Oregon. Highway 99 was paved the entire distance. Will planned to keep Lizzie moving at thirty-five to forty miles per hour and calculated the trip would take them three days with minimal stops. Everyone was cranky, including Will, by the time they reached Los Angeles. The boys were awestruck by the tall buildings, hundreds of cars, and people bustling around like ants on an anthill. Buildings in Tucson rarely reached above two stories. Here, some buildings looked like they might topple over from their height of twelve stories and more.

Will took a short side trip to show them the famous Los Angeles City Hall, towering twenty-eight stories into the sunny sky. They were close to the Pacific Ocean, and Bill said, "Pa, can we please go see the ocean?"

Six days cooped up in a car is a lot of ask of boys accustomed to running, playing, and exploring. Will was weary and badly wanted a drink. He had confiscated Faye's bottle of whiskey and hidden it away under the rear seat of the car. To his credit, he hadn't once pulled it out to slake his thirst.

Once Bill lodged his request, Aaron and Lynch chimed in, bouncing up and down and tugging on the back of Will's seat, saying, "Please, Pa. Please." Will drove west toward the ocean. He turned north along Highway 101 toward Santa Monica. He'd heard about the huge pier built there in 1909 and wanted to see it himself.

The beach at Santa Monica was spectacular. Will parked the car where he could keep an eye on it from the sandy strand and let the boys run and splash on the ocean's edge. He dug out the bottle of hooch and pulled the cork, tipping the bottle to let the amber liquid slide down his throat. Then he put it away, took off his shoes and socks, rolled his trouser legs, and ran down the long expanse of sand to catch up with the boys.

An hour after they set foot on the warm shore, Will got a blanket from the car and spread it in the sun. They all collapsed and let the warmth of the rays and the gentle ocean breeze put them to sleep.

Will awoke with a start and sat up, staring at an expanse of blue ocean with white froth rolling up the sand, reaching closer and closer to their blanket with each breaking wave. The sun was sinking low on the horizon. Will roused the boys and shook the blanket before saying, "Race you to the car. Loser has to drive."

They all took off running and piled into the car, rested, warm, and hungry. Will opened the basket of food Faye had packed and gave each boy an apple. They'd eaten all the sandwiches long ago. Bologna didn't keep long in the heat, and peanut butter melted into the bread making it a gooey mess. They had carrots, prunes, and apples. Will counted his money and calculated they could afford to buy hot dogs at a stand near the pier. It was a splurge, to be sure, but he thought the boys deserved it. I knew they did.

With full stomachs, warm but no longer roasting, tired from an afternoon of vigorous activity and salt air, they climbed into the car and promptly fell asleep as Will drove east to find Highway 99 north. This was his first opportunity to drive at night, and he was anxious to put a few miles between him and the Oregon border. I knew he was in a hurry to get there and couldn't afford to be out of work much longer, but I was comforted that he took the time to let the kids have a little fun and exercise. Hot dogs at Santa Monica Pier and playing on the beach were something they would remember for the rest of their lives.

Will pulled through Corvallis, Oregon, at eleven o'clock at night, four days after they left Los Angeles. He had pushed the car over the summit of the Cascades on the third day and stopped for the night at a city park in Ashland, Oregon. Green grass, cooling shade trees, and a lovely creek ran through the park. Will and the boys pitched their tent, and the boys agreed this was where they should live.

"It's nice," Will said, "but there's nobody here to fix meals for you, and it doesn't look too promising for work."

"Can't we just stay for a few days and camp here?" Bill asked, hope radiating from every tired, dirty pore.

"Sorry, son. We need to get on up the road to your Uncle Irvin and Aunt Beulah's place. They're expectin' us."

"But we don't even know them," Bill said.

"You'll know them soon enough. I think we can make it all the way to Corvallis tomorrow if we get an early start."

"Pa, can we go swimming in the creek?" Aaron shouted, running toward Will from a scouting trip to the creek bank.

"Let me finish tying these tent poles to the stakes, and we can all take a swim."

"Yay!" Aaron shouted, and Lynch bounced up and down, clapping his hands.

"Get your trunks on," Will said. "Soon as you're dressed, we'll go in, and Bill, grab a bar of soap from the car. At least that way, you'll arrive smellin' good."

And they swam, and splashed, and dunked each other until they were worn to a frazzle. It was the most fun and joyful time they'd had together since we left the Sabinal country. Will produced the bar of soap and gave each boy a good scrubbing from the top of his head to the bottoms of his feet.

It was now mid-October, and autumn was bringing cool nights to the foothills of the Cascades. When the boys climbed out of the creek, they stood shivering in their swim trunks until Will wrapped them in turn in their one towel and ruffled their hair as dry as he could. When he got to Bill, the towel was nearly as wet as the boy he was trying to dry.

They ran to the tent and slipped into the opening, chilled, clean, and happy. Will tossed their pajamas to them, and they put them on before they emerged, saying, "Pa, we're hungry," in a chorus of voices through chattering teeth.

"We don't have much left," Will said, rustling through the food box. He came up with a few limp carrots and three slices of store-bought white bread that sagged when they put bologna on it. They had purchased the meat earlier in the day in Redding, California, on their last pit stop before the Oregon border. Will got water from the creek, and that was dinner.

Will didn't eat. He rolled a smoke and sat outside the tent, weary and spent from the long drive and the evening's activity. When he rolled up the tent flap to go inside, the boys were piled together, sound asleep. He lay next to them and threw his arm across Bill and Aaron. Lynch was snuggled against Aaron, sucking his thumb. Will considered pulling it out of his mouth. He had been trying—without success—to break Lynch's habit for three years, but his eyes drooped, and he drifted off before he could make up his mind. His last thought was, "Aunt Beulah will break him."

Will realized it would be midnight before he got to the farm. That was too late to come in on folks. Farmers got up at four to feed livestock, milk the cow, and get ready for the day. Breakfast would be on the table, hot and steaming, at eight when they came inside for the morning break. He still had forty-seven miles to go. He stopped at the city park in Corvallis and parked the car. Bill was flopped down next to him in the front seat, sound asleep. He turned and looked behind him at Aaron and Lynch, curled together like two big pups, their thin chests rising and falling in a rhythmic pattern. They were covered with a warm blanket and sound asleep.

Will slid his butt to the front edge of the seat, pulled his fedora over his eyes, and rested his head against the seatback. They slept like this until the morning sun shone into the car, waking first Bill, then Will.

Aaron and Lynch roused at the sound of voices as Will and Bill discussed their whereabouts. It was already six thirty, and if they didn't hurry, they'd miss the breakfast Will had been looking forward to since his last visit to the Joneses' place the first week in September. It seemed like a century ago. So much had happened. So much had changed.

He hadn't let Irvin and Beulah know Charles wouldn't be coming and Lynch was here in his stead. Charles was old enough to be some real help around the farm, but Lynch would be useless as an extra hand and probably a burden to Beulah. He hadn't had the time nor the inclination to worry about it. Things had a way of working themselves out if you just let them set for a while.

"Hungry?" he asked the three sleepy boys.

"Starved," Bill said.

Aaron said, "Yes," through a mouthful of sleepy, and Lynch just nodded.

"We're almost there, boys. We'll get a couple of gallons of gas and be on our way."

Will drove to a service station at the junction of Highway 99 and Highway 20. He told the boys to use the bathroom, wash their faces, and brush their teeth, handing them their toothbrushes, a washrag, and the lone bar of soap. "Bill, you help Lyn," he said, officially appointing our second eldest son to replace the missing Charles.

When the boys returned from the toilet Bill asked, "Pa, what town are we going to?"

"Toledo," Will said. "Uncle Irvin and Aunt Beulah don't live in town in the summer, though. Their farm is out aways at a place called Mary's Peak. They were still there when I visited. I haven't been to the place in town yet."

"Is that where we can hunt and fish?"

"Yep. Mary's Peak. That's the spot. There are big stands of timber full of deer and elk. Little Elk Creek runs right through the place. A lot like the Sabinal did through our place in Utopia."

I thought I heard a catch in his throat, and I saw glistening in his eyes. He shoved the hose back into the gas pump and tightened the cap. "Get in the car," he said, a little too gruffly. "We've gotta make some time here. Aunt Beulah's breakfasts are worth the long drive from Tucson."

They were buzzing down the highway by seven, looking forward to their first real meal in a long time. Aaron had grown very quiet. Will watched in the rearview mirror and saw him twisting his hair and staring out the window at miles of green grass, tall fir trees, and orange, yellow, and red leaves on the trees closer to the highway. He turned his head and said, "Hey, old man, why are you lookin' so solemn?"

"I don't want to go," Aaron said.

"Why not?"

"I'm scared."

"Nothin' to be scared of where we're goin'. Just wide, open spaces to hunt, fish, and explore when you finish your chores."

"That's not it, Pa. I'm afraid because Charles isn't here. When is he coming back?"

Will and I thought it was Lynch who would miss Charles the most. We were wrong; it was Aaron.

"I'm not sure, Aaron. You'll have Bill to help you navigate the new family and school, won't he, Bill?"

"I guess so," Bill said, sounding as insecure and uncertain as Aaron.

"We talked about this. Didn't we? You're in charge of both your brothers now that Charles is sick."

"Charles is sick?" Bill asked. Will had slipped and spilled the beans when he'd meant to keep it to himself, not to worry the boys. "What's wrong with him?"

Will slapped his thigh. He was angry at himself for letting the cat out of the bag. "Damn," he exclaimed.

"Pa, what's wrong with Charles? How come you didn't tell us he was sick?"

"I guess I'm tellin' you now. He has to stay in San Antonio because he needs a new test for tuberculosis every three months. If nothing bad shows up in a year, I'll go get him and bring him up here."

"What's tuber-losis?"

"It's a sickness in the lungs. It makes it so it's hard to breathe. The doctor didn't think the wet air up here would be good for healing. He isn't supposed to be around other children for a while. That's why he's staying with Aunt Julia."

"Is Charles going to die?" Aaron asked.

"No," Will said, "he's going to take some time to get over his cough. Then we'll bring him back to live with us."

"Pa, I want to go home," Aaron said.

"Me too," Lynch said.

"We should go back and get Charles," Bill said.

"That's not happenin', son. You boys should be thankful you will have a roof over your head, a bed to sleep in, and a woman to cook your meals. Your aunt Beulah is goin' out'a her way to make a nice home for you. It will be better than lettin' Mrs. Bailey adopt you out to strangers."

"Are you going to live there too?"

"No. I need to find work in one of the mills up here. Your uncle Irvin will need you boys to help on the farm, and he doesn't want me underfoot."

"Where will you live?"

"Don't know yet. After you kids are settled, I'll find a place as close by as possible. I may be camping out for a while in that tent we brought. I think Irvin will let me set it up on his property."

"Pa, do you like Uncle Irvin?"

"He's my brother, Bill. Of course, I like him. It's just that there's eight years between us, and he left Texas when I was still your age. I never knew much about him after that."

But I knew. I watched him raise the strap to his sons, Calvert and Marshall. I watched him beat them until they bled. I couldn't stay and watch this. My abilities were waning every day, and I had a daughter and a son in Texas I needed to watch over in whatever time was left in this state of existence.

PART TWO

OREGON

1930-1937

CHAPTER THIRTY

Will

The sign read **WELCOME TO TOLEDO**. I shifted down and pulled over to dig in my pant pocket for the address my sister-in-law had given me. Both Aaron and Lynch hung over the back of the front seat, trying to see where they were going to end up. Bill clung to the door handle on the passenger side, peering intently at the unfamiliar scenery.

A large lumber mill spread out along the Yaquina River and bustled like it was in full swing. A small sign on the side of a building said C.D. Johnson Lumber Company. Everywhere my eye fell, things seemed to be thriving. The imposing Victorian houses that emerged as we passed the lumber company were unlike anything I'd ever seen in Utopia or Tucson. Maidee would have been thrilled. Eula and Fred's two-story house in San Antonio was the grandest house she'd ever seen. Some of these houses were four stories high and built from lumber milled right here in the foothills of the Coast Range. Even Faye's sizable house in Tucson paled in comparison. There wasn't a drop of adobe anywhere. Every house had bright green grass planted in front and was well-kept.

I held the scrap of paper with one hand and gripped the steering wheel with the other, trying to spot an address to tell me where we were. We reached the end of the impressive houses and entered a more modest area right before the main street of downtown Toledo opened in front of us.

The boys stared in wonder at the new sights. People walked along the street, going in and out of stores, carrying bags of merchandise and groceries. The business district was humming. If I didn't know there was a depression gripping the country, I wouldn't have guessed it from this town.

We left the city limits two blocks on and passed a sign that said, **LEAVING TOLEDO, COME BACK SOON**. I slowed to a crawl, looking for the house Beulah described. "It's on a sidehill," she'd said, "and the driveway is real steep. There's a gray barn on the other side of the highway. You'll see it right after you pass the city limits sign."

Beulah and Irvin raised milk goats in the winter months, and Beulah made the best cheese I'd ever tasted. I was sure the boys would be happy here. I almost missed the driveway but spotted the dented mailbox that said JONES, listing sideways at the base of the incline, just in time to make the turn uphill.

The house had been white at one time but was splattered with mud and had a creeping brown stain around the bottom about three feet aboveground. Smoke curled out of a chimney near where I stopped and set the hand brake. A door opened, and a boy about Bill's age poked a curious face out. I opened the car door and said, "Calvert?"

The boy grinned and stepped onto the small porch. "Hi, Uncle Will," he called back. "Come on in. Ma's waitin' breakfast for y'all."

I hadn't heard folks using the familiar Texas "y'all" greeting in a long time. It sounded good to me. Texas seemed a long way away at that moment. Hearing the familiar pattern of speech brought a flood of memories rushing in. Some good. Some bad. This would be a new start for me and the boys. I sure hoped it worked. We'd been through enough changes in the past four years. I looked at the grinning boy standing on the porch, with prominent Jones ears like mine, and said, "Come on, let's go meet your cousins."

Three skinny, scared, shy Texas boys clambered out of the car and stood shoulder to shoulder, waiting for instructions. I walked around the car and said, "Let's go. Bacon's cookin' and biscuits are waitin'. I can smell 'em from here."

The boys shuffled their feet and stared at their cousin, inching their way forward. I stepped behind them and put one hand on Bill's back and the other on Aaron's. When we reached the porch, I lifted Lynch and set him down on the landing. His eyesight was so poor that even a short flight of stairs often caused him to trip and fall. I didn't want to embarrass him.

The kitchen was warm and welcoming. Beulah dropped her spatula and threw her arms around my neck. "Welcome, Will. We've been lookin' for you for the past three days. So, these are your boys?" She spotted Bill and said, "You must be Charles."

"No," he muttered. "Charles couldn't come. I'm Bill."

Beulah shot me a questioning look and said, "Well, I'm glad to meet you, Bill. And who do we have here?" she asked, bending down to look at Aaron.

"This here's Aaron," I said, "and the one I'm holdin' is Lyn."

"Lynch?" she asked. "I thought you were goin' to find another place for him. He's too little to help out on the farm, Will."

"Let's get some warm food in their bellies, and then we can talk," I said, avoiding her look. "Where's Irv?"

"Across the road at the barn," she said. "He already ate and got right back to the milking. Have a seat and get your boys situated. I'll have biscuits and gravy in front of you before you can say, 'Don't you do it.'"

"Calvert, these here are your Texas cousins. Make 'em feel at home. Go find Marshall and have him get Dad."

"That's okay, Beulah. I can find my way to the barn after we eat something. No need to disturb him when he's workin'.'"

Beulah put plates in front of us piled high with biscuits and gravy, cured pork strips, and a big glass of fresh milk for each of my boys. The boys' eyes went wide and landed on me, waiting for me to take the first bite.

I loaded my fork with a big bite of biscuit soaked in the best pork gravy I'd ever tasted. I closed my eyes and said, "Mmm. If that isn't the best food I've tasted since Maidee died, I don't know what is."

The boys followed suit and ate at a steady pace until there was nothing left on any plate. Beulah beamed with pride and said, "Would you like more? There's plenty where that came from."

I could have eaten three more platefuls of the delicious food, but I thought it best to show some restraint in case Beulah got the idea these boys would eat her out of house and home. "Not right now," I said. "We'd better save room for lunch."

Bill looked disappointed but pushed his plate back just as I had. One thing I was thankful for from their time with Mrs. Bailey was their impressive manners.

"If you don't mind, I'll go see if I can find Irv. There are a couple of things I need to get clear with him."

"You go right ahead," Beulah said. "Calvert, did you find Marshall?"

"No, Ma. I think he must be over at the barn with Dad."

"Well, then, you take these boys upstairs and show them where they'll be sleeping. I'll finish clearing up down here."

I thanked Beulah for the fine breakfast and went to find my brother. She was right. He was milking goats. Not my favorite job.

Irv stood when he saw me and put his hand out. We shook, and he said, "Glad to see you finally made it."

"Yeah, it took a lot longer than I figured. Travelin' with three kids takes time you weren't plannin' on. I need to talk to you before you see for yourself."

"What about?"

"I couldn't bring Charles, and I know you were countin' on him bein' a help to you."

"You did say three kids, right? Does that mean you brought the blind one?"

"He isn't full blind. He can see to get around on his own pretty good. He made it through first grade okay."

"That don't mean nothin' to me if he can't pull his weight around here."

"He's small for his age, Irv. He isn't goin' to be any help to you on the farm."

"He can't stay then. You'll have to find another place for him. I've already got four mouths to feed. Six when you add your other two."

"We're family, Irv. Doesn't that mean anything?"

"Not much. I left family behind when I left Texas."

"I don't have a job or a pot to piss in. You goin' to turn me away with no one to look after my boy?"

"Beulah says the state has a boardin' school for blind kids. Take him there."

"He wants to be with his brothers. Isn't it enough that he lost his mother?"

"I didn't have nothin' to do with that. You asked me to take three of your boys, and I agreed because I need extra hands around the farm. This ain't no charity we're operatin' here. If he can't help out, he has to go."

I bit my tongue to keep from sayin', *You're just like Pa,* and walked back to the house. My only hope was that Irv's wife was a whole lot nicer than he was. Beulah was outside hanging laundry on the line when I trudged up the drive from the highway.

"You find him?" she asked.

"Yeah. I found him. Same old surly son-of-a-bitch I remembered."

"What happened? Did you two get in a row already? Brothers." She snapped a sheet and pinned it to the line.

"He says Lyn can't stay if he can't help out on the farm."

"I was afraid of that."

"He says you think the state has a boarding school for blind kids. That right?"

"Yes. I read about it in the *Toledo Sunday Times* a couple months back. It's fairly new."

"Where is it?"

"Salem. On Church Street. Near downtown."

"Mind if I use your phone? That is unless you're willing to take my boy on."

"Sorry, Will. He seems like a sweet little boy, but you can see from the layout of this place and all the stairs in the house that it wouldn't be a good idea. If the other kids were in school, he'd just be underfoot, and I don't think I could manage. Besides, if Irvin says no, there's no arguing with him."

"He'd be in second grade. He wouldn't be underfoot all day."

"If they'll take him at the blind school, Will, you should get him up there right away. It's free. There's bed and board and the right kind of instruction for a damaged child."

"He's not 'damaged,' his eyes are bad. Where's the telephone and the phone book?"

Beulah nodded sideways toward the house and said, "In the front hall."

I made the call. I dreaded it more than almost anything that had ever happened. How could I keep my promise to Maidee if I farmed Lynch out to a boarding school?

CHAPTER THIRTY-ONE

When Monday morning rolled around, I had a pit in my stomach like a wad of unchewed stale bread. I put Lynch in the front seat beside me and drove to Salem to find the blind school. It was a new yellow brick building on a large campus spread over almost eight acres. The administration building was easy to spot from Church Street south of the capitol building. I took my boy by the hand and walked him inside.

"Where we goin', Pa?" he asked. I couldn't look at him for fear I'd lose my courage and bolt.

"We're goin' to look at a new school for you."

"I don't want to go to a new school. I want to go where Bill and Aaron go."

"I know you do. It's just that this is a special school for boys like you who have a hard time seeing."

Lynch clutched my hand and kept pace. He didn't say anything more. I found my way to the administration office at the end of a long hallway. Floor-to-ceiling windows lined the corridor, making it bright and cheery.

After we'd walked some distance, I heard a small voice say, "Is Mrs. Bailey's office down here?"

I lifted Lynch off the floor and rested him on my hip. "No, son, Mrs. Bailey isn't here. This is a school, not an orphanage."

"I like Mrs. Bailey. She's nice to me."

"I'm glad to hear that. But Mrs. Bailey is in Arizona, and we're in Oregon now."

We entered the door with Administrator etched in gold leaf on the obscured glass. Soft colors and comfortable chairs decorated the outer office. A large, gruff-looking man sat in an interior room.

"Excuse me," I said, and he looked up. A warm smile smothered his jowly cheeks, and he stood and motioned us into the inner office.

"How can I help?" he asked.

"I heard you have a boarding school here for children who can't see too good."

"Well, that's almost correct. We do have a boarding school, and it is for the visually impaired. Most of our students are legally blind, some partially blind, and all handicapped by their condition. Is this young man in need of services for the blind?"

"He might be. We think he gets along okay, and I don't think his brothers or I consider him handicapped, but he can't see like the others."

"What's his name?"

"Lynch Davidson Jones."

"And you are?"

"I'm his pa. William E. Jones—Will."

"Pleasure to meet you, Mr. Jones. I'm Wilfred Summerfield, headmaster here. Would you like me to have his eyes tested? If he meets the legal standard for impaired sight, we can go from there. Has he had any schooling?"

"Yes. He finished first grade at the Arizona Children's Home in Tucson. The teachers were nuns. They were very patient with him. He can see some. They taught him to read."

"So, you're new to the state?"

"Yes. We got here last Friday. His mother died in twenty-six. I don't have any way to care for him, and my brother and his wife won't let him stay with them on account of his eyes bein' bad. They told me to bring him here."

"Are there other children in the family?"

"He has three brothers and a sister."

"Are they all sighted?"

"Do you mean can they see okay?"

"Yes."

"They all have eyes like a hawk, near as I can tell."

"Where are they now? I hope you didn't leave them in the car." He smiled and looked out the window.

"No. The girl—she's youngest—and my oldest boy are in San Antonio with relatives. The other two boys are with my brother and his wife in Toledo. They agreed to let them stay until I find work up this way."

"Well, it sounds like you have their care under control. That's a good sign. So many who stop here are only looking for food and shelter for their children. Of course, we provide that for our resident students, but they must meet the legal requirements for blindness to live here. Let's get your son tested. Follow me."

I followed Mr. Summerfield out the door and down another long corridor.

"You know, Mr. Jones, we do much more here than meets the eye. We teach the students how to use and walk with a tapping cane, we teach reading and education with Braille, we help students adapt to the loss of sight with counseling, and we have active living and sports programs, among other things."

"What sort of things?"

"We teach vocational skills and help our students find employment when they're ready to graduate from high school. Some of our students will enter at kindergarten age and exit at the end of their high-school years."

"Do the ones who can see some, like Lyn, learn to read regular, without Braille, I mean?"

"Of course. If a student is partially sighted, their education program is quite different from those who are totally blind."

"You said you have sports programs. What kind of sports?"

"Oh, yes. We're very proud that our students participate in sports. You'd be amazed at how good they are in close-contact sports like wrestling and chess. Sports where something is coming at them are not recommended, but swimming, diving, running, and some track and field events are very popular."

"I think Lyn would be good at wrestling—he's had lots of practice holding his own with his brothers."

"I'm glad to know that. If he qualifies, and with your permission, I'll get him started right away. Did I mention that our campus is a full eight acres? Many vocational training opportunities are scattered around the campus, from a carpentry shop to a small farming operation. We have a sewing program for the girls and a kitchen skills program for both boys and girls. So, when I say there is more going on here than meets the eye, I'm not pulling your leg."

"I didn't think you were, but I'm glad there is more for the kids to do than learn to read and use a cane."

"The state legislature funded and built this facility with the express intent that students would graduate with the skills necessary to live a full and productive life. That is our goal."

I was impressed by all he shared and secretly hoped Lynch would qualify. This looked to be a fine place for him. The only downside was they wanted all students to go home to their families on the weekends if possible. I didn't have any place for myself, let alone one where I could bring Lynch. Mr. Summerfield did say that on occasion they allowed students to remain over the weekend if the family home was too far away or the family had no means to take the student home. I figured I'd find a way to make our circumstances fit their rules. If I could visit Lyn at the school on the weekends, I was pretty sure I could make it work if he tested blind.

We entered a large, brightly lit room with an odd piece of equipment in the center. I now knew our host was actually *Doctor* Summerfield. He took Lynch by the hand and led him to a large chair with all sorts of contraptions attached to it. Lyn looked at me and I could see he was terrified. I followed close behind, and when the doctor lifted Lyn into the oversized chair, I stood beside it and held his hand. His chin trembled, and I could see tears threatening.

"It's okay, Lyn," I said, dabbing his eyes with my handkerchief. This won't hurt. Dr. Summerfield is going to test your eyes to see what you're missing out on."

He dimmed the lights in the room to near zero. I was rocked back on my heels as the testing continued and I realized how bad Lynch's eyesight was. I honestly didn't know how he had gotten along as well as he had. It made me even more proud of Charles, Bill, and Aaron for the way they watched out for him. Maidee would have been shocked by what I saw firsthand.

When the testing was over and Dr. Summerfield brought the lights back up, I lifted Lyn out of the chair and held him close. I knew the verdict, and I didn't want to hear it. My boy couldn't see his hand in front of his face. The doctor caught my eye and nodded toward the door.

"Let's go to my office, Mr. Jones. No point in dragging this out. I'll see if we have an open bed. We need to get this young man into the program as soon as possible."

"I can't leave him today. He needs to be able to say goodbye to his brothers. Besides, I need to think about it."

"Mr. Jones, I understand your feelings. Truly I do. But this child is in danger every minute of every day. The services we offer, the training to help the students gain an education and learn how to navigate the world could save his life."

"I don't know. I promised his mother I'd take care of him. I don't know if I can leave him." I clutched Lyn to me and didn't move.

"Daddy, I want to go home."

I was incapable of thinking straight. I was fighting tears. I was angry. I wanted to hit something. How could this be? I don't know what I thought would happen. I had brought my boy here because my brother and sister-in-law wouldn't let him stay with them. I didn't expect to turn him over on the same day. Maybe I wanted the test to turn out different. Maybe I wanted to believe it wasn't as bad as everyone thought. I didn't know where to turn. This was worse than leaving them in an orphanage. At least there, Lyn had his brothers to look out for him. Here, he'd be alone. The panic in my gut made bile rise in my throat. The guilt I felt almost brought me to my knees.

"Mr. Jones, are you feeling okay?" The doctor's kind voice brought me back to the room.

"I…he…we…" I stammered. I didn't know what to say or do. I set Lyn on his feet and took his hand. "We have to think this over," I said. "I need to let him have a proper goodbye with his brothers."

Dr. Summerfield said, "I understand. I wouldn't expect you to leave him with us today. A proper goodbye to his family is essential. I need to meet with the staff and go over his tests first. That allows us to develop an education plan and one for accommodation. There is much to do before you bring Lynch here as a boarding student. I think a few days would give us both time to prepare. Perhaps a week from today—next Monday? How does that sound?"

My panic subsided. My jaw unclenched, and I was able to take a deep breath. "That sounds better," I said and attempted a smile. "That'll give me a few days to talk it over with my other boys and my family. How about I call you Friday and let you know for sure if I'll be bringing him back to stay?"

"Certainly," Dr. Summerfield said. "I know this is a lot to take in all at once. The test results alone are enough to put anyone off balance.

That, coupled with the idea of separation, is often more than parents can absorb in the first meeting."

"Tell me again how it works if the student can't go home every weekend," I said.

"Of course. Students who board with us full-time go for family visits as often as the parents can arrange it. When they must stay over the weekend, they are allowed to have visitors, but only the immediate family—parents, siblings, grandparents—no cousins or young children. We try to keep distractions to a minimum so the students can practice some of the skills they have learned with other family members. We even hold classes on the weekend in the accommodations part of the curriculum, so family members become familiar with the physical implements we use and are exposed to sign language."

"Why sign language? Isn't that for deaf people?"

"Yes, it is, but many of our students are both deaf and visually impaired, and for our students to socialize and communicate with each other, we teach sign language for the deaf to our blind and near-blind students."

"That sounds like something my boys and I would benefit from. How do we find out what classes you have and when?"

"We communicate regularly with a weekly news update through the mail. We call if we ever need to reach the family outside of those updates."

"I don't even have a place to live, let alone a telephone."

"I'm sure you'll get settled soon. In the meantime, since you have told me your other boys will be living with your brother and his wife, perhaps we could call and leave a message for you with them?"

"Okay. I'll ask about that. But I can visit every weekend, can't I? And I can bring his brothers?"

"We would prefer that. I'm glad you recognize the importance of maintaining close contact with Lynch and between Lynch and his brothers. Shall we go to my office then and complete the admission request?"

What could I say? My youngest son was blind as a bat. He was going to need everything they offered at this school. I couldn't work and take care of him on my own. He couldn't be left to fend for himself, and Bill and Aaron shouldn't be saddled with the responsibility. My heart ached for Maidee. Why did she have to leave me? The thought of her made my eyes water, so I looked away. "Sure. I guess now's as good a time as any."

CHAPTER THIRTY-TWO

Lynch and I returned to Toledo in silence. He sensed my mood and curled against my side in a way that comforted me. It seemed I'd had more leavin' of these boys than any man ought to have in a lifetime. I admit I struggled to keep my promise to Maidee to take care of her babies. They were my babies, too, even if they were half-grown. If I'd been a prayin' man, I'd have prayed Bill and Aaron had safe harbor with my brother, but my gut told me otherwise. I knew that situation would merit close attention. I had to find a job and a place for myself next.

Beulah met us at the door. "Well? What was it like? You still have him. Are you going to be able to leave him there?"

I couldn't tell from her voice if she was hoping I would leave him or wouldn't leave him.

I said, "It's a nice place. Nice people runnin' it. I couldn't leave him without a proper goodbye with his brothers."

"Come on in. I'm getting dinner on, and Irv's gonna show up any minute wanting to eat." She disappeared into the house and left the door standing open.

I carried Lyn up the steps and into the kitchen. "Where can I put him? I'll help you get things on the table."

"Is he asleep?"

"No, just tuckered out. We had a big day."

"Put him in the front room on the sofa. You can see him from here."

My brother sauntered into the kitchen as I put plates around for everyone. I watched him counting with his eyes to see if I'd gotten rid of Lynch. "He's in the front room. I'm takin' him back in a week as a student and full-time boarder."

"Oh, that's wonderful," Beulah said from the stove. "Will you be stayin' with us until then?"

"If you'll have us."

Irv made a guttural sound in his throat, but Beulah said, "Sure. We'd be happy to have ya…both of ya, that is."

Irv pulled out his chair and sat. "Quit yer jawbonin', woman, and git me some grub. I got work waitin' on me."

"I thought you was through for the day. What happened?"

"Nothin' happened. Them two young 'uns Will brung is worthless as tits on a boar. They don't know nothin' about farmin'. Takes more time to show 'em ever' little thing than it does to do it myself."

"Where are they?" I asked.

"Sweepin' the goat barn, last I saw. Told 'em they couldn't come up to dinner 'til they was done."

A coldness swept through me. It was just the way Pa talked to me, like I was useless and worthless. "I'm going to check on them. They'll be anxious to know if Lyn came back with me."

"Best not interrupt what they's doin', I say. Leave it be. We'll see how they are at followin' directions."

I didn't respond. I headed out of the house and down the driveway toward the barn.

I found Bill and Aaron wielding brooms bigger than they were against a wet concrete floor. Aaron had tears rolling down his face, and Bill looked like he could tackle a bear.

A broom handle hit the floor with a loud whack when Aaron spotted me. "Pa," he cried, "where were you? We didn't know if you were coming back."

Bill leaned his broom against a stall door and stomped toward me. "Pa, this ain't going to work out. Uncle Irvin's meaner than a rattlesnake. We already cleaned this floor twice, and he's making us miss dinner to do it all over again."

"Don't say 'ain't,' Bill. I've told you enough times already. Go pick up Aaron's broom. Lean it up next to yours and come with me. Dinner's about on the table. I'll talk to Irv about this." I took out my handkerchief and wiped the tears off Aaron's face. "You boys are going to need to toughen up real fast. I don't have any other place to keep you right now, understand?"

"But, Pa, he's mean!"

"I can see that, Bill. I said I'd talk to him, and I will. You boys just keep your heads down and do as he tells you until I can find another place for us. Got it?"

"Where's Lynch? Did you leave him off somewhere? Aunt Beulah said you were taking him to another town to go to school and he might not be coming back."

"I took him to a special school for kids with poor eyesight. It's in Salem. They gave him some tests, and it looks like he'll be able to go there. It's a boarding school, sort of like the orphanage, only none of the kids there are orphans."

"Will we ever be able to see him again?" The pain in Aaron's voice near broke my heart.

"Sure. He'll stay during the week, and then on the weekends we'll all go visit him, just like when I came to visit you every weekend at the children's home."

"Promise?" Bill said.

"Yes, I promise. I'd never put him somewhere we couldn't see him when we wanted. He'll get special help in this school. I think it's the right thing to do. Now, let's get us some of Aunt Beulah's good cookin' before it's all et up."

I left the barn holding Aaron with one hand and Bill with the other. These boys were my heart and soul. The thought of Irvin being mean to them rankled me. I'd soon have that talk with him.

We tucked around the table in the three empty places. Beulah had collected Lyn and had him situated between Calvert and Marshall, her and Irv's two boys. Everyone was subdued. I suspected Irv was responsible for that. I could see he wasn't happy I brought the boys up from the barn with me.

"You finish the sweepin'?" he asked, fixing a mean glare on my boys.

"They did what you told them. Seems like three sweepings ought to be enough for one day."

Irv fixed his eyes on me. "You'll make pansies out'a 'em if you let 'em off the hook ever' time they get assigned a chore."

"You let me worry about that. I didn't bring them up here so you could treat them like low-hired hands. You treat them right, and they'll do right by you. Won't you, boys?"

Aaron and Bill nodded, but their eyes told a different story.

Irv settled on the front porch with a tobacco pipe after dinner. I decided now was as good a time as any to have the talk I promised the boys. "You know, Irv, I can understand you bein' disappointed that Charles couldn't come to help out, him bein' older and all, but that's no reason to take it out on these two. Bill and Aaron are both good boys. They'll do you right if you treat them right. The way Pa treated us wasn't right, and you know it. Now I see you usin' the same sorry ways with my boys. We agreed before I brought them, you wouldn't use the strap on them, and they say you haven't, but it's only been a few days. I just want to be sure we're clear on that."

"Yep."

His response didn't inspire much confidence, but I had to take him at his word. "Good. Well, I'll be huntin' a place to live and lookin' for a job this week. Can you relax your edict about Lyn bein' here with Beulah for a few days? I'm puttin' him in the Oregon State School for the Blind next Monday. They ran some tests, and he meets the legal requirements for being blind. He's going to be livin' at the school. I'll take the boys to visit him most weekends, so you'll need to get along without them one day a week."

"Yep. Won't be no problem."

Sweet-smelling tobacco smoke drifted around us, reminding me of Uncle Robert. The surprise memories flooded through me and almost brought me to tears. "Well, thanks then. Keep in mind these boys lost their mother, and now they've lost their sister and two more brothers. If they're a little difficult sometimes, that could be the cause. Bill's pretty rugged, but Aaron's still feelin' raw. He relied on Charles more than Bill did, and he's closer in age to Lyn and Maisie, so I think he feels it worse."

"Yep. Beulah done drilled it into me already. You goin' to be around in the evenin's?"

"I suspect so. At least for a few days until I find a place and get situated with a job. Any suggestions where I should start lookin'?"

"Nope. The mill you passed comin' into town may be takin' on a few now that the Japs have all gone away."

"Why'd the Japs go away?"

"It was a while back. People just didn't want slant-eyes workin' their jobs. They run 'em out 'a town."

"Has this depression slowed the work down much around here?"

"Sure has. Might not be any jobs. Could be you'll have to go on down to the coast and try the mills there."

What Irvin told me about the Japs turned out to be true, only it happened in 1925. The Japanese mill workers and their families were run out of town by an angry mob, and the mill moved them all to Corvallis.

I decided to try my luck at the C.D. Johnson Lumber Company and got hired on the spot. I'd never worked in a lumber mill, or any mill for that matter, but my mechanical engineering degree from A&M brought a glimmer to the eye of the guy doing the hiring.

"We could use a good millwright," he said after looking over my application. "You have any interest in that?"

"What's a millwright?"

"Mechanic. He keeps all the saws and mechanical equipment in working order. Seems like it might be right up your alley."

"I'd be right pleased to take that job," I said. "I've never worked on this kind of equipment before, only farm equipment and automobiles, but if I can have a little time to get accustomed to it, I'm sure I can figure it out."

"Pays twenty-five dollars a week. That work for you?"

"Sounds just fine."

"The hours can be a little irregular. If something goes down on graveyard or swing, you'll get called in to fix it. Stay sober and close to your telephone. You have a telephone, don't you?"

"Not at present. I don't even have a place to live yet. Just got into town four days ago."

"We've got a vacant houseboat down on the river if you want to stay there. It isn't much to look at, but it has everything you need to set up housekeeping. You're single, right?"

"Yes. Widowed. I've got three boys, but they're living with my brother and his family. Would I have either of the weekend days off? I have one son who will be living in Salem at a special school for kids who don't see too well. I need to be able to visit him one of the weekend days each week."

"That's fine. We'll make sure you're covered. No kids on the houseboat, though. Too dangerous. If you decide to take it, I'll get a phone put in right away. Rent's four dollars a week."

"Can I take a look at it before I decide?"

"Sure." He scribbled the location on a little map and said, "Slip B. Space three."

I took the houseboat. Boat was a loose description because it was mired in silt from the river. I didn't know if it would float or not. I soon discovered that sleeping on a bunk on a boat in a tidal river was an unexpected adventure. Every time the tide went out, the boat listed to the right, and I rolled out of bed.

It was cold. Cold in a way I'd never felt before. Beulah said the "coastal climate" made it seem cold even when it wasn't on the thermometer. I rolled out of bed the first night and hit the floor with a thud. I was treated to a cold draft blowing up from the part of the boat stuck in the mud, half in and half out of the water. I soon learned that I would need to sleep in my long johns and wear warm socks to bed.

Beulah gave me a couple of heavy quilts and an old dirty pillow with one pillowcase. Not what you'd call fancy living, but at least it was a place to lay my head and keep from irritating my brother with my presence.

I stopped by to see the boys every day. They never seemed happy, but they were warm, dry, and well-fed. I didn't have even that to offer them.

We'd been living like this, in two separate places, for about a year when it happened. Roused by a soft scuttling on the deck topside, I went to see what or who was on my boat. Bill and Aaron stood shivering in the moonlight, shoeless and coatless. I could see Aaron had tears in his eyes.

"What happened? Why are you here?" I sounded accusatory, and I didn't mean to. It was just so unexpected, and it scared me to see them here in the middle of the night.

"We ran away," Bill said. "Every time Aaron wets the bed, Uncle Irvin takes the strap to him. When he peed the bed tonight, we decided to leave before he found out."

"Wets the bed? Strap? Come below deck and get out of this chilly night air. You can explain once you're warm." I herded them toward the hatch and down the short flight of stairs to my sleeping quarters. I dried them off, wrapped them in one of the two quilts, and put them on the lower bunk. I sat on the end of the bed and said, "Now, tell me what happened."

Bill's blue eyes sidled toward me. His voice was a whisper, "When Aaron gets sad, he has bad dreams. When he has bad dreams, he wets the bed. Aunt Beulah washes the sheets and tries to hide them from Uncle Irvin because it makes him mad and he puts the strap to Aaron's backside."

"Did he put the strap to you tonight, Aaron?"

Aaron shook his head and looked down.

"Aaron, I'm talking to you. I want to see your eyes. When was the last time he took the strap to you?"

"Yesterday," he said, his voice a swallowed whisper.

"Crawl out here and drop your trousers. I want to see."

"Nooo, Daddy. I don't want to show you."

"You're going to show me whether you want to or not. Now get out here."

"I'm sorry, Daddy, I won't do it again. I promise."

"Aaron, I'm not going to hurt you. I need to see what's been done to you, is all. If he left marks on you, I'll take care of it with him."

Aaron reluctantly climbed out of the warm bed and stood in front of me. I pulled his pajama bottoms down and saw the raised red welts lacing his white bottom. I pulled his pajamas up and took him onto my lap. "Aaron—and you hear this good, too, Bill—you don't ever have to stay where someone is taking a strap to you. Especially when it's for something you can't help."

Both boys nodded, and Aaron said, "Can I get under the covers? I'm cold."

"Yeah. Sure. Bill, how long has this been going on?"

"Ever since you left us there. Aaron's been sad."

"Why have you been sad, Aaron?"

"I miss Charles…and Lynch."

"What are your bad dreams about?"

"I can't remember."

"Are you doing well in school?"

"Yes. I like school. It's Uncle Irvin I don't like."

"He sleeps on the floor most nights to keep from peeing the sheets," Bill piped in. "Our room doesn't smell so good."

"Thanks for telling me. I'll get your things in the morning. You'll be staying here now. Oh, and when the tide goes out, the water drops, and the boat leans to one side. Hang on to each other until I can get a strap rigged to hold you in the bed." I tucked the quilt under the mattress nice and tight to keep them from rolling onto the floor. "Now, let's get some sleep."

"Pa, what if he pees this bed? It will get all over me."

"Let's just hope being out of reach of that strap will ease his mind enough to let him sleep until morning. If it happens, we'll wash the mattress as best we can and get something to put over it."

We didn't need to worry. Once Aaron and Bill were on the houseboat with me, Aaron never wet the bed again. What I did to my brother more than made up for the strappings he gave my boy. Some sins cannot be overlooked in the here and now.

I promised Maidee I'd never hit one of the boys, and as far as I was concerned, that promise meant no one else got to either. The stories Bill told me about how Irvin treated them were enough to make me want to commit murder, and I came close.

CHAPTER THIRTY-THREE

My life on the houseboat with Aaron and Bill was an adventure none of us much enjoyed. It was cold, cramped, uncomfortable, and dangerous. My work at the local mill meant I had irregular hours and got called in on whatever shift they needed me—sometimes, it meant working part of all three. I was terrified of leaving the boys alone on the boat, but I didn't have much choice. The mill boss had made it clear there weren't to be any kids on the houseboat. I lived in constant fear I would be busted.

I had to rely on the boys to get themselves up and off to school most of the time. We figured out that if they were up by the road by 7 A.M. they could get a ride with a passerby most days. Bill had turned twelve just before Christmas, and Aaron was ten. They were too young to do so much on their own, but I didn't have many options.

The only upside to my circumstances was that having them there kept me out of the bar at night. I had to be home with them, so my nightly habit of hanging out in the tavern at the top of the hill was severely curtailed.

One night, about a year after the boys came to live with me, I decided to stop in after an emergency swing-shift repair and have a beer. The barkeep greeted me and motioned for me to lean over.

"Some dish was in here earlier lookin' for you," he said under his breath.

I looked around to see if anyone was listening. No one appeared interested in our conversation, so I said, "Did she give a name?"

"May or Gaye—somethin' like that," he said.

My heart nearly stopped. Had Faye made good on her threat to follow me to Oregon? I never expected that, but the thought that she might be here and might have a place to live popped right to the front of my mind. We were still married. I'd never been able to cobble together enough money to pay her back what I owed or file for divorce.

I leaned over the bar and said, "Give me a piece of paper and something to write with. If she comes in again, give her my note and tell her I'll call if she leaves a number."

"Good lookin' gal," the barkeep said. "Can't say as I blame you for wantin' to get in touch. I told her I thought I knew who you were, and I'd let you know she was lookin' for you."

Faye called me the very next night. Luckily, I was home. I wasn't sure I wanted the boys to know Faye and her kids were in town until I knew if there was any chance we might be getting together. I pretended it was a call from work and said I had to leave for a while. When I told them I needed to be gone for an hour or two, Bill said, "Dad, can I go out for the baseball team?"

"Let's talk about it later," I said. "I need to get to the mill now."

Both boys screwed up their faces.

"Don't go topside unless you have to pee, and stay as far away from the side of the boat as possible, ya hear?"

"When will you be back?" Aaron said.

"I'm not sure, son. I'll make it quick." I jumped off the houseboat and ran up the hill to the tavern.

Faye was waiting for me. She looked mighty good sitting on that bar stool. When I walked in, she turned her head and flashed a big smile.

"When did you get here?" I asked.

"Two days ago," she said. "I finally sold the house and gathered enough courage to bring Rosemary and Favel and strike out for Oregon. I wasn't sure you'd be happy to see us since I never heard from you."

I reached for her hand and squeezed it. "I'm very glad to see you," I said. "Surprised, but glad. How'd you know where to find me?"

"I didn't. I just knew you were heading to your brother's in Toledo, so that's where I started."

I told her about my job at the mill and my living situation. I filled her in on why the boys were with me and why Lynch was in the school for the blind. Her eyes filled with tears when I described the houseboat and how worried I was all the time about one of the boys falling overboard or me getting canned for violating company policy.

"Where are you staying?" I asked.

"We took a room for three nights in a boarding house so I could look for you. Thank you for leaving me a way to reach you."

"I guess looking for me in the local bar was your first idea of where you'd find me," I sneaked a glimpse of her out of the corner of my eye. "Are you planning to stay in Toledo?"

"That depends on you. I have enough money to buy a house here or rent something to see how we like it."

"I think renting makes better sense. This depression has everything so upside down it's hard to know what's coming. I'm lucky to have a job from one day to the next."

Faye stole a glance at me, and her voice caught when she said, "Would you be interested in finding a house together?"

My stomach lurched. Was this the solution I hoped for? Could I live with Faye again? The kids were older now. Would they still get along? I knew I didn't love her. I'd never missed her a single minute of a single day. I still missed Maidee all the time. Her presence hung over me like a fine mist. I could feel her but never see her. I cleared my throat and stared at the bar. "Right now, that sounds pretty good. But I don't want you to think my situation is a good reason to try living together again. It didn't work for us before. I'm not sure things would be that different now."

"I'm willing to chance it if you are. I miss you, Will. As far as I know, we're still married. I can't think of a good reason not to give it another go. I can't move on in this limbo, and neither can you."

"I never wanted to move on. I'm sorry I couldn't be a decent husband and a dad for your kids. I guess it was just too soon after Maidee died for me to try marriage again."

"How about this? I'll start looking for a place that's big enough for the six of us, and if I find something, you and the boys can take a look at it before I make any decisions."

"Sounds like a plan." I wrote my telephone number on a scrap of paper and handed it to her, forgetting she already had it. "Call me when you have something. We can go from there."

I slipped off the stool without even taking a sip of the beer I'd ordered. My gut churned, and my head swam. What had I just agreed to? Maybe a safe place to finish raising Bill and Aaron, but would I be able to hold up my end of the bargain as a husband to Faye? I patted Faye's hand and squeezed her shoulder. "Gotta run," I said. "Can't leave the boys alone on the houseboat much longer."

Our reunion was so brief I wasn't sure I hadn't dreamed it. I don't know why I bolted out of the bar so soon after getting there. The idea that I might have a safe place for the boys was uppermost in my mind, but I got cold feet when I thought about what it meant for me as a man. I hadn't even asked Faye about Rosemary and Favel. I needed to do some serious head-clearing before I heard from her again.

I rushed back to the houseboat and immediately realized something wasn't right. A sheriff's car was parked near the dock, and a small gathering of people stood nearby. Our boat was still and quiet, so I thought the boys had the good sense to stay out of sight. I moseyed over to the small crowd and said, "What's happened?"

"Some kid took a dive off that houseboat there," a man said, indicating my place with his thumb.

The panic in my voice and the stomach-churning fear I'd dreaded all these months rose as a tide. "Where is he? Is he okay?"

The man looked hard at me. "Easy, man," he said. "Someone downstream fished him out. The sheriff has him wrapped in a blanket down there by his car."

I bolted. Covered the short distance from the houseboat to the sheriff's car in record time. The officer looked into my terror-filled eyes and said, "This your boy?"

Aaron looked up at me, guilt, shame, and fear written all over his face. "Sorry, Daddy. I slipped when the boat rolled."

I grabbed Aaron away from the officer and pulled him tight to me. "Where's Bill?" I said, imagining him in the water, trying to catch up with Aaron as he slipped downstream.

"He's hiding."

"Where is he hiding?"

"I don't know." Tears filled Aaron's eyes, and his slight body trembled with the wet and cold of the January night.

"Tell him it's okay to come out. I'm not mad. Nobody's going to get in trouble. It was an accident. You're okay. That's all that matters."

Aaron turned his face up the hill and called, "Come out, Bill. Daddy's here, and he ain't mad."

"'Ain't' isn't a word, Aaron."

"Sorry. I forgot."

The officer stepped up to me and said, "So, I guess this is your kid?"

"Yes. He's mine. I left him on the houseboat while I went to fix a machine at the mill. I'm back now. I'll take him."

"Okay. But you know I need to report this to the mill. The boat he fell off belongs to them."

"Please don't. I have a new place for them—for all of us; this was temporary. I can't afford to lose my job."

"You come on down to the office in the morning. We'll talk to the sheriff and see what he wants to do. I can't afford to lose my job either, you know. I need your name and a way to reach you before I let you go."

"Sure. Fine. Name's Will Jones. My telephone number is five-five-two. I guess you know where I live."

Out of the corner of my eye, I saw Bill slip out of the bushes along the riverbank and crawl over the side of the houseboat. He disappeared down the stairs.

I put my arm around Aaron's shoulders and guided him toward the boat.

"Where's Bill?" he asked, with a tremor of fear in his voice.

"He's on the boat," I whispered. "Let's go. You can tell me what happened after we're inside."

"Daddy? I'm sorry. Will we have to move now?"

"Yes, we'll have to move, but I have a plan. Don't worry."

CHAPTER THIRTY-FOUR

I called the mill office and told the girl who answered that I had a personal emergency and would be about an hour late. I dropped Aaron and Bill at the school and went straight to the sheriff's office. I needed to get out in front of this thing before I lost my job.

Sheriff Long shook my hand and told me to wait on a bench in front of the office. "I'll be right with you, Mr. Jones," he said. "One of my deputies had an incident last night he needs to review me on before he takes off for the day."

"That incident may be what I'm here about. I'd appreciate you hearing me out before you let your officer explain what happened."

"That wouldn't be standard procedure. I need to see his report first."

I watched his back disappear down the hallway with my heart in my mouth. I realized I was clenching my teeth and making the cords in my neck pulse the way Maidee always said I did. "Help me here," I whispered to her. "I need this job." I felt the slightest touch of a breeze brush my cheek. I'd have thought she was here if I didn't know better.

I didn't have long to wait until the sheriff leaned out of a room halfway down the hall and hollered, "Mr. Jones. You can come down here now."

My gut churned. I had to find a way to get him not to report the incident to the mill. I believe my legs wobbled when I stood.

"In here," the sheriff said, motioning me into a small office. The officer from last night was seated in front of the desk. Sheriff Long motioned for

me to take the chair next to him, and he stepped behind and sat in a swivel
oak desk chair that threatened to dump him on the floor. He grabbed the
edge of the desk to steady himself and said, "Goddamned chair. Gets me
every time." We all laughed, and it lightened the atmosphere.

"Now, let me see if I understand what happened here," Sheriff Long
said, looking at the report. "You had a kid on the houseboat that belongs
to the mill, and he fell overboard. Is that right?"

"Yes. But I wasn't there when it happened."

"So, it's against company policy to have kids on the houseboats, and
unattended kids are even worse. Is that about right?"

"I guess. I got called away last night but was only gone for about half
an hour. I told him not to go topside unless he had to pee."

"And he had to pee. And he fell overboard when the boat slipped
with the ebb tide. I see all that here. The question is whether or not we
have to report this to the mill. Right?"

"If they find out I had a kid on the houseboat, I'll lose my job. I've
made other livin' arrangements, but we can't move for a few more days.
I'm askin' you to cut me a break here. I got three boys to raise and no one
to help. One of them is in the blind school in Salem. The other two are
with me on the boat. I just found out last night we have another place to
live. I can move them in a couple of days. That's why I was called away,
to make arrangements for them."

The sheriff smoothed the papers in front of him. He looked down at
his hands. He turned and gazed out the window. I thought I was going to
toss my breakfast on his desk. Finally, he said to the other officer, "Mac,
I'm goin' to let this be your call. No harm, no foul, in my opinion." He
twirled the chair around so his back was to us and stared at the wall.

The officer sitting next to me squirmed in his chair. He cleared his
throat. "I'll write a warning for a safety violation and send it over to the
mill. I won't mention the particular nature of the violation. If they want
to pursue it, that's their business. If Mr. Jones here pays the fine today, I
can show it as settled in the report."

"How much?" I asked.

"Two dollars," he said.

"Done," I said, reaching for my wallet.

Sheriff Long turned around to face us again. "Nice to meet you, Mr.
Jones," he said. "Try to keep those boys out of trouble."

I stood to shake his hand before I beat it down the hall and out
to the parking lot. I heaved a big sigh of relief and climbed into the

car to go to work. I'd need to think of what kind of safety violation I might have incurred before the office called me to account. This whole incident had spawned more than a few little white lies. I reasoned one more wouldn't hurt.

I wasn't home an hour before the phone rang. Faye had a house for us to see, and it wasn't just any house. One of the stately Victorians that lined the main drag coming into Toledo was available. It had enough rooms for all the kids, and if Faye and I shared a room, it left two rooms for her to rent out. Given my close call, I would have been hard-pressed to turn her down. I gathered the boys and told them Faye and the kids were in town and wanted us to look at a house with them.

Bill scowled and clenched his jaw, just the way I do.

Aaron's eyes were full of wonder, and he said, "Wow! A real house? Are we going to live with them again?"

"I think we might," I said.

"Do I have to share a room with Aaron and Favel?" Bill asked.

"I don't know yet how it will shake out, son," I said. "Let's go take a look. You might even get a room all to yourself."

"Yes!" Bill said, punching a fist into the air.

The boys scrambled off the boat and hightailed it up the hill to the car. I handed Bill the paper with the address and told him to be on the lookout for a tall white house with blue trim.

We cruised slowly through the downtown to the more prosperous side.

Bill yelled, "There it is," and bounced so hard in the seat that his head hit the roof.

I pulled to a stop in front of an imposing house sitting back from the street, farther than the houses on either side. The sloping lawn was terraced three levels to the front steps.

I had to make this work—no matter what my feelings were. We climbed out of the car and started for the front door. It burst open, and Rosemary and Favel darted out to greet Aaron and Bill.

All four kids stopped just short of each other and stared. They'd all grown. Rosemary, now eleven, had developed into a very attractive young lady. Favel, at ten, no longer looked like an undersized runt, and was square with Aaron eye to eye. Bill and Rosemary were the same height, and Bill took a sudden spell of shyness when he saw her.

Faye stood on the porch in the waning light, wearing a clingy blue dress that spilled easily over her nice figure. I took a long look. This was going to be different. I had plenty of responsibility already; adding a wife and two more kids gave me pause.

I waved to her, and she motioned us up the walk to the open front door. I gave her a brief hug when I reached the top.

She said, "I could probably afford to buy it, and it was for sale until just recently. The owner has decided to rent for now, so I thought it might be a good way to see if we like living together again before I jump into anything permanent." She stepped out of my embrace and turned toward the open door.

"Let's have a look around," I said. When I stepped into the entry, I could see that there was already furniture in the rooms. "Furnished, too?" I asked.

"Yes," she said, "that's one of the best things about it. I sold everything I owned with the Tucson house, but this one is ready to go." Her warmth and excitement were music to my ears.

I was warming to the idea of living with Faye again, and the house was a perfect solution to an otherwise unsolvable problem. I couldn't stay on the houseboat and keep the boys with me.

This house had six bedrooms. Faye chattered merrily away as we walked from room to room. "I thought if you are open to the idea, we could have this larger room at the top of the stairs. Favel and Aaron could have the room next to us, and Rosemary just across the hall. There is a bathroom between these rooms and the other three. Bill could have the room on the other side of the bathroom from Rosemary. That would leave the two rooms at the end for us to rent out. What do you think?"

None of the kids had followed us into the house yet, and I reached for Faye. I pulled her close to me and kissed her hard and deep. She deserved better than a down-on-his-luck millwright who drank too much and had five kids. I could try to make it up to her by being affectionate and acting interested. When I let her go, she took a step back and looked at me. Neither of us needed to say anything. We both knew there was nothing there. I might as well have kissed the wall for all the excitement I felt. Poor Faye smiled and said, "Well, that was a surprise."

Indeed, I thought. Honestly, I had expected to feel something. It had been so long since I'd been with a woman I wondered if I'd ever feel excitement again. This foray into married bliss wasn't an auspicious beginning. We would move into the house and attempt to make a go of a marriage that should never have been in the first place. I felt awful. I had to make myself *feel* something for this woman. She was my salvation, and I owed her.

The silence between us had reached the awkward stage when all four kids thundered up the stairs, pushing and shoving and saying, "This is my room," and "No, it's not, it's my room," and "You can't have the biggest room 'cause you're not the oldest." The diversion was welcome, and both Faye and I stepped into the fray to settle the first of what would prove to be many controversies.

CHAPTER THIRTY-FIVE

The next three years were a tangle of drama and conflict. It wasn't only the kids who had difficulty adjusting. Faye and I struggled to find comfort in each other's presence. As was my habit, I began spending more and more time in the bar at the other end of town. I wanted to make Faye happy, and I couldn't find any fault on her part that would spell failure for our relationship. I take all the blame if blame is to be laid. I didn't love her the first time I married her, and I didn't love her this time.

It wasn't anything I could put my finger on, except that there was no spark in our physical relationship. My mind would drift back to the many loving occasions and times I spent with Maidee. There was always an attraction, an urgency, a need to be together. Even when Maidee went through her dark time, the slightest contact with her body aroused me. I couldn't help touching her even when I knew she was going to recoil.

I had to force myself to touch Faye, who was always willing and available to satisfy my needs. It felt like a duty to me, never the magical tender experience of real love.

We had been living together for about a year when I got the call saying Charles's most recent test was positive for tuberculosis. The news was devastating. I couldn't afford to go to San Antonio to see him, and I refused to take solace in the comfort Faye offered. I turned to the bottle to dull the pain and came home less and less often when my regular shift at the mill ended.

Faye frequently came looking for me and tugged my sleeve to get me to climb down from the bar stool. I was drunk—or near drunk—almost every night. I can't say I was very pleasant *to* her, and I'm sure intimacy wasn't very pleasant *for* her, with a boozed-up husband, reeking of alcohol, fumbling about in the dark, making a feeble attempt to be interested.

The same ache I felt when Maidee died reinhabited my soul. I slept, I worked, I ate, and I drank. The routines of managing Bill and Aaron fell entirely on Faye.

It wasn't until the night she stormed into the bar in a fury and grabbed hold of my sleeve that I knew something was about to change.

"Get off that bar stool and come with me right this minute," she said through gritted teeth. "I've had enough. There's trouble at home, and I need you to sort it out—now."

Faye hauled me out of the bar and shoved me hard in the middle of my back toward the car.

"How'd you get here?" I asked, fumbling in my pocket for the car key.

"I walked," she said, putting a period on it. "I walked, and you are going to drive me home, too drunk to drive or not."

"I'm not too drunk to drive," I said, opening the car door. "What happened at home?"

"Bill happened," she said. "Bill and Rosemary happened."

I wasn't following very well. "What'd they do?"

"I caught them playing house in Rosemary's bed. I want you gone, and I want him gone. This is more than I can stand. You're never home. I have to manage all four of the kids by myself. You drink up everything you make, and we've gone through most of my savings from selling the house. I mean it, Will, I'm done. The last thing I need is a pregnant fourteen-year-old and another baby to raise."

"Whoa, there. Don't you think you're getting a little carried away just because two kids engaged in a little hanky-panky? I'll talk to Bill and tell him he needs to take his urges elsewhere."

"No. I want you both out of my house."

Something in her voice said she meant it. I had no idea where I'd go or how I could afford a place to live. What was now called The Great Depression had deepened, and my hours at the mill had been cut back. I still had two growing boys to feed. Things did not look good.

When we got back to the house, Faye bolted from the car and left the passenger door open. She ran up the front walk and took the stairs two at a time. There was no mistaking that she was in a hurry or feared what she'd find behind the front door.

I closed her car door and followed at a hurried pace. Faye flung the door open and shouted, "Rosemary? Bill? I hope you are both where I left you, because if you aren't, there is going to be hell to pay around here." She ran up the stairs and flung open Rosemary's bedroom door.

I was right on her tail, and I saw the girl curled up on the bed like a kitten, her head buried in her arms and crying.

"Don't move," Faye said. "I'll be right back." She rushed down the hall to Bill's bedroom door and grabbed the knob. It didn't turn. "Bill Jones, you open this door right now."

I heard a rustling within, and a minute later my son opened the door a crack and peered through. When he saw me, he stepped back and let Faye open the door the rest of the way.

I pushed past Faye and said, "You want to tell me what's been going on here?"

"Not really," he said.

"Let me put it another way," I said, "What in the H-E-double L have you been up to?"

"Nothing."

"Nothing, my eye. You know perfectly well what your mother walked in on. Have you lost your mind?"

"She's not my mother."

"Bill, I wouldn't start that right now if I were you. Faye cooks for you, cleans up your messes, and looks out for you when I'm not here. She's as much a mother to you as anyone ever has been."

"Doesn't matter. She's still not my mom. And Rosemary's not my sister."

"Oh, I get it. You think because you and Rosemary aren't blood, you can mess with her any old time you feel like it?"

"It's not like that. We like each other."

"I don't care if you like each other or not. You are fifteen years old, and Rosemary's barely fourteen. If you get her pregnant, who do you think is going to pay for your rent and your food? You aren't even finished with school yet."

"Like you should talk. Mom was only fourteen when you married her."

"That was different. We were in love, and I was already through college and had a going business. I could take care of her."

"If you'd been taking care of her, she wouldn't have got murdered."

"Stop, Bill. This isn't the conversation we need to be having right now. I need to know if there is any chance you could have gotten Rosemary pregnant tonight."

"No. We didn't go that far."

"Are you sure?"

"I'm sure. Ask Rosemary."

"Oh, I will. And I'll ask Rosemary whose idea this was. And if she says it was you, there will be some serious trouble around here."

"She wanted it. I wasn't doing anything to her she didn't want."

"We'll see about that. As for tonight, you stay in this room and don't leave it for any reason. Hear?"

Faye and I started back down the hall to Rosemary's room. I said, "She seems awful shook up. Could we wait until morning to talk with her?"

"Not if you're going to get up and go to work in the morning. I want you here for this. He's your boy, and you need to take care of it. Besides, I want you and Bill out of here in the morning. I know he goes to school, and you go to work, but I want you to promise me you will spend every waking hour you aren't working looking for a place to stay."

We stopped, and she opened Rosemary's door. "Rosie, honey," she said gently, shaking the girl's shoulder, "Will and I need to talk with you."

"Go away. I don't want to talk."

"I know you don't. I know you're embarrassed. But we have to know a couple of things."

"What?" Rosemary raised a red, swollen face with snot running down her chin. It wasn't a pretty sight.

"We need to know if you and Bill—you know—had intercourse."

"I don't know."

"Do you know if he got far enough that you could get pregnant?"

"I don't think so."

"Did he do anything that hurt you?"

"How do you mean?"

"You know. Did he put his penis inside you and it hurt?"

"I don't remember."

Faye turned to me and said, "I think she'd remember if he had succeeded in taking her virginity."

I stepped over to Rosemary and said, "Was this tumble you two were taking something that has happened before?"

"No."

"Did Bill come into your room and suggest you get your clothes off together?"

"No."

"Then how'd you come to be naked together in the bed?"

"I can't remember."

"Come on, Rosemary. What's done is done. I'm just trying to figure out if this has been going on for a while or if this was the first time you two got together like this."

"It was the first time. He wanted to kiss me, and I wanted him to. I don't remember what happened after that."

I believed the girl. I thought I'd have noticed if she and Bill had been sparking. Sometimes, these things just happen so quick-like there isn't time to decide if it's good or bad or right or wrong. I leaned down and patted Rosemary. "It's okay. I'm sure he likes you. You *are* growing into a real looker. I'm not excusing him. I'm just saying sometimes boys let their feelings get out in front of their good sense. You should try to get some sleep now. I don't think you need to worry about Bill coming in to bother you anymore."

"Mom, are you going to kick me out?"

"No, Rosemary. I'm not going to kick you out, but I have told Will he needs to find another place for him and the boys to live. I can't have this kind of thing going on right under my own roof. If you and Bill want to get together when you're older, I won't try to stop you, but you're way too young now."

"I'm sorry. Please don't make them move. It won't happen again."

"Get some sleep. You have school tomorrow."

CHAPTER THIRTY-SIX

Bill's foray into Rosemary's bed was just the beginning of a long list of issues and crises caused by or participated in by my second oldest son. I had to respect Faye's edict that we move, so I contacted the mill about the houseboat. It was available, but word had gotten back to them that I had kids on it the last time, so the manager was less than eager to fulfill my request. I had to show proof that the boys were living elsewhere, with sworn statements from the folks they were staying with that the arrangement was permanent.

Faced with living in a Hooverville or hobo camp on the railroad tracks, I approached my sister-in-law, Beulah. She was happy to take Bill back under her wing, but my brother refused to let Aaron into his house. He knew he could get a day's work out of Bill, but his misgivings about Aaron couldn't be resolved. I chose not to fight him on the issue, and Aaron came up with his own solution.

He had a good friend at the high school, whose mother took pity on him and offered him a place in their home until he graduated. So, I let Aaron go live with strangers, Bill went back to Irvin and Beulah, and I moved onto the houseboat.

The weekend after we moved out of Faye's house, I took the boys to Salem to visit Lynch, the one bright spot in our lives. He had gone out for wrestling and was considered an up-and-coming athlete at eleven years old. He loved the Oregon School for the Blind and had adapted well. Each time we visited, he proudly showed us around the campus and explained everything he was doing. This time was important for him as he'd been promoted to sixth grade and made the wrestling team. I think his brothers were a little envious of his pleasant and secure living conditions.

"I'm going to Mary's Peak with Calvert and Marshall," Bill said. "Uncle Irvin says there's great fishing up there, and I can even hunt deer and 'coons."

"If you can stay out of reach of his strap," Aaron said. "I'm going to live with Jeff Davis's family in Toledo. They have a telephone, so I can call you."

"I don't have a telephone," Lynch said.

"I could write to you," Aaron offered. "I suppose that would be best. I'm better at writing. I can't ever think what to say on the telephone."

"Besides, it costs a lot of money to telephone," Lynch said.

A sullen Bill said, "I went out for the baseball team, but Dad couldn't afford the uniform, so I had to quit."

"They give us our uniform for wrestling. It doesn't cost anything," Lynch said.

"Do they have a baseball team here?" Bill asked.

"No, stupid. Standing around and having somebody throw something at you when you can't see wouldn't be fun."

"Don't call your brother stupid, Lyn. It isn't nice, and it isn't true," I said.

"Sorry, Pa," Lynch said.

"Don't apologize to me, Lyn. Apologize to your brother."

"Sorry, Bill."

"It's okay, Lyn. It *was* stupid."

"Well, boys, I think we'd better hit the road. It isn't far, but it is long, since I have to deliver Bill clear out to Mary's Peak."

We said our goodbyes and Bill and Aaron climbed into the car without arguing about who got to sit up front. That was something new. I didn't mention it because I didn't want to break the spell.

I knew it would be harder and harder to get the boys together now that we would be scattered around the county like vagabonds. My heart always pinched when I had to leave Lyn behind. This time was worse than ever.

I dropped Aaron off first at the Davises' and then drove out the long dirt road to Mary's Peak to help Bill settle in. The uneasy feeling that crept up my spine when I saw Irv emerge from the big barn gave me pause.

"Bill, if he ever takes that strap to your hide for any reason, you find me. I'll finish what I started."

"No need, Dad. I'm almost as big as he is now. If he decides I deserve a strappin', I'll probably have it comin'. If I don't think I have it comin', I'll fight him or run away."

Faye took Rosemary and Favel and moved up the coast to Astoria. I had no reason to go home at night, so I spent more time in the tavern than ever. I missed the boys, but I never thought about Faye. Out of sight, out of mind applied to our relationship more than it ever had. I still missed Maidee every day and even more at night.

I struggled with the notion that Aaron lived with people I barely knew, but they were always good to let me know when he needed anything. I'd stop by their place from time to time to satisfy myself that he was safe and happy.

I rarely saw Bill. It was too uncomfortable for me to be around my brother. He'd never forgive me for beating him half to death for strappin' my boys, and I'd never forgive him for the strappin's. Bill appeared to be holding his own in the Jones household. They let him go out for baseball, and he let me know when he had games in case I could come. I didn't ask how he got a uniform, and he didn't say. When I did see him, it was because he needed my permission for something that required a parent's signature.

Bill spent a happy summer working, fishing, and hunting on Mary's Peak. He shot his first buck in the fall. He and his cousin Calvert were best buddies, and I thought he had adapted well to being with family. Things were running smoothly until very late one night when the sheriff knocked on the houseboat door.

I'd been at the bar drinking until midnight. I finally reminded myself I had to work in the morning and stumbled down the hill to the river. I had just crawled into bed when I heard someone stomping across the deck, and soon realized they were pounding at my door.

I tried to make sense of it in my alcohol-addled brain when someone yelled, "Jones? Mr. Jones? Are you in there? This is the sheriff."

"Yeah. Yeah, I'm here. Hold your horses. I'll be right out." I pulled my pants on and staggered to the door. "What?" I said, pulling it open. "Has something happened to one of my boys?"

"You might say that. I've got a young fella named Bill Jones in custody. He yours?"

"Sure. Yes. He's my boy. What'd he do?"

"Robbed the post office from what we can tell. Him and a couple of his buddies thought it would be a fine idea to have them 'gimmie' checks that got delivered today. We caught 'em red-handed. Still inside the building, with two paper bags full of checks they stole from the mailboxes."

"How'd they get into the mailboxes? Aren't they locked?"

"Sure, they're locked. Seems your boy here figured out a particular way of hitting the box that makes it pop open. They just reached in an' took 'em."

"Where is he?"

"Jail. This here's a federal crime. We're just holding the kids until the Feds show up to get 'em. They'll take 'em to Salem to the state lockup until the trial. You should come with me now if you want to see him before they get him."

My head was spinning, and it wasn't just from the alcohol. Bill wasn't quite seventeen yet. It was possible he could get out of this as a minor.

"I'll get my shoes and follow you to the station."

"Not a good idea if what I think I smell is comin' from you. I'd have to take you in on a dooey. You can ride in the patrol car. I'll bring you back when you're done visitin'."

I hesitated and then went inside for my shoes. I followed the deputy to his car and climbed into the front seat as directed.

What in the hell was he thinking? Why would Bill do something like this? He knows better. I went over everything in my mind, but I couldn't figure any logical reason for what the deputy said happened. I fluctuated between angry and scared spit-less. When we pulled up in front of the jail, I bailed out of the car like my pants were on fire.

"Hold on," the officer yelled. "You can't get in without me, and I can't move as fast as you. Besides, you aren't his lawyer, so you can't see him alone. I need to be there."

Once we entered the small building, I saw three jail cells down the narrow hall. I started in that direction, and the deputy grabbed my arm.

"Hold on, Bucko. I'll go first and let you know when you can step up to the cell. From here on, you don't make a move or do anything without my say-so, okay?"

"Yeah, sure," I mumbled, wrenching my arm away. I felt angry and embarrassed to be seeing my boy behind bars. I followed the deputy as close as I dared. I wanted to see Bill's eyes before we talked. I'd know how he was feeling from the look on his face. When the deputy pulled up short, I smacked into his back.

He turned and gave me a shove. "Stay back," he barked.

I obeyed and stepped back while he peered at the three boys sitting on a bench inside the cell.

"Jones. You got company. Step up here."

Three pairs of eyes shifted my way. Bill stood and shuffled to the barred door, head down and shoulders slumped. My heart lurched. He hadn't looked so defeated since the night his mother was shot.

"You," the officer said, "you have ten minutes with him." He leaned toward the cell and said to the other boys, whose eyes were riveted on Bill's back, "The rest of you stay put. Don't get off that bench. Don't try to hear what's bein' discussed. You'll get yer turn when I'm done here. Capisce?"

Two heads nodded, and four eyes dropped.

I stepped up to the cell door and met Bill's eyes. He looked both chagrined and defiant. I knew this wasn't going to be a welcome discussion. I wanted to pull him through the bars and hug him almost as much as I wanted to reach in and cuff him upside the head.

I said, "Well, this is a hell of a note. Robbing a post office. Whatever possessed you to do a thing like that?"

Bill shrugged and turned away.

"Bill, you can ignore me if you want to, but I think you'd better look me in the eye and tell me what happened. Why were you in town in the middle of the night? Why weren't you out at the ranch?"

"Uncle Irvin kicked me out. I didn't have any place to go."

"Why'd Irv kick you out? And who are these other two yahoos?"

"I was supposed to be pitching hay, and I sneaked off to go fishing."

"And these two? Where'd you meet up with them?"

"At the school. They sleep in the doorway 'round back. That's where I figured to spend the night."

"So, they don't have folks?"

"No. Their dad left to find work, and they didn't go. They're on their own. They go to school to get out of the cold. At night, they hang out wherever they can to keep from getting caught."

"Damn this depression. That still doesn't tell me why you decided to rob the post office."

"No reason. Just something to do, I guess. I knew I could make the boxes pop open if I hit them a certain way, and I was telling them how to do it. They thought it would be fun to learn how, so we walked over there. The lobby's open all night, and it's warmer in there than the door well."

"So, you were just trying to stay warm?"

"Yeah. I guess so. Once I showed them how to pop the boxes and we saw the gimmie checks, it just sort of happened. I don't remember whose idea it was to take some. We were probably just stupid enough to think we could cash them and get money to eat."

"Bill, when folks are on the dole, they have hungry kids at home. After all you've been through, would you take food out of a kid's mouth?"

"No. It was stupid, and I'm sorry. We didn't have time to try to cash any of the checks. We were just killing time and trying to stay warm."

"You realize this is a big deal, right? Robbing a post office is a federal crime with a long prison sentence. I don't know how I'll get you out of this mess. I can't afford a lawyer. Hell, I can't even afford a place for you to live."

"I'm sorry, Dad. I'm sorry I got kicked out of Uncle Irvin and Aunt Beulah's place, and I'm sorry about this trouble."

"I'll stay in touch with the sheriff and find out where they take you. If I can get off work, I'll come talk to you there."

"Dad, please don't tell Aaron. He'll be embarrassed, and I don't want him to find out."

"I suspect he'll find out at school. Stories like this don't stay quiet long when kids are involved. They spread like wildfire. I'll try to catch him before school tomorrow."

CHAPTER THIRTY-SEVEN

It didn't take long before the Feds took Bill and the other two boys to lockup in Salem. I got a call the next day. He would be a resident of the Marion County correctional facility until his court date. They let me talk to him for a short three minutes and told me visiting hours were Friday between three and four o'clock and Saturday between ten and eleven in the morning—no exceptions. I told him I'd come Saturday since I could also visit Lyn on Saturday, and gas was expensive.

Bill had a defiant streak, and I was scared spit-less he would appear arrogant and unrepentant in front of the judge, but when I saw him locked in a jail cell for the second time, I realized how shaken he was by this experience. He looked like a skinny kid caught cheating on a test, ashamed and mortified that I had to see him this way.

"I'm sorry, Dad." He shook his head sideways and let his eyes fall everywhere but on me.

"Bill, this isn't the time for sorry. We need to figure out how we're going to get you out of this fix. I can't afford a lawyer, and I'll lose my job if I miss any more time at the mill. There are plenty of men out of work who would be happy to step into my shoes."

"I know. What's going to happen to me?"

"That, I don't know. The lady at the desk out front said the judge would hold the first hearing Wednesday of next week. I think she called it the arraignment. It's where they explain the charges and you plead guilty or not guilty."

"What should I do?"

"Decide whether or not you intended to cash those checks, and if the answer is yes, you need to plead guilty. If the answer is no, you can plead not guilty and hope the judge will let you explain."

"What if I don't know?"

"This is the part where you have to man up. You're the only one who knows what was goin' through your mind that night. I can't help you decide if you are guilty of a federal crime or just caught up in some mischief you didn't know was serious. All I can do is be there and hope the judge will release you to my custody."

"You're going to come to the hearing?"

"Damned right, I'm comin'. You're my boy. Whatever happens in court isn't going to change that one iota. You're also sixteen and still a minor. I'm hopin' the judge will agree that you're my responsibility. If I could go to jail for you, I would."

"They don't let people do that, do they? I mean, serve somebody else's time?"

"No, they don't. I'm just sayin' *if* it was possible, I'd do it for you. You wouldn't be in this fix if I'd been a better provider. The way I see it, this is as much my fault as it is yours."

"It's not your fault. If I hadn't gone fishing, this never would have happened."

"Well, you did, and it happened. So, now we need to keep our fingers crossed that the judge will go easy on you. I'm sorry, I can't afford a lawyer. I don't have anybody I can borrow from now that Faye's gone. We'll have to roll the dice and hope for the best."

"Dad? Thanks for coming. I'll see you Wednesday, right?"

"Right." I stuck my hand between the bars, and we shook. I know I held on longer than I needed to, but it was hard to let go. His eyes glistened, so I dropped his hand and walked away. I knew he didn't want me to see him cry, and I didn't think I could take it if one of those tears escaped before I got out of there.

God, Maidee, what am I going to do? Our oldest is dying from tuberculosis, and now our second is in jail, looking at a long prison term. I've failed at everything I've tried since you went and left us. I've tried to keep the boys together. I've tried to quit drinkin'. I've tried to forget what it was like loving you so I could love someone else who could help me with the boys. None of it worked. None of it. Help me, Maidee. Tell me what to do.

I drove to the school where Lyn lived, but I couldn't make myself park the car and go inside. Seeing my youngest son in an institution was more than I could take today. It was just one more reminder of all the ways I'd failed as a father.

I noticed the superintendent's car in front of the mill office when I got back to Toledo. I pulled into the mill yard and parked. *Might as well get it over with. I need time off Wednesday.*

"What's up, Jones?" he said when I opened the door and stepped inside. "Somethin' break down out there I don't know about?"

"Naw. Nothin' like that. I need a word."

"It about your boy?"

"Yeah. How'd you hear?"

"Case you hadn't noticed—this is a small town. Ever'body knows ever'thing."

"Right. Well, his hearing is Wednesday in Salem, and I need to be there, him bein' a minor and all."

"Got it. I'll get somebody to cover, but this is the last time."

"Thanks." I plunged my hand in his direction, and he ignored me. I let it fall and walked to the car.

Wednesday rolled around, and I dressed in the only suit I owned, the one I wore when Maidee and I got married. I was even skinnier now than I was then, so it hung on me like an empty gunnysack. My neck was too small for my shirt collar. I hadn't prospered, and it showed. I drove as fast as I could and still kept the car on the road all the way to the Salem city limits. It was only by an act of God that I didn't get stopped and fined for speeding or reckless driving. I parked in front of the courthouse on Court Street. Nice name—makes it hard to get lost. I hadn't ever been in a courtroom. The closest I'd come was when Maidee and I got married, and that was in the judge's cramped office. This room was spacious, with high ceilings, and gave the impression of being very important. Lives change forever in a place like this. I looked around in awe.

Poor Bill. He'll be scared witless in here. The thought had no more than left my head before a side door opened. Bill and his two partners in crime were led into the room and seated in front of the railing that separated the judge's stand from the part where I was sitting.

The uniformed bailiff escorted the boys in. Once they were seated, a door opened and the bailiff said, "All rise."

An oversized, very stern-looking man with spectacles perched on his nose walked in and sat behind the elevated podium. "What do we have today?" he asked the bailiff.

"Robbery of a federal building."

"Now, that's a new one," the judge said, looking over his spectacles at the three boys. "How old are these young men?"

"Two are sixteen, and one's seventeen."

"Who's the youngest?"

"William Echols Jones, Junior, Your Honor."

"Is there a parent present in the courtroom?"

I raised my hand and was halfway out of my seat when the judge glared at me and said, "No need to get up yet. I'll call you when I need you."

I plopped back onto the bench.

Bill turned around and looked at me. Relief flooded his face. I nodded to him before he turned back when the judge said, "You. William Echols Jones. Step to the front."

I started to stand, and the judge said, "Not you. The boy. Is there an attorney representing you, young man?" He peered down at my son.

"No, Your Honor," Bill said. "My dad can't afford one."

"Is that man who raised his hand your father?"

"Yes, sir… I mean, Your Honor, sir. Excuse me."

"Easy, son. Sir, or Your Honor—either is fine. You don't need both."

"Sorry, sir."

I thought I saw a faint smile flicker across the judge's lips, but he quickly looked down at the papers the stenographer had handed him. He studied the papers and then, looking directly at me, said, "Are you William Echols Jones, Senior?"

I didn't know whether to stand or sit, so half out of my seat, I said, "Yes, Your Honor."

"You can come up front here next to the boy, now," he said.

I scrambled to my feet and walked down the two steps to the little gate that separated me from the front of the courtroom. It squeaked when I pushed it open, and Bill turned around to look. Our eyes locked, and the fear in his made me want to wrap him in my arms like I had when he was a little kid.

I came to a stop shoulder to shoulder with my son. The judge peered over his specs at us and said kindly, "I'd like to hear from Jones Junior what happened to bring him here."

Bill gulped and glanced at me. He cleared his throat and said, "Um."

"Yes?" the judge said, "Um, what?"

Bill told his story about running away from Irvin to keep from being strapped to teaching the other two boys how to pop open a locked mailbox. He didn't mention stealing the welfare checks.

The judge looked down at the charging papers in front of him. He read for what seemed like an eternity. Finally, he looked over the big podium again and said, "It says here you stole recently delivered government checks out of the boxes. Is that true?"

I leaned against Bill's arm to let him know I was standing with him, whatever he had decided to do.

"Yes, Your Honor, but I didn't try to cash any of them. I never meant to take anything out of the boxes. I don't know whose idea it was, and I'm sorry. I'm real sorry."

"Are you aware of the penalty for this crime you didn't intend to commit?"

"No, sir." Bill's chin was almost buried in his chest.

"You need to look at me when I tell you, son. The penalty for stealing mail is up to five years in a federal penitentiary and up to twenty-five thousand dollars in fines. Do either of those sound like things you'd like?"

"No, sir."

"How long do you think it would take to pay off a fine that size?"

"I don't know. The rest of my life, I guess."

"Would your father be able to pay off a fine for you?"

"No, sir. He works in the mill, but only part-time, and he has to send money to the blind school for my brother and to my aunt to take care of my other brother."

"I see. Mr. Jones, Senior, it's your turn. Why was this young man not living with you and under your care?"

"I had my hours cut at the mill and couldn't afford a house. The mill lets me stay on a houseboat on the river, but I'm not allowed to have kids there."

"Is that where you're living now?"

"Yes, Your Honor."

"How many children do you have?"

"Five."

"Five? Where are the other four?"

"My girl lives with my sister in Alpine, Texas. My oldest boy has TB and lives with his aunt in San Antonio because he can't be around other kids. My fourteen-year-old lives with a family in Toledo and goes to high school there. My youngest son lives at the Oregon State School for the Blind."

"Where's their mother?"

"She died in twenty-six. Murdered."

"Well, Mr. Jones, I hate to be the one to add to your long list of burdens, but what this young man did is considered a serious crime by the United States Government. It doesn't sound like you can take responsibility for him, so that doesn't leave me many options."

"I'll take responsibility for him. I'll take him and leave the state if I have to. Somehow, I'll find enough work to support us. I'm askin' you to give him another chance. He isn't even seventeen yet. Prison will only teach him worse. Please, Your Honor, he's just a kid."

The judge glared at me. His face turned red, and I could see he gripped the papers in front of him tight enough to bend them. This did not look good.

I waited. Bill waited. The judge glared. Finally, he leaned toward me and said, "You, Mr. Jones, Senior, approach the bench."

I looked around the room, but I didn't see any bench. He could tell I was confused, and I saw him smile before he said, "I mean for you to come up here and stand close to me so I can talk to you eye to eye."

I hurried forward and stopped just short of his podium thing. I guessed that was what he called a bench.

He spoke very softly when he said, "I've given your circumstances some serious thought here, Mr. Jones. I'm going to give your boy another chance. Listen carefully because these are my conditions. You take him and leave the State of Oregon within three days. If I ever see the whites of his eyes in these parts again, I will send him up the river for a very long time. Do you understand?"

I blinked back tears of relief. "I understand, Your Honor."

"Good. Now go get your boy and let me explain to him what I expect."

I went to where Bill stood rooted and said, "The judge wants to talk to you. Go up there where I was and pay attention."

I don't know what the judge said to Bill, but when they finished talking, the judge said, "This case, The United States Postal Service against William Echols Jones, Junior, is dismissed. The defendant is free to go. Next."

Bill didn't even glance at the other two boys sitting alone at the table in front of the barrier. We pushed open the little gate and took the stairs out of the courtroom three at a time. I pushed Bill by his back toward the outside doors and kept my hand firmly planted until we reached the car.

"We need a plan," I said. "First, I think we should go tell Lyn we're leavin' Oregon for a while and make sure the school will let him stay. Then we'll talk to the Davis family to be sure they will let Aaron live with them while we're gone. I'll pick up my things from the houseboat and stop at the mill long enough to give notice and pick up my check. We have to let Beulah and Irv know where you are, and you probably want to say goodbye to Calvert and Marshall."

"Dad. I'm sorry for what I done. I don't want to leave Aaron and Lynch. The judge said I can't ever come back to Oregon."

"Yeah, he told me the same. I figure after you're eighteen, he wouldn't be able to stop you as long as you kept your nose clean and didn't get in any more trouble."

Bill nodded. He looked small and pitiful. Defeated. There was no sign of the usual blustery self-confidence and defiant attitude when he said, "Dad? Where are we going?"

"Don't know. I think we'll just hit the road and see where we can find work. If we can make enough to keep gas in the car and food in our bellies, we might make it back to Texas to see Charles and Maisie."

"I'd like that. To see Charles and Maisie, I mean."

"Me too. It's been too long."

CHAPTER THIRTY-EIGHT

Three days to get everything in place for an earthshaking shift in our lives wasn't enough. It might have made a difference if I knew where we were going. The most troublesome for me was the state-run school where Lynch lived. They were not happy I was moving out of state.

The headmaster said, "Mr. Jones, the Oregon State School for the Blind is for residents of Oregon. If you move to another state, we won't be able to keep Lynch with us. Are you certain you want to do this? He is doing so well here."

"I don't want to do it. I don't have a choice. I have a son in Texas I haven't seen in six years dying from tuberculosis. I have a judge's order to take Bill out of state and keep him out. I can't throw him to the wolves by sending him off alone when he's barely sixteen. After he turns eighteen, he's on his own. I won't be gone any longer than I need to be to keep him out of trouble." My voice rose with growing frustration until I sounded angrier than I intended.

"Mr. Jones, I appreciate your dilemma, I do. But we have rules. As you know, we've conformed to your circumstances by not sending Lynch home every weekend. I'd lose my position if anyone higher up got wind of this. I have a family to think of, too, you know."

"Let's say it's an emergency. My son is dying. I'll be back as soon as he passes. No need to put the reason in writing. I'll stay in close contact, and if you need me to be here, I'll head straight back to Oregon."

"So, you are going to Texas to be close to your son, who is ill?"

"Yes. That's it—and I'll be back as soon as possible."

"Swear?"

"Yes, I swear. Aaron will still be in high school in Toledo, and my brother and his wife can serve as contacts."

"Would they be able to exercise guardianship rights for Lynch? That would make it all on the up and up."

"We don't have time before the deadline to get Bill out of the state."

"But you could begin the process before you leave, couldn't you?"

"I can't promise. My brother might put his foot down about that. He doesn't want responsibility for any but his own. Our being here caused him enough trouble."

"Please tell me you will try. Talk to your brother. If someone who is a permanent resident takes guardianship, my decision will be much easier."

"Okay. I'll try, but no promises."

"Understood."

Bill and I piled our belongings into the Lizzie and headed south. I had my final check from the mill, a box of home-canned food Beulah slipped me when Irv wasn't looking, and enough gas in the car to make it out of town. There wouldn't be any Hoovervilles until we made it to southern California.

In a rare act of generosity, Irv threw an old, battered tent at me and said, "Here. I ain't usin' it anymore since we moved into the old schoolhouse."

The tent had been their "summer house" on Mary's Peak until the school was abandoned due to so many families leaving to find work. Logging work had all but dried up. People with kids were forced to vacate the logging camps and find other work. Most moved east to pick fruit in the Willamette Valley or south to the orchards in the Rogue Valley.

We only stopped long enough to pitch camp and sleep one night near Medford. I was tempted to seek work picking fruit, but my orders were "out of the state of Oregon."

As soon as we settled into the tent for the night, Bill said, "Dad? Are we going to see Charles?"

"I hope so. I'm not sure we have enough money to make it to Texas, but I'm sure as hell goin' to try."

"I want to. I miss him."

"Me too, Bill, but your shenanigans have put us in a tough spot. I can't take permanent work, and you need to be in school."

"I don't want to go to school. It's boring. I haven't learned anything since fifth grade."

"That kind of thinkin' won't do you any good. if you ever want to make anything of yourself, you have to graduate high school."

"If we aren't going to Texas, where are we going?"

"As far as our money takes us. If we can find enough work to buy gas and make it back to Arizona, I'll be happy."

"I want to go to Texas."

"Wantin' and doin' are two different things. We'll do what we can with what we've got."

Bill grumbled something and rolled away from me. Considering our predicament was all his doing, his insolent attitude nettled me. "Watch your mouth, buster. Remember whose fault it is we're even on this trip. I didn't ask for this, and I'm not takin' any cheek from you when things don't go the way you want." I got no response and hoped Bill took my words to heart for a change.

CHAPTER THIRTY-NINE

Bill and I traveled south through the rich agricultural valleys of southern Oregon. We looked out the window at flourishing crops and orchards full of ripening fruit with families of pickers working the harvest. It was hard to imagine the depression affecting these busy people the way it had folks in the timber country.

A tension was building between us that made for poor travel companions. I was snappish and irritable. Bill was sullen and withdrawn. When one or the other of us attempted to fill the long, quiet stretches, we met with snarls, grumbles, and silence.

I thought about the promise I made to Maidee all those years ago to keep the kids together and care for them. I had failed miserably. Guilt swept through me like a meal of rancid meat. My gut churned, and my eyes teared. I had abandoned Aaron to the care of strangers and Lynch to the State of Oregon. Charles was dying, and Maisie, my sweet, cherished baby girl, wouldn't even know me if I showed up on Eula's doorstep. I drank too much, earned too little, and now chafed under a judge's order to leave the state we'd called home for six years. I resented Bill and his shenanigans. Being civil to him got harder as the miles went by.

When we crossed the border from Nevada to Arizona, I breathed a sigh of relief.

Bill sat up straighter, and his face relaxed in a lopsided grin. "Well, it ain't Texas, but it's close," he offered in a conciliatory tone.

"Don't say 'ain't.' You know the rules."

"Jeez, Pa, are you going to hound me about that now? I'm almost seventeen. When can I stop living by your rules?"

"When you grow up and act like a man instead of a stupid kid. We're out of money and out of work. The first thing we need to do is find someone to hire us. Then you need to show me you mean to make a man-sized effort and contribute to your well-being. Talkin' like a hick isn't goin' to earn you any points when you're lookin' for work. Stand up like a man and sound like a man. With luck, somebody will hire you to do a man's job."

"That and when I'm eighteen. When I'm eighteen, I'm leavin' and never lookin' back. I'll get Aaron and Lynch, and we'll make our own way. You can stumble around some farmer's field behind a mule plow or scrap for fruit in an orchard all you want. I'm headin' for Oregon and a different kind of life."

"You sure do talk big for a boy who turned our world upside down by bein' stupid. It's your fault, and no one else's, that Aaron and Lynch are left behind. I don't want any lip either, so let's decide right now that what you make belongs to me, and what I make belongs to me until I say different. We have to send money north for both your brothers' keep, and you're goin' to pitch in. Capisce?"

"Capisce," Bill grumbled in defeat, but I knew better than to think this was the end of it. We rumbled south toward Mesa, where there were citrus orchards and melon fields. If we got work picking fruit, I thought we might earn enough to buy a train ticket to San Antonio to visit Charles. I pulled into the first field with a Help Wanted sign at the entrance.

The field agent motioned us over, and before dark, we were hired and had picked several boxes of oranges. The pay was meager, but we could eat that night. He told us to come back at daybreak and he'd put us on steady. I asked if we could pitch our tent somewhere nearby, and he pointed to a bleak area outside the protection and shade of the orchard. I nodded but thought we'd pitch our tent in the shade of an orange tree after he left.

Christmas came and went, and Bill turned seventeen. We worked in the orange orchard for the next seven months, earning fifteen cents an hour. If we weren't harvesting oranges, we were pruning trees and clearing undergrowth. We saved every cent, except for what we spent on food—and the bottle of whiskey I managed to hustle off a Jewish trader who took reject oranges and traded them to the Indians for blankets. He took the blankets to Mexico to sell.

Bill and Hiram the Jew got to talking one night, and the trader figured out Bill spoke a few words of Spanish that might be useful to him on his next trip south. He offered to take Bill on for two dollars a day if he'd make the next run to Mexico with him. The harvest season was ending, and Bill was excited to think he could make more money doing something fun, instead of strapping on a heavy sack and carrying a ladder from tree to tree. The backbreaking work hadn't done much to improve our relationship, but it had made us stronger than we'd been in quite a while.

"Dad, please let me go. You could head out to San Antone and visit Charles and Maisie, and I could follow as soon as I get back."

His plea and the suggestion that I take our earnings and visit Charles while he was gone were irresistible. I agreed to let him go with the Jewish fruit merchant, who assured me he'd be safe and back in Mesa in two weeks. The next day, I approached the field boss to let me park the car at the orchard for a couple of weeks. I packed everything we owned inside and thumbed a ride to the railroad station with Bill and the trader.

"I wish I could go see Charles," Bill said, and I suspected he already felt sorry for his bargain. "Tell him I'm coming to see him when I get back from Mexico."

"Well, maybe you will and maybe you won't. We barely have enough money for one round-trip ticket, and you only agreed to work for this guy for the next two weeks. Maybe, if you hang on to every dollar you get paid."

"Tell Charles I miss him and I'll come as soon as I save up enough money."

"Will do. I might make it in time for his high-school graduation. I'd like to be there for it. You work hard now and do what your new boss tells you, hear?"

"Yeah. See you in a couple of weeks." Bill climbed into the front seat of Hiram's rickety old truck and waved to me.

I headed straight for the ticket window and laid down what pay we had left for a ticket to San Antonio. It wasn't until I was seated in the car and we started rolling that I heard Maidee say, "How could you let him go off with that man? You barely know him. Isn't it enough that you left Aaron with strangers and Lyn boarded out? How will you ever find him again?"

My imagination and guilty conscience were ganging up on me, but I swear she hovered right behind my left ear when she spoke to me that way. I shook my head to clear her voice and said, "He's near grown now, Maidee. We can't keep him on a short leash forever."

The woman sitting next to me turned her head and said, "Pardon?"

The train lurched, and I looked out the window to avoid answering.

CHAPTER FORTY

I slumped in the seat and let my head rest against the window on my rolled-up jacket. The railcar reeked of unwashed bodies and dirty upholstery. I wasn't riding first class but was relieved to be out of the hot sun and the backbreaking work of picking oranges. The rhythmic rocking of the train lulled me to sleep, with visions of my oldest son and baby daughter swimming through my addled brain.

Julia and Sam met me at the station and took me straight to the house. Charles was waiting for me, but seeing him so frail and sickly made my heart ache. We had known for some time that he had tuberculosis, and close contact with others was discouraged. I couldn't help myself and swept him up in my arms.

"Pa," he said, "where's Bill?"

My eyes swam, and I grabbed my handkerchief to blot my nose before it spilled over. "Bill took a job with a Jewish fruit salesman and is on his way to Mexico. He'll be gone two weeks, and I need to get my visitin' in and head back to make sure he's still in one piece. He gave me strict orders to tell you he misses you and will come as soon as he has enough money for a ticket." I blew my nose and wiped the tears away. I hadn't expected to be so emotional, but seeing my boy again after all this time upended me.

"I'm graduating this weekend, Pa. They're going to let me walk across the stage with the other kids to receive my diploma if I keep my face covered and promise not to shake hands. I have to wear gloves too. Aunt Julia bought me a new linen suit. It's swell, Pa. Will you come?"

"Wouldn't miss it for the world. I'm proud of you, and I know your ma is looking down with a big ol' grin."

"I wish she was here. I miss her."

"So do I, son, so do I. But I know she's watching over you, and that settles my mind. Your brothers would give anything to see you, but this damned depression put us in a bind. With you being sick and all, well, we just couldn't work it out."

"I know. It's okay. Living with Aunt Julia and Uncle Sam is fine, but I miss Aaron and Lynch real bad. They write to me, and that helps. Pa, do you think Bill will really come see me?"

"Yes, I do. If this job pans out, he'll be making two bucks a day. He'll have enough for a train ticket in no time. It might take two or three more trips south of the border, but he'll come."

Charles's graduation was terrific. He cut a handsome figure in the cream-colored linen suit Julia bought him. It reminded me of the one Eula bought me when I graduated from A&M. Maidee would be beaming with pride. He wasn't allowed to sit with the other students, so when his turn came, they brought him out from a side room off the school gymnasium and helped him up the stairs.

Julia had concocted an ascot to complement his suit and shirt and he had it pulled up over his nose and mouth to keep from contaminating anyone. He wore white gloves and saddle-tan shoes and was by far the best-dressed young man in his class.

My chest swelled, and Maidee's presence seeped around us like a vapor. After the ceremony, we stood outside the building, and Fred took photographs of Charles and me together. He was barefaced, and we stood apart. I'd hugged him the one time when I first saw him at Julia's house. It was hard to keep from doing it again. I wanted to wrap him in my arms and squeeze him till his eyes popped.

It didn't seem possible that eighteen years had lapsed since that first overwhelming burst of joy I had at seeing my new son, a tiny, frail infant, now thin and infirm in a body wracked with consumption. It wasn't fair. I'd have given anything for Maidee to see him graduate. She would have that look of love radiating from her face like when he was a newborn. She feared she might lose him in those early days, and I feared we were losing him now.

I still needed to make it to Alpine to visit Maisie. Fred's health was poor, and he and Eula had moved to the small community to provide a cleaner climate in the high country air. They thought it would be better to raise Maisie in a smaller place where they could keep a close eye on her and bought a little farm where she would have animals and lots of space to roam. It was a long train ride, and I was running out of time.

Fred met me at the station, but Eula and Maisie stayed home fixing our evening meal. My beautiful daughter was now a willowy girl of nine. With her crop of dark curls, she could have been a brunette Shirley Temple. I couldn't believe my eyes when she greeted me, shy and unsure who I was. I hadn't seen her in all the years since we left for Oregon.

Eula said, "Give your daddy a hug, Maisie," but when I reached for her, she slipped behind Eula's plump figure and stuck a finger in her mouth. Her eyes shifted up to meet mine ever so briefly before she turned her head and buried it in Eula's side.

Eula tugged her free and gave her a little nudge toward me. Maisie pulled back, and I said, "Just let her be. When she's ready."

We all went into the big white farmhouse to one of Eula's delicious meals. It reminded me of when Maidee and I showed up on their doorstep in San Antonio when we were runaways looking to get married. It seemed like a century ago, but it was just shy of twenty years. How could so much good and so much bad happen in such a short time?

Maisie glanced at me during dinner, raising her liquid green eyes to mine and then darting them away when I made contact. It amused me, but it hurt my feelings, too. I understood why she was shy around me. I was no better than a stranger. How could I have failed her like this? I had longed for a daughter, and when the good Lord gave me one, I was overjoyed. She reminded me so much of Maidee. Her eyes were that same emerald shade, and her face was as beautiful as her mother's. She was a mix of the two of us, where the boys all favored the Jones side of the family.

With her head bowed and her eyes lowered, she lifted my empty plate from the table and whispered, "Mama says you're my daddy. If that's true, why don't I live with you?"

Stumped for an answer, I turned away. She called Eula "Mama," and had grown up as their daughter. What right did I have to swoop in and expect her to love and remember me?

"It's complicated, Maisie. I was your daddy once upon a time, but I wasn't doing a very good job of it, and Eula and Fred stepped in and rescued us. We both owe them. It's best you think of Fred as your daddy. I won't be around, but I still love you very much. And your brothers, Charles, Bill, Aaron, and Lynch, all remember you and love you, too. Did you know you have four big brothers?"

"Yes. Mama showed me a picture of them. She said they live far away. Once, she even showed me a letter from one of them."

"From Charles? He's the oldest and the letter writer in the bunch."

"No. I don't think it was him. I think it was Aaron."

"Aw, yes. That might be the case. He's another one who writes letters. He's a little closer to you in age and crazy about you. Did you write back to him?"

"I can't remember. I'll ask Mama." And she slipped away as quickly as she'd appeared.

The next day, as I packed to catch the train back to San Antonio and on to Mesa, she slipped up next to me again. "Can I give you a hug to give to Aaron for me? Tell him I'll write him a letter soon." And with that, her skinny little arms wrapped themselves around my waist and gave me the best squeeze I'd had since Maidee died.

Tears wet my cheeks as I stroked the top of her curly head, resisting the urge to lift her into my arms and never let go. She had a home with a mother and father who doted on her. I couldn't ask for more, and I couldn't offer anything like it. I patted her back and hugged her as much as her awkward embrace allowed.

"You betcha. I'll deliver that hug to Aaron. It would be my pleasure."

Maisie tipped her angelic face up at me and said, "If I didn't have Papa Fred, I'd want you for my daddy."

Tears plopped onto my vest, and I stooped down to take her in my arms, knowing it would be a long time before I saw her again. "You'll always be my daughter, Maisie, no matter if you love Fred best."

She pulled away and bolted from the room, calling to Fred, "Daddy, can I go to the train to say goodbye to Mr. Will with you?"

If hearts sing, mine was an entire chorus.

CHAPTER FORTY-ONE
Maizelle

By the time Will returned to San Antonio, Charles had taken to bed. Our beautiful boy lay listless and pale against the cool sheets Julia replaced every few hours. Spasms of coughing wracked his frail body. Julia bathed his forehead with a cool towel and wiped away the blood-infused spittle that erupted unbidden from his mouth.

My childless sister administered the most loving and tender care this side of heaven. I should have been the one to comfort him and tend to his needs. My heart ached.

As Charles's condition worsened, I couldn't comfort Will or Julia. My sister would sooner die herself than lose my beautiful boy. They both lamented that it was a mistake for him to take part in the graduation ceremony. The additional exertion seemed to have taken whatever wind he had left in his sails and squeezed it out of him.

Charles took his dying breath with Julia holding him in her arms. Will huddled next to the bed stroking his blond hair, and Sam stood in the doorway of the bedroom with a bewildered look on his face.

I knew Sam was anxious about how Julia would react when her beloved nephew passed. She had all but abandoned Sam in the past six months. He feared she would be inconsolable, and he was right.

When Charles slumped against the pillows and his head lolled to the side, the first of many tears slid off Will's hollow cheeks. Julia buried her face in Charles's chest and wept like never before. Sam approached and attempted to lift her away from the body, but she flung an arm back to brush him away.

"Not yet," she said, choking on her tears. "Not yet. Leave me be."

Will closed Charles's eyes, pulled the sheet over his face, and stood.

"Can I get you anything?" Sam asked.

"No," Will said. "I need to be alone."

"Of course," Sam said. "When you're ready to let him go, I'll call the funeral home."

Will left Charles and Julia and went outside to light a cigarette. He couldn't figure out what to do or how to do it. I could tell he was in a state of shock and disbelief. He had come to see our son graduate from high school, not watch him die. His mind whirled in confusion. Where's Bill? Why did Charles have to die? What should I do next? Where should I be? Should I call Aaron and Lyn?

He couldn't go back to Arizona until after the funeral. What if Bill comes back from Mexico and I'm not there to meet him? How can things have gone so wrong so fast?

As for me, I was worried sick about Bill going off with that Jewish fruit merchant—or blanket trader—or whatever he called himself. The man was a total stranger, and Will had abandoned our son without a solid plan to reconnect. Charles's death would delay Will's return to Mesa, and he had no way to contact Bill. I made a hard decision. I put myself in motion to find our son.

As much as I wanted to stay with Will to comfort him when they laid Charles to rest, I couldn't. My ability to make my presence known had grown weaker as the years passed. Traveling between San Antonio and Alpine to look after two of my children had drained my resources. I needed to remain vigilant about what I could influence on the earthly plane. My eldest was dead. I couldn't bring him back but I would be here to welcome him. I had otherworldly obligations to discharge before I moved on permanently.

I arrived in Mesa and waited near where Will had parked the car. He didn't know it yet, but migrant workers from Mexico had confiscated everything he left in the back. The tent was gone, the blankets were gone, and anything they hadn't taken with them was now in use by someone else.

Bill and the Jewish man, Hiram, were nowhere in sight. I drifted south into unfamiliar territory, hunting for them. The fruit-picking season was over, and I had no more ideas about where to look. I searched the reservation and rested for a while. Listening to the Indians tell stories and sing songs to the skies and the animals brought a sense of peace. I gained more strength, and once I felt stronger, I traveled south into a foreign land called Mexico.

It was a good thing I did. I found Bill wandering alone along a train track. He was dirty, crying, and very angry. He cursed Hiram and damned him "to hell." I touched him on his shoulder, and he raised his arms and shouted into the night, "What?! That lying SOB didn't pay me. He dumped me in the middle of the night and drove off. I don't have any money. I don't know where the hell I am. What am I supposed to do, laugh about it?"

There was nothing I could do but stay with him, try to calm him with my presence, and listen while he ranted into thin air. If only I'd been able to let him see me. My presence calmed him, even though he didn't understand why.

He walked most of that night without knowing where he was headed. Just before dawn, a bright light lit up the tracks behind him, and a low rumble shook the ground. Bill jumped out of the train's path and crouched as the train rumbled toward him.

My heart lurched with fear. Everything about this looked dangerous. I wanted Bill to move farther away—lie down in the shallow ditch—but he crouched like a cat ready to spring. The train rumbled past, shaking the ground, making Bill's clothes billow around his thin form, first sucking to him, then lifting away like he might take flight. When the caboose appeared, he stood and raised his arms.

I wasn't prepared for what happened next. He leaped forward and grabbed a narrow railing, clinging to it with white-knuckled ferocity until he got one foot onto something solid and pulled himself onto a small platform.

He maneuvered himself over the side rails and flopped onto the wood flooring. He crawled to a sitting position and flattened his body against the back of the train car. I stayed with him, although it took all my strength, and I had no idea where we would end up.

When the brakes squealed, and the train began to slow, Bill stood and looked around. His legs were cramped, and he was cold. He had no earthly idea where he was. His stomach growled, and his mouth was dry.

His uppermost thought was unslaked thirst. He had to get off this rolling train and find water. Food would be welcome, but water was urgent.

It was dark of night, and the temperature had dropped uncomfortably low. The railcar he was on came to life. Men talked, lanterns glowed from the interior, and the aroma of food cooking wafted through the night air. Bill pondered whether or not he should push his way into the car. He could have both water and food while warming himself against the coal-fired potbelly stove he glimpsed through the dirty rear window.

Desperation makes people do desperate things. He realized he had two choices: jump from a moving train and disappear into the night or face the wrath of the railroad men and be thrown off the train. He decided on the latter.

"Excuse me," he said, pushing the door open and stepping inside.

One of the men whirled in his direction, slopped hot coffee over his hand, dropped his tin cup, and bellowed, "Sonofabitch! Where'd you come from?"

Bill was relieved that the man spoke English, even if it was threatening and angry. "Sorry to bother you, but I need a drink of water real bad."

"I'll bet you do. How many of you managed to sneak onto the train? Are they clinging for life on the roof?"

"There's no one but me. A guy I was traveling with in Mexico dumped me and drove off. I hopped the train a long way back. Alone."

"Ain't often we see white kids on this train. Where'd you hop on? Where's your folks?"

"I think it was in Mexico. Where are we now?"

"We just crossed the border into Cal-i-for-ni-a. We'll be cleared at the border and take on more freight and fuel. Where's your folks?"

"I don't got any folks anymore. My ma's dead, and my pa's in Texas. Like I said, it's just me. Could I please have a drink of water?"

There were three men in the caboose. The one standing over the stove cooking reached across his enormous belly, poured water from a brown jug into a tin cup, and handed it backward toward Bill.

Bill stepped toward the cup, and the first man moved between him and the outstretched arm.

"Just a minute there, hotshot. You'll get water if and when I say you get water."

The fat cook's arm rotated back to the counter and plopped the cup down with a bang. Water sloshed over the side, and Bill's mouth watered at the sight. He struggled to keep his feet planted.

"Please," Bill said, and then, overcome with hunger and thirst, he slumped to the floor.

Two of the three men rushed to help him back onto his feet. The third worker, who, up until now, hadn't uttered a sound, said, "Mac, give the kid a drink of water. We can decide where to toss him off the train after."

"Cookie, hand me that cup," the man called Mac barked in a gruff voice.

The cook handed over the cup, and Mac foisted it on Bill.

Bill gulped the contents without taking a breath and handed the cup back. "Thanks. I needed that."

My heart lurched. What were these three going to do to my boy now? He needed food. He needed to get warm. He needed more water. Would they really throw him off the train?

CHAPTER FORTY-TWO

The three men inside the warm caboose argued about what to do with Bill. My heart was in my throat, waiting for them to decide. I was unable to do anything to affect the outcome.

"I say we just toss him off the back," the man called Mac said with a growl.

"No," the fat cook said. "He's just a kid. And he's American. Not one of those Mexicans looking for a way into the country."

The third man, whose name turned out to be George, said, "I'm with Cookie. When we get stopped at the check station, why not just let him jump off and disappear?"

Mac grumbled something unintelligible, stepped toward Bill, and shoved him backward. Bill landed on his bottom with a thud. "He ain't goin' to get far if'n he can't even stand up to a little push."

"Let me get some more water and food into his gullet. He'll be okay. He's just weak from hunger."

"Yer a soft touch, Cookie. We can't save 'em all, ya know. The fact he's a white kid, and American, is the only reason I'm goin' along with ya."

I'd been holding my breath, waiting for the decision. I relaxed momentarily until the questions invaded my mind. What would Bill do? Where would he go? How would he survive? I had no choice but to travel with him and make sure he was okay.

The train ground and screeched as it came to a stop before inching forward at a snail's pace. The small caboose jerked when the train began to move and dumped Bill onto his butt again. All three of the grown men threw back their heads and laughed.

"That's your first lesson, hobo. When a train's about to move, you'd best be hangin' on to somethin' bigger and stronger than you," Mac said.

"Come 'ere boy," said Cookie. "I've got a bowl of stew for you. Eat fast. You're goin' to be on the road again soon."

Bill rolled to his knees and grabbed a chair bolted to the floor. He pulled himself upright and said, "Thanks, man. I'm so hungry I could eat a horse or its saddle."

The three men chuckled as the cook plunked a bowl of beef stew in front of my son. Bill grabbed the big spoon and wolfed the meal down. The train came to a complete stop again, and he looked up with fear in his eyes.

"That's right, boy. This here's the end of the line for you," Mac said.

"Here, take this," George said, tossing a well-worn blanket in Bill's direction, "you'll need it."

Mac scowled but let it pass. He reached for Bill's arm and said, "Time for me to escort you off this train. Good luck. You'll find a hobo camp not too far up the line. I'd advise you to stop there and make a few friends. They'll show you the ropes." He guided Bill out the back door and said, "Jump now, real easy like. When you feel the ground under your feet tuck and roll."

I hovered over Bill, doing everything in my power to protect him from harm. I drifted under him and let him roll over me. If it softened his landing, I couldn't tell. He scrambled to his feet, rubbed his knees and elbows, jumped off the tracks, and disappeared into a long, dark side yard of parked and abandoned railcars.

It wasn't long before he found the hobo camp. Six derelicts sat hunched over their knees around a low burning campfire. Each held a ragged-edged can of Dinty Moore beef stew, opened with a jackknife and dogged determination. Each used the same knife to spear the morsels from the gravy and drop them on an eager tongue. As Bill approached, four pairs of eyes drifted his way, but none stopped eating.

"Mind if I join you?" Bill sauntered up using all the insolent courage he could muster. Each man noticed and logged his attitude and manner. No one looked at him, and no one spoke.

"I'd like to warm my hands if it isn't too much trouble."

One of the men scooched over, and Bill crouched next to him. "Name's Bill. I could use a little advice if you have any to spare."

"Advice about what?"

"Oh, how to get on and off a movin' train. Where you grub for food. Stuff like that."

"You runnin' away from somethin'?"

"No. I got on a train in Mexico by accident and didn't know how to get off again until it stopped here. I was lookin' to meet my pa in Arizona, and I think I overshot the mark."

"That where you're headed?"

"No. I thought since I was this far, I might try makin' it back to Oregon."

A voice from across the fire pit said, "That home?"

"Has been for the past few years," Bill said, watching red cinders pop out of the fire.

"What brought you down here?"

"Oh, you know, lookin' for work, like everybody else."

One of the other men in the circle cleared his throat and tossed his empty stew can into the fire. "No work around here. Maybe up north a ways."

"Yeah, I'm not lookin' for work now. I plan to hop the rails back to Oregon to see my brothers."

"How old are you?"

Bill shot a look at the man's face and then lied. "Eighteen."

"You don't look eighteen. You sure about that?"

"Yeah. Why? Does it matter?"

"Matters to me. I don't want no entanglements with the law over harborin' an underage runaway."

"I told you, I'm not a runaway."

"Right. And I'm King Edward."

All the men chuckled and one by one tossed their empty cans onto the fire.

Another one spoke. "Sorry, we didn't know you was stoppin' by for dinner or we'd of saved you some." More chuckles rippled through the small circle.

"I already ate. Thanks anyway."

It could have been his nonchalant arrogance or his naturally chatty nature, but before another hour passed the four hobos were giving Bill instructions on how to hop the rails and get off without getting injured or caught. They told him about the hobo camps along the tracks from California to the Canadian border. They laughed, poked fun at one another, and accepted him into a friendly family of kindred spirits.

I didn't like it one bit. All of it sounded dangerous, and having my son traveling alone with characters like this made me more anxious than ever. I needed Will to be here. He never should have let Bill go off with that man. Now, I had no choice but to abandon my dead son to protect my errant one.

CHAPTER FORTY-THREE

Bill didn't have any money, but that didn't stop every hobo between the California border and San Francisco from shaking him down. Every time they came up empty, someone thought punching him in the stomach or the face would be a good idea. I suffered each of those punches as if they were given directly to me. Bill shrugged them off and continued his integration into the various camps.

One night, around a camp near San Francisco, the men talked about a Yard Bull throwing a couple of kids out of a boxcar, and one died. "Those kids wouldn't have been where the Bull could see 'em, except they were tryin' to get away from a chicken hawk," one of the men said.

Everyone around the cooking pot nodded their heads and looked glum. Bill looked from one to the other, trying to figure out what a chicken hawk was and how a bird could cause such panic that the boys would show themselves. The small circle of men had grown unnaturally quiet. One of the men kept shaking his head as if by saying a silent no, he could change the outcome.

"What's a chicken hawk?" Bill asked, his eyes darting uneasily from one grim face to another. Everyone froze. Mouths in mid-bite stopped chewing. Four pairs of white eyeballs rolled in his direction, then quickly shifted away.

The oldest hobo in the group squirmed and hung his head. One of the other seasoned veterans finally lifted his eyes and looked at Bill. "A chicken hawk is a scumbag who thinks skinny kids, like yourself, make just as good screwin' as a broad. They's sweet as sugar to ya—might even offer ya somethin' to eat to soften ya up. But then—look out—and don't never turn yer back 'cause what's comin' for ya ain't somethin' ya want. Get my drift?"

It was Bill's turn to squirm. He looked around the circle, gulped, and said, "Thanks. Any tips on how to spot one?"

"Oh, you'll know. Some of 'em ain't even subtle about it. The wolf offers you food or loans ya a jacket or blanket. Some ask if they can sit close to ya to get warm. Next thing ya know, they's warming their hands between your thighs. Ya get a feel for it after a while. I'm surprised you ain't already had the experience. The chicken hawks just wait 'til they get ya alone in a boxcar and take what they want."

Bill gulped again. "Na. Nothin' like that so far. Just lucky, I guess."

"Lucky or smart," another man said. "Steer clear of the sweet talkers and the ones with somethin' to eat. They come in all shapes and sizes, but the big ones are the worst 'cause they can pin you before you even know what's comin'."

Another husky voice broke into the night. "They hunt for the sparrows. Sparrows are girly boys ready and willing."

Bill gagged. The conversation upset him. His food churned in his gut as he pictured what he'd do to any man who tried any monkey business with him. It would be the last night he slept with any ease on any car of any train.

When dawn broke, Bill roused from his spot on the ground, grabbed his bundle with the tattered and worn blanket the man on the caboose had tossed to him, and headed out to find an O&C Railroad car. He figured if he took the Oregon and California, he would eventually end up back in Oregon. He had panhandled on the streets in San Francisco until he had three dollars in change.

He still couldn't eat anything after what he'd heard the night before, and he knew getting on a train with money in his pockets was a sure invitation to be shagged and robbed. He removed his worn shoes and stuffed in new cardboard to cover the holes, placed the coins between that layer and a second layer of cardboard and, using care not to disturb the coins, slipped his feet inside. The gnawing discomfort in his gut was a ball of pure fear. So far, he hadn't had anything worse than a knife put to his throat when a "road yegg" tried to shake him down, but the fear of being assaulted hung over him heavy as chain mail on a warrior.

The thought of my son going through anything like the assault I had endured by the man who eventually took my life was more than I could bear. I hovered and fussed and tried to imprint myself on Bill. Of course, my presence agitated him, and not knowing what annoyed him made it all the worse. We moved as one through the rail yard, looking for the O&C designation. I spotted it first and got behind Bill to steer him in the right direction. Floating above the terrain had its advantages. When Bill turned in the wrong direction, I tumbled some crates into his pathway.

"Crap!" he said, banging his knee against one of the falling containers. "Shit, damn, hell!" He bounced around on one foot holding his injured knee up in the air.

I disapproved of his language, but I understood his frustration.

"Why can't I just find a train to take me home? Why do I have to keep taking detours?"

Bill rounded a corner toward the O&C line and a Yard Bull spotted him and shouted, "You there. Where do you think you're going?"

The Bull took off running in Bill's direction, and Bill hightailed it out of sight. He slipped between two freight cars and spotted the O&C letters two rows over. He took off running like a spring flood on the Sabinal, darting between cars, slithering his slender frame beneath them to hide in the small space between the bottom of the car and the railroad ties. The Bull gave up the chase when he figured the vagrant wouldn't try to jump a car on his train.

Once Bill thought the coast was clear, he crawled from under a car and sneaked to the O&C yard. He was in luck. The first empty car he found was an unlocked grain car. In the last camp, Hobo Joe had told him that the grain cars were the best on the O&C because pigeons flocked in to pick up the grain spilled from the off-loaded sacks.

"If you're smart, you'll get on early, hide in a corner, wait until the Yard Bull does his inspection, slide the doors shut, and whack a few pigeons for dinner. You show up at the next camp with a string of dead pigeons, and you'll have the best mulligan stew you ever tasted and friends for life."

Bill was not given to prayer. Like his father before him, he was a believer, but he didn't take much to the rituals nor ask permission from

God for his day-to-day living. Today was different. Today, he prayed. He prayed he would be alone in the grain car. He prayed he wouldn't get caught and beaten by the Yard Bull. He prayed the car would be too dirty or unappealing for a chicken hawk to jump. As he prayed, he was overcome with the urge to sleep. The car was dark in the far corners, and he slipped down on his haunches to rest his eyes, his back pressed against the tightly fitted boards, thinking if he stayed crouched, he'd be better prepared to run if the need arose. Soon, his legs went limp, and he slumped to the floor. His night of terror and worry about the dangers he had yet to encounter had exhausted him.

The soft cooing and rustling of the pigeons scavenging loose grain was a lullaby that put Bill into a contented slumber. He was in this state of half-sleep when a loud rumble shook the rail yard. Men shouted, and feet stomped on the gravel as they ran, banging on the sides of railcars— the racket shot shock waves through him. The Bull, he thought and plastered himself as far into the corner of the door side of the grain car as possible. It was the best position to escape discovery as the Bulls flashed their lights into the far corners first, and then the corner to the car's rear, skimming past his hiding place where he was partially concealed by the door. His heart pounded, and the sudden rush of adrenaline from waking so suddenly left him taut and alert. He glanced around the railcar to see if he could see anyone else. His eyes had adjusted to the dark, and all he saw were the pigeons returning to get more grain after being frightened off by the commotion. He lowered his eyes so the Bull's flashlight would miss the glow.

Whatever had caused the loud rumble and the hubbub stopped as abruptly as it had begun. Bill waited while his heart slowed to a more regular rhythm, and when nothing else seemed to be happening, he slid along the wall toward the sliding door of the car, inching it closed so as not to disturb the remaining birds.

A hand appeared around the door from the outside, pushing it back toward Bill. He froze as a pair of legs flung into the car and a man materialized.

Bill waited. The new passenger didn't move. The pigeons flapped wildly, banging into the car's sides, hitting the ceiling with a loud thud, and falling back to the deck stunned. Bill almost had the door closed before the new person pushed it open far enough to squeeze himself through the crack. The body rolled onto its back and scooched away from the opening toward the other end of the car. Bill slithered down the side wall and curled himself around his drawn-up knees. He reached for the big door and continued inching it closed.

A dazed pigeon lay at his feet. He grabbed the bird and twisted its neck. Dinner, he thought. He rolled forward and reached for a second bird that spun in a circle just out of reach. It had a broken wing. When its wild flailing launched it closer, he snatched it and twisted its neck. For two, he thought.

The car jerked and a loud bang rippled through the air. *Coupled. We're underway.* The new stowaway moaned.

It hadn't occurred to Bill the person might be injured. He peered into the dark and said in a low, husky voice, "You need help down there?"

"I'm shot," a detached voice said into the dark. "I don't know how bad, but it hurts like hell."

"That what all the commotion was about?"

"Yeah. The Bull from the Northern Pacific caught me tryin' to jump the oil car."

"Why'd you pick an oil car? They're dangerous."

"It was handy."

"Handy wouldn't be good enough for me. You got somewhere you need to be in a hurry so you couldn't wait for something better?"

"Na. just stupid, I guess."

"Or desperate. Was the Bull chasing you?"

"Yeah. There was some kind of explosion down at the far end of the yard, and I was running to get away from it. The Bull saw me and probably thought I'd caused it. Wasn't me, though."

"Where you shot?"

"Shoulder."

"Makes it hard to jump a car with a bum shoulder, I'll bet."

"Yeah. I wouldn't have made it onto this car if it had been rolling."

"What's your name?" Bill asked.

"Ronnie. You?"

"Bill. Where you headed?"

"Home. To God's country."

"Oregon, then?"

"Yep. Can't wait to see them big 'ol Doug fir trees again."

"This should be the train to get us there if we don't get busted. Once we're rollin' I'll light a match and take a look at your wound. Too risky yet. I don't want the Bull to have any reason to open this car."

"That's right neighborly of ya, Bill. Where you headed?"

"Anyplace in Oregon I can find a little work. I'm flat busted."

"Ain't we all?"

Bill bit his tongue to keep from saying, "Don't say 'ain't.'" I chuckled to myself. It seemed unlikely this injured person would be able to harm Bill. I think we both drew in a breath of relief.

Ronnie Miller turned out to be the same age as Bill and just as eager to get back home to Oregon. He was from the coast and had been hoboing for two years since the cannery in Astoria shut its doors. "I been all the way to the east coast of the United States and haven't found anyplace I'd rather live than Oregon," he said. "Maine was real pretty, and their fisheries were still operating, so I had a short stint of work there. It wasn't enough to keep me, though. I miss my brother, and I miss my girlfriend."

"What about your folks?" Bill asked.

"Yeah, them too, I guess," Ronnie said. "My dad drinks too much and beats on my mom, so it ain't too peaceful around there. That and work is why I left in the first place. You got folks in Oregon?"

"Two brothers. One in Toledo and one at the blind school in Salem."

"No folks?"

"My mother's been dead since I was five. My dad drinks too much, too, but he doesn't have anybody to beat on."

"Where's he?"

"Not sure. We were working in Mesa, Arizona. I went to Mexico with a trader, and he went to San Antonio to visit my sister and brother. I got separated from the trader and hopped a freight back to the US of A. My dad could be waiting for me in Arizona for all I know. I don't have any way to get ahold of him or find out where he is."

"That's messed up," Ronnie said.

"Yeah. But I'll connect with him again once I get back to Oregon and get enough money to make a few long-distance phone calls. Mostly, I just want to be sure my brothers are okay."

"You have a sister and another brother, too?"

"Older brother and baby sister. They live with relatives in Texas."

"Is that 'cause your mother died?"

"Yeah. My sister wasn't even two yet, and my brother got TB, so he couldn't be around the rest of us. I haven't seen them for almost seven years."

"Sorry, man. That's the shits."

"Not so bad anymore. It was hard in the beginning, but I sort of got used to it."

Bill asked the question that was burning a hole in his brain. "You ever run into a chicken hawk on your travels?" He gulped and stared at his feet, afraid to hear the answer.

The dark car grew quiet. Bill could hear Ronnie breathing, but he wasn't saying anything. The silence spoke louder than his voice. The train rocked in a steady rhythm as it rattled along the tracks. Daylight crept in through the slit in the door, and the atmosphere grew heavy.

"Can't say," Ronnie finally said.

"Can't say or won't say?" Bill asked.

"A little of both, I guess. I shoved one fellow off a boxcar we was in. Could be he was one. I didn't let him stick around long enough to find out."

"Sounds like you had good reason to help him find another means of transportation."

"Yep."

The silence broke, and the boys visited like old pals for the next few hundred miles. When the train pulled into Klamath Falls, Oregon, they slipped out of the car and realized this wasn't a rail yard. It was a grain silo, and the car they had been riding in would soon be home to a few tons of wheat. Ronnie's wound needed attention, and Bill felt bound to help him. The boys wandered into the small downtown, looking for a doctor's office. Between them, they had less than twenty dollars and no idea how much a doctor would charge.

CHAPTER FORTY-FOUR

Ronnie Miller and Bill Jones were two of the hungriest young men on the planet. Ronnie suggested they find something to eat before they searched for a doctor, and Bill said, "No way, man. That shoulder wound is lookin' worse and worse every day. We need to get you checked out. If you still have shot in there, it has to come out before you get some serious poisoning or worse."

"I hear you," Ronnie said, "and I appreciate your concern. Ain't nobody but my ma ever give a shit whether I lived or died."

"I'm not sayin' I love you like a mother. I'm just sayin' I don't want you getting' any worse and makin' it harder for us to stick together. It's been good havin' a buddy to ride with."

"Yeah. I think so, too. Less to worry about when there's two of us."

The boys wandered through the town, and near the end of the long main block, they came across an office that said, "Physician and Surgeon" in gold letters on the window.

"Looks like we're in luck," Bill said.

"Maybe," Ronnie said. "Unlikely any doc is goin' to look at me for what I've got in my pocket."

"Only one way to find out," Bill said, pushing open the door.

Both boys stepped over the threshold into the small waiting room, where a kind-looking woman sat behind a window. She glanced up with a look of surprise mixed with fear, assessing whether these scruffy strangers were a danger to her. "May I help you?" she squeaked.

Bill spoke. "My buddy got himself shot awhile back, and it looks real bad to me."

"Has he seen a doctor?" she asked.

"No. We came in on the O&C from San Francisco. You might say there weren't many doctors along the way."

"I see." She sniffed. "I'll see if Doctor Hall has time to take a look."

She went into the back of the building, and when she returned, she said, "Can you pay?"

"Not much," Ronnie piped up. "I've got two bucks, if that will do."

"I think that will do very nicely," she said. "Come with me."

Both boys started after her, and she stopped. "Just the injured party, please. The examination room is small."

"Will the doc tell me how to care for his wound? We're travelin' together, and I'm the one who needs to know what to do."

"I'll let Doctor Hall know. You take a seat in the waiting room, please." She dismissed Bill with a nod, turned, and marched down the hall with Ronnie close on her heels. When she returned, a white-faced Ronnie followed at her heels like a puppy.

Bill jumped to his feet and said, "What happened? You all right, man?"

Ronnie staggered toward him, and his knees buckled as he reached Bill. Bill's arms shot out and wrapped around Ronnie, half carrying, half dragging him to a chair.

The woman said, "Oh dear. I think he's feeling faint from shock. Doctor Hall removed several shotgun pellets, and there was both pain and blood. Some folks don't take to either of those too well. We had to do it without anesthesia due to the patient's limited funds. When was the last time he ate?"

"Ate?" Bill asked. "Far as I know, it's been more than two days. Neither of us had anything to eat on the train."

"I should have known," the lady said. "I'll call the café next door and tell them to give you the Blue Plate Special. Can you help him over there? I think all he needs is some food in his system."

"I can help him over there, but we don't have enough money to pay for a meal."

"It's on us," she said. "You young fellows need nourishment. His wound won't ever heal if he isn't eating regularly."

"Thank you, ma'am, that's mighty nice of you," Bill said. "Is there anything else I need to know about taking care of his wound?"

"Doctor Hall gave him a package with fresh dressings and an anti-infection salve for you to apply. The bandage needs to be changed every day."

"How many days?" Bill asked.

"When you don't see any more seepage or blood on the dressings, you can quit."

"Ma'am, we're goin' to jump the next railcar out of here. I don't know how many days it will be before we get where we're goin'. Will it hurt if I can't change it every day?"

"It could. He's at risk of severe infection in a wound like that. I'll ask Doctor Hall to give you enough dressings for five days. Will that do?"

"I hope so," Will said, uncertainty creeping into his voice.

"You go get something in your stomachs now. I'll come over in a few minutes with additional dressings."

Bill put his arms around Ronnie's midsection and pulled him to his feet. Ronnie swayed like a willow tree in a stiff breeze. "Easy, man. Just lean on me, and I'll get you there. I promise not to drop you."

The two boys shuffled out of the doctor's office and went to the Coffee Cup Café next door. A waitress ambled over and said, "You two the ones Doc Hall's buyin' the special for?"

"I guess so," Bill said, looking at the tabletop and avoiding eye contact.

"Well, is you, or ain't you?" the waitress said.

"Yeah. That would be us," Bill said. "My buddy's weak from hunger and shock. Could we get some water?"

"Comin' up," she said. "Where you boys headed?"

"Home," they said in unison.

"Where's home?" she asked.

"Waldport," Ronnie said, and "Toledo," Bill said.

"Can't say as I've ever heard of either of them," she said, walking toward the kitchen.

The Blue Plate Special turned out to be roast pork, mashed potatoes and gravy, broccoli, and a fresh baked biscuit. The boys ate like starved men, enjoying one of the best meals they'd had in the past several years. Neither of them especially liked broccoli, but they ate every morsel as if it were their last meal.

"How's your shoulder feel?" Bill asked, putting the last bite into his mouth.

"Hurts like hell," Ronnie said. "No. Maybe worse than hell. Maybe double hell."

"Sorry," Bill said. "Maybe we should stick around here a few days to be sure it's safe for you to hop a rail."

"Yeah, I couldn't hop a rock in the road right now," Ronnie said. "It's okay if you want to go on without me."

"Not happenin'," Bill said. "We're doin' this together. Capisce?"

Ronnie looked at Bill, and their eyes locked. An understanding went from one to the other, and a deep friendship was ignited and acknowledged at that moment.

CHAPTER FORTY-FIVE

Bill and his new friend stayed in Klamath Falls for a week. The accessible lake provided several spots to camp in the tall grasses without being seen. A couple of cafés near the station had prime pickings, and they scrounged from the scrap barrels every evening. No one bothered them, and they took advantage of the opportunity to fill their bellies and rest up while Ronnie's wound healed. I swelled with pride over my son taking care of his friend and was relieved they weren't in danger on another train.

It didn't take them long to figure out the train they hopped took a few spur lines to get from San Francisco to this spot in Southern Oregon. They asked around among the other vagrants and hobos they spotted, and chatted up locals to get a fix on what kind of railcar they should be on to get to the other side of the state. They were anxious to get back on the tracks again and head home.

Not many trains stopped at this outpost. It was day eight before they spotted the train they needed to reach the state's western side.

"You think you can use that arm to grab a handhold?" Bill asked Ronnie.

"Won't know 'til I try."

"If you miss, I'll catch you," Bill said.

"No, man, you should go first. Then there'll be someone to pull me up if I need help," Ronnie said.

The boys scouted the yard and knew there wasn't a Bull behind every car waiting to snag them. They only saw one in seven days, and he had come in on a Pacific Northern that didn't stick around long. He left when the cargo was loaded.

"Let's do a practice hop," Bill said. "I'll do the first jump and then you. We'll see how it works. If you aren't on, I'll jump off again."

The boys picked out an empty boxcar, and Bill ran alongside the slow-moving train. When he was ready, he grabbed a metal railing on the side of the sliding door and pulled himself up.

Ronnie gripped the rail and swung his body over the edge. Only one leg found purchase, and he started to slide off as the train picked up speed.

Bill flattened himself on the boxcar floor and grabbed Ronnie with both hands—one on the arm with the injured shoulder—and Ronnie shrieked in pain.

"Pull your leg inside!"

"I can't. The wind's got me."

"This will hurt. Get ready," Bill said, pulling Ronnie's body with all his strength and sliding one hand down to grip a pant leg. His fingers grasped the fabric and pulled.

Now free of the pain from Bill gripping his injured arm, Ronnie tried to scoot farther into the car.

Bill let go of the pants and thrust his arm across Ronnie's butt, pulling and rolling him into the boxcar.

Once Ronnie was aboard, both boys collapsed, laughing and crying, exhausted from the effort.

"Where you fellas headed?" The voice came from somewhere in the bowels of the dark interior and shocked Bill and Ronnie speechless. They held their breath. They weren't alone.

Bill scrambled to his feet and peered toward the unwelcome voice. "Home," he said. "Both of us. You?"

"Oh, you know. Anywhere the wind blows. That was quite a little mount you did there. Your friend new to this method of travel?"

"No," they chorused.

"I have a bum shoulder," Ronnie said. "I didn't get a strong grip, and the wind caught me."

Bill's heart was pumping so hard I could see his chest rising and falling. I could tell he was scared.

"We been doing this a long time," he said with bravado. "We know the ropes."

"Good to hear," the voice said. "Why don't you come on in and make yourselves comfortable? I even got a blanket."

The train was picking up a head of steam. Bill felt a tug on his pant leg, turned, nodded, and slipped down. The boys put their legs out of the boxcar and jumped.

They rolled down the embankment, and only the tall reeds along the shore stopped them from falling into the lake. When they came to a stop, Bill said, "You okay? How's your shoulder?"

Ronnie winced and then giggled.

Bill said, "What's so funny?" But then, Ronnie's mirth turned contagious, and the two of them flopped over on their backs, howling with laughter.

When they got their nervous hysteria under control, Ronnie said, "That was a close call," as they watched the caboose of their ride west fade into the distance.

"Might not'a been anything at all," Bill blustered.

"My ma always said, 'Better safe than sorry,'" Ronnie said, giggling again.

"Stop it now! Just stop!" Bill said. "It isn't funny. He could'a been a chicken hawk. Sure did sound like it. Anyway, you're the one who thought we should jump."

"Yeah, but I didn't notice you hesitatin' none."

"We need to get back to the station and scout us another train headin' west or north before it's too late."

"Won't be another 'til tomorrow or the next day, from what I heard," Ronnie said.

The boys stood and clawed their way up the embankment to the now silent tracks.

Once they were back at the Klamath Falls yard, they decided to scrounge the back of the Easy Street Café for dinner. They were in luck and filled their bellies before crawling into the tall grass along the lakeshore to sleep.

Dawn broke with the sound of a woeful train whistle in the distance, and Bill was on his feet in a hurry.

Ronnie crawled upright. His shoulder pained him something awful since his roll down the rail embankment, and he hadn't slept well.

The boys shook themselves awake, rubbed the sleepy sand out of their eyes, and hightailed it toward the station. They had discussed the various types of cars they could hop and decided a flatcar might be a better choice—one with a light load of cargo they could hide behind.

Luck was on their side, and they hopped a flat roller loaded with small containers tied down with ropes and straps. There were no chicken hawks to worry about here, plenty to hang on to, and many spaces in and among the crates where two skinny kids could hide.

The train crossed the mountains and picked up a main line heading north near Gold Hill, Oregon. They spent three days and nights on this flatcar, never sure where they were or how long it would take to get somewhere near where they wanted to go. The train stopped at several small outposts along the way. They saw signs that said Dillard, Roseburg, Yoncalla, Eugene, and Millersburg.

Millersburg looked promising. His stomach growled, and Bill said, "I think I'll get off here. One side of my gut is gnawing on the other side."

The country around the rail station reminded him of Toledo and Corvallis, with low foothills and vast fields of farmland running the width of the valley.

Bill fidgeted with his clothes and picked at his cuticles. I think he felt uneasy about returning to Oregon. The judge's order loomed over him.

"Yep," he said, "here's where I get off. It looks like home, and it smells like home. I could get a job around here doing farm work."

"Want company?" Ronnie asked.

"Sure, if you think this is close enough for you. It's not Waldport, though."

"I know. But I'd like to work for the summer and have a few shekels in my pocket when I get there."

"Sure then. It would be a lot more fun with somebody I know than somebody I don't know. Let's go."

I watched them slip off the side of that flatcar like a pair of cats slinking down an alley wall. They jumped over the rails going the opposite direction, slid down an embankment and into a brilliant green field. They skirted the edge, heading toward some equipment on the southeast side.

The man operating a big tractor-like rig caught sight of them from the corner of his eye, stopped the machine, and jumped down. He started toward the boys with his shoulders hunched up by his ears, his jaw set, his fists doubled, and ready for confrontation.

"What the bloody hell do you think you're doing?" he shouted.

"Looking for work," Bill said. "Me and my buddy just got here from working farms in California, and we need work."

"Well, this here ain't no charity farm for hobos. You say you got experience?"

"Yes, sir," Bill said, with false bravado, "we got lots of experience. What you farming here?"

"Mint," the man replied. "We harvest it for the oil. That's what that rig is. We process the leaves through it before they get distilled in those buildings over yonder. Finest mint oil in the Willamette Valley."

"You needin' a couple of hired hands right now?"

"You know, we might. We had a couple 'a young bucks movin' irrigation pipe, but they ran off a few days ago. Would you be interested in somethin' like that?"

"Heck, yeah. We'd be interested in just about anything you got right now, including a meal. Are meals part of the package at this farm?"

"Yep. Quarters ain't much, but the chow hall is okay. You wantin' bed and board plus wages?"

"If that's the package, we'd take you up on that deal."

"Like I say, the quarters ain't much, and the wages ain't much either— dollar a day plus bed and board. Take it or leave it."

Ronnie and Bill spoke as one, "I'll take it."

"Head on over to the buildings you see yonder. Ask for the foreman. I'll be along after I finish this row."

As they drew closer, they saw many men swarming around the buildings, in, out, and in again, carrying things and moving equipment. It appeared to be a bustling place with much to do. Neither Ronnie nor Bill had any experience working on a farm like this. They exchanged glances, and an unspoken pact was welded in place: Act like you know what you're doing, watch the other guys and do what they do, never let on that you haven't done it before, keep your head down and your shoulders square, talk little and stay alert.

Bill stopped the first man he saw and said, "Can you tell me where the foreman is?"

The man used his head to point toward a man counting containers.

"Thanks," Bill said, walking toward the foreman.

The man raised his head as the boys approached. "Lookin' for work?" he asked, sizing them up.

"Yes, sir," Bill said, and Ronnie nodded.

"You got any experience?"

"We just finished the harvest season in California. You tell us what needs doin', and we'll do it. The guy on that rig out there thought you might be lookin' to hire a couple of strong hands to move irrigation pipes."

"That we are," the foreman said. "If you're up for the job, you're hired. You can start right after dinner. Make yourselves at home. We eat at seven. We work as late as the light lets us. This is the spring planting, but as the days get longer, so does our workday, and yours will be even longer."

"Why's that?" Ronnie asked.

"Because you need to move the irrigation pipes about every two hours around the clock. The evening rotation usually starts around nine. You already met Big Mac. He'll show you what to do and how to do it tonight. Then, you're on your own."

Bill and Ronnie shared a shack with hay-stuffed canvas pallets for beds. They were so tired at the end of each day they wouldn't have minded if the canvas had been stuffed with rocks. They were too tired to go anywhere in the few hours a week they had off and managed to save almost every dollar they earned. Their arms grew strong, and their legs even stronger. Ronnie's shoulder no longer troubled him and the physical exertion that was difficult in the beginning came easy. The man wasn't kidding when he said the chow was good. They ate their fill at every meal and looked forward to the next.

With the spring harvest over and the fall planting in the ground, both boys felt drawn to, if not greener—for there was little greener than a mint field—then different pastures, and they told the foreman they were moving on.

They left the way they came, only this time, they would hitchhike to Corvallis.

"I'm going to join the Civilian Conservation Corp," Bill said, and Ronnie said, "If you're joining the CCC, then so am I."

"Do you think they will let us go to the same camp?" Bill asked.

"How the hell would I know?" Ronnie said. "I don't know any more than you do. That guy we talked to at the farm seemed to think it was the best idea for guys like us."

"I want to go to Salem and see my brother before I do anything else," Bill said, "but I can't show my face where people know me until I turn eighteen."

"When's that?"

"December the fifteenth," Bill said, "and I can't wait."

How well I remembered. December fifteenth, 1919. Katherine and I were alone in the living room, trying to decide if we should send Will for the midwife. My pains were coming faster and faster until it was too late, and Katherine had to deliver Little W.E. all by herself. It seemed like yesterday, and here he was, a grown man, no longer little and no longer W.E. He adopted the name Bill as easily as putting on a sweater. It took me a while to think of him as Bill.

"Why can't you show your face?" Ronnie asked.

Bill pulled a toothpick out of his mouth and twirled it between his thumb and forefinger. It was clear to me he didn't want to share his past troubles with Ronnie, but their friendship had grown beyond the point of keeping secrets from each other.

"I was a stupid kid. Got in some trouble, and the judge told my dad to get me out of this state and keep me out. I took a big risk coming back. Don't dare press my luck."

"What kind of trouble?" Ronnie asked, sliding a sideward glance at Bill.

"Nothin' you need to worry about, buddy. Just shenanigans. When we get to Corvallis, I'll find a phone booth and call him. I need to call my other brother, too. And my dad."

"I'm not callin' nobody. I'll just show up, and if they let me in, great. If they shut the door in my face, I'll just keep movin'."

"Do you think they will have a phone we can use at the CCC camp?" Bill asked.

"Doubt it," Ronnie said. "They don't want guys callin' mama and cryin' about how bad things are."

Bill laughed. "Well, they don't have to worry about that with me. My mama's been gone so long I almost forgot what she looked like."

My heart clutched. It never occurred to me the boys would forget what I looked like.

"Was she good to you?" Ronnie asked.

"The best. One thing about my mama was she always loved on us. She had long hair that shined when the sun hit it. I remember that. And she was gentle. She never raised her voice or a hand."

"You're lucky. My ma beat on us ever' time our pa beat on her. The more he drank, the more he beat on her, and the more she beat on us. I think she felt real bad about it though, 'cause she always wanted to hug on us after."

Bill and Ronnie reached the highway's edge and turned to face the oncoming traffic. They stuck their thumbs out and waved to get someone to stop. No one appeared to be in the mood to pick up hitchhikers, and by late afternoon, with no luck, they had walked over six miles to the exit sign to Corvallis. Another four miles and they entered the sleepy town, looking for any sign of the CCC office. No people were around, and streetlamps blinked to life as dusk fell.

"Hey, look," Ronnie said, "there's a park over there. We could rest until somebody comes along we can ask."

"You hungry?" Bill said.

"Yeah, but I don't see no place around here to eat."

"There has to be a restaurant someplace in a town this size," Bill said.

Ronnie said, "I'm too beat to walk another block. I'd rather find a bench and lie down for a while. Then we can search for food."

"I'm too tired to eat," Bill mimicked. "Pansy."

"I ain't no pansy. We've been walkin' for four hours. I'm tired."

"Okay, little girl, let's go find you a beddy-bye."

Ronnie doubled his fist and punched Bill in the arm. Bill grabbed Ronnie's wrist and twisted his arm behind his back.

"Ouch! Stop."

Bill let go and turned toward the park a block away. "Let's go."

The boys found a long bench under an oak tree with a sprawling canopy. It looked safe, dark, and quiet.

Ronnie crawled underneath onto the grassy cushion and bunched his bundle for a pillow.

Bill plopped onto his side and stretched the length of the bench, his knees curled and his bundle tucked under his head.

They were asleep within minutes. I watched over them throughout the night. It made me uncomfortable to think somebody could rob them of their hard-earned money. I couldn't do much to protect them, but I could find a way to wake them if necessary.

CHAPTER FORTY-SIX

Ronnie felt the toe of a boot kicking at his legs. Bill struggled to sit up with someone's hand pressed hard against his shoulder.

"What you two doing loitering in a city park? Don't you know loitering is against the law here?" The brusque male voice broke through their sleep and roused their brains to high alert.

Bill was poised to do combat until he saw the uniform. "Let me go," he said, twisting away from the man's grip.

"I'll let you go, alright, as soon as you tell me what you're doing here sleeping in a city park at five o'clock in the morning."

Ronnie shoved the man's boot away and tried to roll out from under the bench.

"You stay put," the man barked at him. "I'll deal with you soon as I find out what your buddy here is up to."

Bill sat up and rubbed his eyes. It was just beginning to get light, and the man in the uniform appeared very official and very stern. "Nothin'. We aren't doin' nothin'. Catching a little shut-eye while we wait for the CCC office to open."

"The CCC office? What you boys want with that pussy outfit?"

"We just finished workin' on a mint farm in Millersburg, and some guys there said the CCC was lookin' to take men in and teach them a trade. We plan to join up."

"How old are you?"

Bill pondered his options and decided once again to lie. "Eighteen."
"Your buddy, too?"
"Far as I know."
"Well, I want you both on your feet and at attention. I've got a better deal for you than the CCC could ever come up with."
It was then Bill realized the uniform wasn't that of a policeman. This guy was in the Army. "What kind of a deal would that be?" he asked.
"The kind that gets you three squares and a bed every day while it's teaching you how to be a man. How does that sound?"
Ronnie cleared his throat and squirmed. "I don't know," he said. "I think the CCC does that for you, plus teachin' you a trade."
"That's what they claim, but I got more recruits coming in trying to figure a way out of the CCC than I got coming in to join the Army."
The boys exchanged glances, and Bill shuffled his feet as he tried to inch out of the man's reach.
"Where you think you're going? You leave when I say you can leave. The way I see it, you've got two choices. Come with me and hear what I have to say, or I take you by the collar and deliver you to the local constabulary for loitering. What's it going to be?"
Bill couldn't risk a run-in with the police. They would discover his trouble in Toledo and send him up the river. He had to think fast, and before he could stop himself, he said, "I think I'll go with you and hear what you have to say."
Ronnie hung his head and nodded.
"You boys had anything to eat?" the Army man asked.
"No," they said together.
"I'm going to buy you breakfast, and then we'll go to my office and talk. How does that sound?" He turned to Ronnie and said, "Now. You can move now."
They followed the uniformed man with their stomachs in their throats.
"My name is Sergeant Phillips. I'm a recruiter for the US Army. I consider this my lucky day, and when I'm done telling you about the United States Army, you'll consider it your lucky day, too."
The breakfast of pancakes, fried eggs, hash browns, crisp bacon, sausage, and toast boggled their eyes. As far as Bill was concerned, it surpassed even Aunt Beulah's breakfasts. He'd never had anything like it. Ronnie didn't even have something to compare it to. He ate everything they put in front of him and did think this was his lucky day.

Sergeant Phillips handed each boy a bus ticket, shook his hand, and clapped him on the back as they boarded the Greyhound bus for Fort Stevens on the Oregon coast. Bill hadn't been able to call Lynch or Aaron. Sergeant Phillips assured him he could once he got to the base.

Both boys had lied about their age, but the Army recruiter didn't notice. He had a quota, and these two young men were ripe for the picking.

Bill did have the opportunity to call both his brothers after he arrived at Fort Stevens, and what he learned was not good. I dreaded him making those calls because I knew Charles had died. Will was back in Oregon and had been drunk for weeks. Lynch had taken it all in stride, but Aaron was bereft.

"Aaron, it's your brother, Bill." His voice was hesitant, as if Aaron wouldn't know him after all this time.

"Bill? Where the heck are you? Dad said you ran off to Mexico with some Jew, and he hadn't heard from you since."

"Well. Hello to you, too."

"Sorry. Hi. I was just shocked. Did you know Charles died?"

The line was quiet. Unbidden tears welled in Bill's eyes. He couldn't speak.

"You still there?"

A gulp, a swipe at the tears, and a choked-out, "Yeah. Still here. When?"

"Dad said it was right after you ran off. He tried to find you, but no one in Arizona had seen you."

"I wasn't in Arizona, and I didn't run off. I was dumped in Mexico and jumped a freight train to California. Took me a few weeks but I made it back to Oregon. I joined the Army."

"The Army! How'd you do that? You aren't eighteen."

"I'll write you all about it. There isn't time on the phone. How you doin'? Dad helping you with money and all?"

Now, it was Aaron's turn to go quiet.

"You there?" Bill asked.

"Yeah. I'm here. He isn't helping, because he's been drunk ever since he got back. I don't know where he gets the money for booze. He isn't working that I know of."

"You going to finish high school?"

"Yes. I'm going to finish. And try to go to college in Eugene if I can find a job that pays enough for the tuition."

"No worries. I'll send you my paycheck every month. The Army gives me everything I need. You can send part of it to the blind school for Lyn and keep the rest for school."

Now it was Aaron's turn to get choked up. He gulped and said, "Thanks, Bill. You don't have to do that. I'll find a job."

"I'm doin' it, and that's all there is to it. No need to argue. We're family, and family that can't help each other is no family at all."

What I heard pleased me, except for Will's drinking. I knew he was struggling with the loss of our eldest son.

The next night, Bill called the Oregon State School for the Blind and told the secretary he was in the Army at Fort Stevens and to tell Lynch he would write to him. Lynch happened to be walking past the office when the secretary was talking to Bill.

She said, "Wait! Wait! Don't hang up. Your brother is right here." She waved her arms and ran toward Lynch, grabbing his coat sleeve as he passed. "Your brother is on the phone."

"Hello?" Lynch said, unsure which brother she was talking about.

"Lyn? It's Bill. How the heck are you, man?"

"Bill? They found you?"

"Who found me?"

"Dad and Aaron? They said you disappeared in Mexico."

"No. False alarm. I'm in the Army here at Fort Stevens. Up on the coast by Astoria."

"I know where it is. We wrestled in a tournament up there."

"Really? How'd you do?"

"I won. I always win. I'm the Oregon state champion in my weight class."

"No shit! Well, aren't you hot stuff?"

"Yeah. I'm doing pretty well. Wrestling is fun for me, and my schoolwork is easy. I'm learning finish work in carpentry so I can get a job when I graduate."

"That's great. Glad to hear it. Say, I told Aaron I'd send my check to him every month, but he's supposed to share it with you. Be sure you get your share, okay?"

"Okay. Thanks, Bill. Did you know Charles died?"

"Yeah, Aaron told me. He says he cries every time he thinks about it."

"Did you cry?"

"Sure did, buddy. I was planning to go to San Antone to see him after I got back from Mexico, but that got all screwed up and I never made it. Now it's too late. How'd you take the news?"

"I didn't cry at first, but the next day it hit me, and I broke down in class and had to leave. It's hard to believe Charles isn't ever coming back."

"I know. I'll try to make it down to Salem to see you before the Army ships me off to some other place."

"That'd be great. Write to me."

"I will, little brother. I will."

CHAPTER FORTY-SEVEN

Life in the Army suited Bill. The routine and order of each day seemed to be just what he needed to thrive and grow. His friendship with Ronnie Miller deepened, and he had his first true friend. Both joined the Fort Stevens baseball team. Bill was a natural athlete and excelled. When they called for soldiers to join the diving team, he also stepped up for that challenge. Ronnie took a pass on the diving, and Bill would have been well advised to do the same since he broke two front teeth off at a rakish angle on his third time off the high board.

I enjoyed watching him learn new skills, march, take orders, and adapt to a disciplined lifestyle. I hung around much longer than I needed to because it was all so much fun, and watching Will drink himself half to death was something I couldn't tolerate.

The Army gave these young men opportunities they would never have in civilian life. Each week before the United Service Organization show and dance, they offered free lessons to anyone who wanted to learn. Ronnie was awkward and uncomfortable, but Bill took to it like he'd been born to it.

After a few weeks of lessons, he thought he might be ready to ask one of the attractive local girls who frequented the USO events to dance. One girl in particular caught his eye, a Hedy Lamarr look-alike called Dot. She always came with her beau and another couple, but she danced with the soldiers brave enough to ask her. What mother wouldn't stick around to see how it went?

The night of the dance arrived. Bill polished his shoes, made sure his uniform was perfect, his shirt neatly ironed, his tie properly knotted, and his hair swept back and styled with pomade in the day's fashion.

"Whee, whew!" Ronnie wolf-whistled through his teeth and pranced around the barracks like a peacock strutting its stuff. "Ain't you just toooo pretty for us common folk?"

Bill punched him in the shoulder, and Ronnie danced out of reach, cackling like a spooked rooster. "I expect you think you're too good to walk over to the dance hall with me," he teased.

"Put a sock in it," Bill said with a crooked grin. "Just don't step on my bright and shiny shoes."

"Wouldn't think of it," Ronnie said, striking a solemn tone. "Anybody can see this is one important date you're heading for. Only a fool would risk mussing you up." He danced out of Will's reach again and laughed like a crazed person. "Who is she, Bill? Have you set your sights on someone special?"

"None of your beeswax."

"Beeswax? Wow. We're even practicing nicey-nice language. She must really be something."

When the two young men reached the dance hall, locals and soldiers already crowded the floor to the strains of a Glenn Miller-type band. Couples swirled past doing the foxtrot with grace and style. Bill watched for about fifteen minutes, and when the Duke Ellington song "Mood Indigo" ended, he spotted Dot leaving the floor with her boyfriend.

He sauntered in her direction, and when she returned from the ladies' room, he caught her before she sat down. "Dance?"

Her luminous hazel eyes appraised him, and she cocked her head. "You any good at the foxtrot?"

"Shall we find out?"

She smiled assent, and he swept her onto the dance floor. Their bodies melded like two halves of a whole. Any nervous doubt Bill might have entertained flew out the door the minute she stepped into his arms.

They danced to the rising and falling rhythm of Bing Crosby singing, "Too Marvelous for Words." They swirled, they dipped, they swung apart and back together. Their feet glided in perfect time and never missed a step. The music flowed through and around them until the other dancers stopped and cleared the floor one couple at a time. Soon, they were the only couple remaining.

When the song ended, Bill pulled Dot close and planted a kiss on her forehead. She beamed with delight. He whispered in her ear, "You are, you know, too marvelous for words." Then he swung her into his arms for the next dance before her boyfriend or any other desire-filled soldier swept her away.

"Let's take a break," she pleaded after six straight dances with Bill.

He guided her toward the open door, saying, "We'll get some fresh air and cool down." His arm around her waist met with no resistance.

They stood outside and gazed at the stars. The roar of Pacific Ocean waves crashing onto the beach filled the night with a woeful, haunting sound.

Dot lifted her auburn hair off her warm back and let the marine air cool her neck.

Bill watched her and felt his heart lurch.

She was the one. I knew it, and he knew it. He was just like me. When he met the one, he knew then and there she would be his wife.

"We should get back. Freddy's going to be mad enough at me as it is. If I'm gone much longer, he might not give me a ride home." She turned her glowing face to him and parted her lips.

But before she could speak, Bill said, "Which car is his?"

She pointed to the black four-door, 1930 Model A Ford Sedan with oversized white tires shining in the moonlight.

"Cool car. I'll walk you inside. Thanks for the dances. And you are, you know, too marvelous for words."

Dot blushed and turned away. "You're not too bad yourself. I've never danced with anyone easier to follow."

"I wish you'd follow me to the end of the earth," he said. "Come on. I'd better deliver you to your boyfriend."

As soon as Dot was seated next to Freddy again, Bill hightailed it over to a buddy of his who had a car. "Milt, I need a favor. I'll pay you five bucks to use your car for an hour after the dance ends."

"What do you need a car for?"

"You'll see. Is it a deal?"

"Show me the five-spot, and I'll tell you if it's a deal."

Bill rummaged in his pant pocket and pulled out his wallet. He lifted a five-dollar bill from behind a flap in the bill compartment and waved it under his buddy's nose.

"Yeah. Okay." Milt dug in his trouser pocket for the key. "Take it easy with her. She means the world to me."

"Who?" Bill asked, thinking Milt knew who he had been dancing with.
"Bessie. My car, buddy. No monkey business with my girl, okay?"
"Thanks, pal. I'll treat her like a baby."

Bill ran to the parking lot and unscrewed the tire air valves on Freddy's car. The orchestra and the waves drowned out the low hiss that escaped into the night. He sauntered back inside to wait for the dance to end.

I shook my head and smiled. I didn't wait to see what happened. Bill would be all right. Will would have to find his way out of the darkness without my help. Lynch, Aaron, and Maisie were all in safe hands. It was time for me to go.

THE END

EPILOGUE

The Army shipped Bill to the Panama Canal Zone for the remainder of his enlistment.

Dot broke her engagement, and when Bill returned in 1941, he looked her up.

Dorothy (Dot) Reisdorf and William (Bill) Echols Jones, Jr. were married on March 15, 1942, with Ronnie Miller as best man and Rosemary Richey as maid of honor, but that's a story for another time.

Bill and Dot were married for sixty-seven years and had three children: Linda, Gordon Charles, and Jeffrey. Linda is the author of this book and its prequel, *Finding Utopia*. Bill apprenticed as a gun and locksmith in Coos Bay, Oregon, and moved the family to Roseburg, Oregon, in 1951, where they opened the Umpqua Gun Store. Bill died in 2008 at age eighty-nine after a long battle with dementia. Dot died in 2014, two months before her ninety-third birthday.

Will Jones, Sr. died in 1947 from tuberculosis at age fifty-three at Coquille Valley Hospital, Oregon. He contracted the disease from his son, Charles, who died at age eighteen in San Antonio, Texas. Will lived long enough to know his first grandchild, Linda, after whose birth he quit drinking and smoking so Dot would let him spend time with the baby. That ended when Linda tested positive for tuberculosis at age three, a disease which, in her, never materialized.

Will saw Bill established in business and married with two children, Aaron graduate college, and Lynch established in a trade, but he died a year before Maisie married.

Aaron Upton Jones graduated from the University of Oregon with a degree in Physical Education, claiming it was the only degree he could manage while working two jobs to get through school, supporting himself and his sister, Mazie (Jones) Brown, who left high school and joined her brother in Eugene. Aaron became one of Oregon's most accomplished and wealthiest lumbermen, owner of Seneca Lumber Company. He married Jean "Deannie" Bauman, and they had three daughters: Becky, Kathy, and Jodie.

Following their divorce, he married Marie and adopted her daughter, Suzanne. Aaron died from complications of Alzheimer's, September 22, 2014, at age ninety-two, three days shy of his ninety-third birthday. Marie is still living and raises thoroughbred horses.

Lynch Davidson Jones graduated from the Oregon State School for the Blind and pursued a trade as a finish carpenter. In the early 1950s, he moved to Alaska and bought a fishing trawler. He married his partner in the fishing business, June Cook. They married and divorced twice following long seasons together on the boat. In the early 1970s, he returned to Oregon, where he met and married Vonnie. He was one of the first people to wear contact lenses and one of the first people in the country to have Lasik Surgery, which was arranged and paid for by Aaron. Lynch didn't have children and died June 8, 2011, at age eighty-eight, of complications from dementia.

Maizelle (Mazie) Jones Prucha died in 2014 at age eighty-nine, ten days shy of her ninetieth birthday. She married in 1948, had three children, Sharon, George, and Marian, and was widowed on June 8, 1988. Her children still live in Texas.

Maizelle's sister, Julia Clark Magavern, died in her thirties of breast cancer.

The book is a work of fiction, though many of the incidents around which the story takes shape were actual.

As the author, born in 1944, I hope you enjoyed my retelling of my father and his siblings' early lives after leaving Utopia.

Reach me via email at novelistlindaweber@gmail.com or visit my webpage at www.novelistlindaweber.com. Leave your name and email and I will update you on future tales from the Sabinal Canyon.

AUTHOR'S NOTE

Many people who read my first book, *Finding Utopia,* sent me messages pleading to know what happened to Will and the children after Maizelle's murder. Unfortunately, I don't have a good paper trail for those years between her death and my father's enlistment in the US Army. The Jones children had a lost childhood in many respects.

Over the years, I heard my father talk about many of the incidents in this book, and I have put context around story fragments. I have invented characters, imagined dialogue, and relied on old letters miraculously saved, obituaries, and conversations between my dad and his brothers, Aaron and Lynch Jones.

These things are true:

Will moved the boys to Del Rio, where they lived with their paternal grandparents until Mama Sarah's health gave out and she could no longer manage "three rambunctious little boys."

Will placed the boys in an orphanage twice, but I don't know where, when, or the orphanage's name. The boys learned table manners and comportment from "a real nice lady" during those stays. Will paid board for them until his auto repair shop went up in flames.

The children lived for a time in the back of a junked-out vehicle in a wrecking yard.

Maizelle (Maisie) lived with Will's sister, Eula Brown, in Alpine, Texas, and went by the name Maizelle (Mazie) Brown.

The family moved to Oregon, where the boys lived with Will's eldest brother and his wife in Toledo and on Mary's Peak, between Corvallis and the Oregon Coast. They ran away from that home due to physical abuse and lived on a houseboat on the Yaquina River that tipped sideways when the tide went out.

Lynch attended and graduated from the Oregon State School for the Blind, where he was a champion wrestler and learned finish carpentry skills.

Aaron graduated from Toledo High School and was one of only two students to attend college. He was an outstanding athlete and strong academically. He graduated from the University of Oregon with a degree in Physical Education.

Maizelle (Maisie/Mazie) didn't learn about her mother's murder or her heritage until she was in her mid-teens. She somehow made it to Oregon, lived with Aaron, and attended "school"—although whether it was high school or college is unknown.

Bill robbed the post office in Toledo and was banished from Oregon by a kind judge who gave him a second chance. His father took him to Arizona, where they found work on a truck farm. Bill traveled to Mexico with a Jewish blanket and fruit trader, and he and his father parted ways. Bill rode the rails and hoboed his way back to Oregon. He got off the train in Millersburg and worked on a mint farm.

An Army recruiter rousted Bill and his buddy as they slept in a park in Corvallis, waiting for the CCC office to open. They were on a bus to Fort Stevens in Warrenton, Oregon by five o'clock that night.

Will was married briefly to a "nice lady named Mrs. Richey," but where, when, or for how long is lost to history.

Dot Reisdorf met Bill Jones at a USO dance at Fort Stevens, where he did let the air out of her fiancé's tires so he could give her a ride home.

Those incidents are context; the story is fiction.

ACKNOWLEDGEMENTS

The Sisters Writes read and critique group listened and encouraged through every chapter of this book. Their critique was invaluable. Four professional beta readers read the manuscript and offered insightful comments and scores high enough to make me believe the book was worth publishing. I owe them all a debt of gratitude.

My outstanding editor, Susan Buchanan of Perfect Prose, edited with heart and care.

And all those wonderful people who read *Finding Utopia* and asked for "the rest of the story." Without your hunger I would never have written this book. It is character driven with real people whose lives of resilience in adversity tug at your heartstrings.

And for anyone who doesn't believe in ghosts, well, if you had been living inside my skin since the muse first visited thirty-five years ago, logging "coincidence" after "coincidence" that drew me to write the first book, and pushed me to write the second book, you might change your mind!

BOOK CLUB PROMPTS

1. Most of the characters in *Surviving Utopia* were real people personally known to the author. Did you develop an attachment to the characters that carried you along in the story?

2. Did the narration by a disembodied spirit in part one and a portion of part two work for you? Why or why not? When the narration switched to Will in part two did the transition bother you or was it smooth?

3. Had you read *Finding Utopia* before you read *Surviving Utopia*? If not, did the author give you enough backstory to understand why Will and the boys were on this journey and how their struggles came about?

4. Did Will's treatment of Faye Richey seem believable and realistic? Did their relationship add to the story?

5. How did you feel about Will leaving the boys at an orphanage? Was his determination not to let them be adopted a good thing for the children or a bad thing?

6. Do you think the author's depiction of the struggles people endured during The Great Depression gave substance and purpose to the story?

7. Will was a seriously flawed human being. Considering his demons do you think he acted in a manner consistent with expectations for fathers and men at that time? Do you think he loved his children? Did he ever do anything that raised your opinion of him as a man, a father, or a husband?

8. Who was your favorite character in the book and why?

9. Who was your least favorite character and why?

10. If you have read other books set during The Great Depression, such as *Sold on A Monday* or *The Four Winds*, how do you think this book compared?

Praise for *FINDING UTOPIA*

Quotes from verified purchasers on Amazon

"…compelling…a loving, unforgiving, tragic, and violent story…characters are relatable and well developed. The landscape of rural Texas in the early 1900's come to life in the author's vivid descriptions."

"…Brilliant work!…thought-provoking page-turner…explores complex themes…leaves a lasting impression…characters are well developed and relatable."

"Incredible read!…the lives and love of Maizelle and Will were woven skillfully, leaving the reader not holding a book, but inside the story…"

"…Griping and Powerful…expertly told…wonderful details about life 100 years ago…characters that are human and wholly relatable…pulls you in and doesn't let you go until the powerful, emotional conclusion…and not even then!"

"…Attention grabber…pulls you in like you were living there with the family."

"…Exceptional on so many levels…Ms. Weber has a talent for character development…"

"…Characters jump off the page…a real page turner…"

"Finding Utopia is a country song writ large…characters come to life through masterful dialog…This book rocked my world and broke my heart…"

"I couldn't put this gripping tale down…Highly recommended."

"…A great read…So good…Wonderful read!…The characters pulled me into the story…Beautiful, remarkable story…A Must read!…Great storyteller!…Loved this entertaining and warm story!…This is not your typical romance novel!…Rich characters and immersive dialogue.

Reader Views Editorial Review

"Finding Utopia" by Linda Weber is a gripping read rife with unfettered emotion and resilient characters who are well-developed through Linda Weber's excellent writing. By delving deep into the clutches of trauma, family, and a couple's unwavering love, the content explores what it means to be human.

Made in United States
Troutdale, OR
12/12/2024